HOME EXTENSIONS AND CONSERVATORIES

HOME EXTENSIONS AND CONSERVATORIES

DAVID FISHER

DAVID & CHARLES
Newton Abbot London North Pomfret (Vt)

British Library Cataloguing in Publication Data

Fisher, David
  Home extensions and conservatories.
  1. Architecture, Domestic   2. Dwellings——
  Remodelling
  I. Title
  728   NA7125

  ISBN 0-7153-8573-9

Typeset by ABM Typographics Limited, Hull
and printed in Great Britain
by Redwood Burn Limited, Trowbridge, Wilts
for David & Charles (Publishers) Limited
Brunel House   Newton Abbot   Devon

Published in the United States of America
by David & Charles Inc
North Pomfret   Vermont 05053   USA

Contents

1   Home Alterations and Additions   7

2   Preliminary Considerations — Assessing Feasibility   51

3   Building Design Services   63

4   Contracts and Communications   70

5   Insurance — Who Insures What?   83

6   House Construction Systems in the UK   87

7   Building Components, Materials and Service Systems   110

8   Extension Work Affecting Mains Electricity, Gas and Water Connections   182

9   Raising the Wind   184

10   Survival on Site   186

    Appendix 1: Relevant Organisations   187

    Appendix 2: Conversion Factors   199

    Index   203

1
Home Alterations and Additions

Developing or expanding your existing house or flat to cope with your changing living pattern is a course of action that offers many advantages over selling up and moving out to one which is larger, or more suitably divided for your needs. Since both moving and extending entail a fair amount of inconvenience, time, disruption of normal living patterns and — inevitably — expense, it is as well, before deciding to do either, to establish your basic motives for making a change.

WHY STAY?

Perhaps you have no special attachment to the city, district, town or village in which you currently live, no need to stay near a relative or in a good school's catchment area and no personal aversion to a change of scene. You may want so much extra accommodation of one sort or another that an extension big enough to provide it would be well over the size likely to obtain the approval of the planning authorities. The planners may also object to alteration proposals likely to change too radically the character of your home, when a radical change is precisely what you are looking for. In all these cases, a move is the only satisfactory option. Indeed, judging by statistics relating to the length of time the average mortgage contract runs these days in Britain — only seven years — it is a popular option.

Possibly your next house or flat may cost more than your present one can be sold for, but property, if you buy the right sort, normally appreciates in value with time, and you may have a talent for renovating neglected dwellings, thus improving their market price

and giving yourself a good chance of making money by moving. As long as your profit on the sale adequately covers the incidental moving costs — estate agents' and survey fees, bridging loan interest, removal charges and conveyancing costs, not forgetting the expenses of refitting carpets and curtains — moving around once in a while may pay dividends.

THE CASE FOR STAYING PUT

If the sort of home you want is not fundamentally different from what you have, and if you would really rather not move, you should at least investigate the possibilities of reorganising it to fit your requirements before looking for an alternative place to live. Alterations and additions cost money, just as moving does, but the £2,000 to £4,000 it can cost you, in basic terms, to move can go quite a way to paying for the work. The chances are that you will have to spend far less to change or add to your existing home than to fund a sell-and-buy operation, with moving costs on top of the price differential. Provided you take care with the style and quality of the development work, it will increase both the market value and saleability of your property, the value added almost invariably being greater than the amount you spend to produce it.

Living with the disturbance of building work can be trying, but equally, there is a considerable part of your living space that need not be unduly upset — as compared to moving house, an event which can be guaranteed to disturb absolutely everything and everybody.

Figs 1 & 2, Plates 1 & 2 (pp 8–11)
A between-the-wars council house at Stoke Lacey in Herefordshire, bought by its present owners in 1979. Before the extension work — which was carried out, except for the brickwork, by the owner himself — the kitchen was an awkward shape, unplastered and had a bathroom encroaching on it. There was virtually no entrance hall. The downstairs extension provided a more commodious hall and kitchen, plus a garage. Over the garage, it was possible to put a bathroom, toilet and a fourth bedroom. The total extension cost was about £8,000 in 1979. Part of the work was covered by an improvement grant from Malvern Hills District Council *(Christopher Morton)*

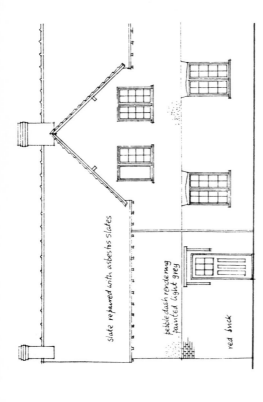

slate repaired with asbestos slates

pebble dash rendering painted light grey

red brick

south east elevation

south west elevation

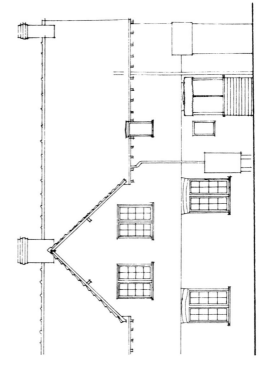

north west elevation

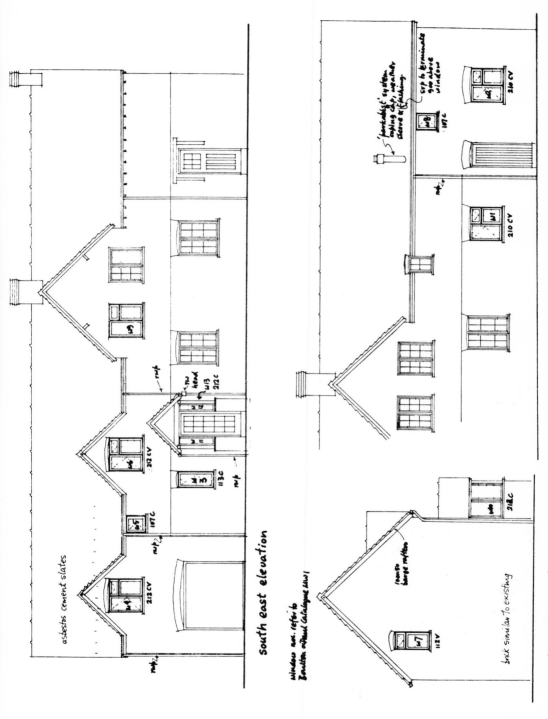

asbestos cement slates

south east elevation

south west elevation

north west elevation

windows nos. refer to
Boulton oPaul Catalogue 1901

brick similar to existing

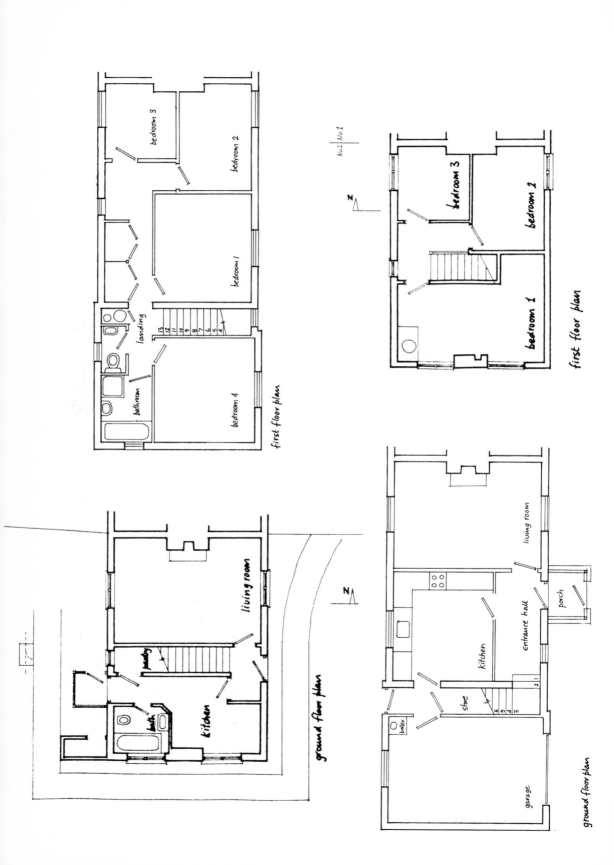

bedroom 3

bedroom 2

bedroom 1

bedroom 4

bathroom

landing

first floor plan

living room

laundry

bath

kitchen

ground floor plan

N

No 2 | No 1

N

bedroom 3

bedroom 2

bedroom 1

first floor plan

living room

kitchen

entrance hall

porch

store

boiler

garage

ground floor plan

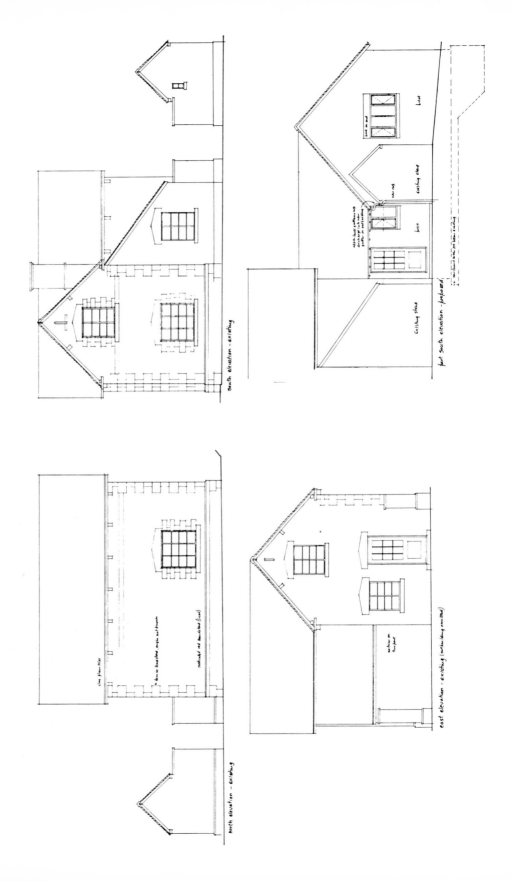

north elevation - existing

south elevation - existing

east elevation - existing (north along overcliffe)

part south elevation - proposed

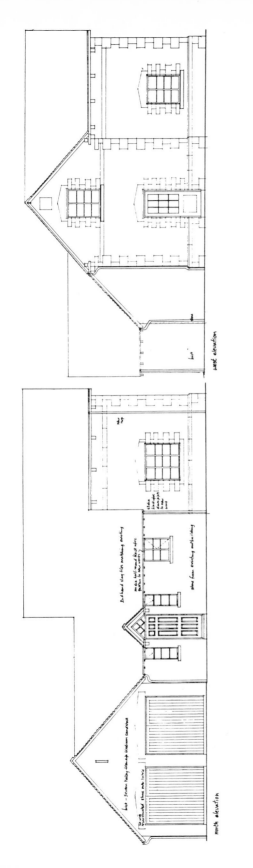

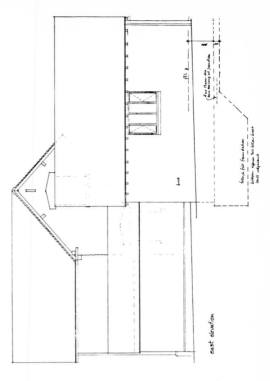

west elevation

east elevation

north elevation

Fig 3 This cottage, on an estate in Herefordshire owned by the National Trust, was originally a gamekeeper's. Its present owner, a car enthusiast on a modest income, needed to extend it, partly to provide a good-sized garage and partly to increase the size of the very small hall. Plans for the extension had to have the approval of the Trust as well as the local planning authority, yet had to allow for economical construction by the owner, with some professional assistance on the facing brickwork. Salvaged clay tiles, matching the existing ones, were used for the roof (*see also Plate 4*) (*Christopher Morton*)

THE FIRST STEP

Well in advance of investigating the practical pros and cons of knocking the homestead into a more acceptable form than the one you have become dissatisfied with, spell out in clear, simple terms your true objective. A great deal of work may be feasible, but if all you truly want is somewhere to change out of wet outdoor clothes before stepping into the hallway, or a kitchen twice the size of the present one so that you can eat meals in it, there is no point in finding out just how far down the garden the local authority will let you build. An outsize extension may give the architect a fascinating project and the builder a fat profit, but their business is to produce what you want at a fair price, and yours is to obtain what you want at a fair price — not to take on greater expense than you need to, just because it would make good overall added-value sense on paper.

Your underlying need may be for a big larder, so you can shop less frequently, or for somewhere to sit in the sun. Teenage children may need a place to be noisy and free from total supervision, whilst you want your own compartment for quieter living. A musical person may need to be hived off, or a studious one provided with desk space and book storage. It may make good sense to give an elderly or handicapped relative semi-self-contained accommodation in your home, rather than need continual visiting miles away.

PORCHES

Many older houses, and some not so old, have open porches at their entrance doors, or no porch at all. A porch is more than a privacy shield — or can be, if it is enclosed and the doors into and out of it draughtproofed, so that it acts as an insulating air-curtain between the warm interior and cold exterior atmospheres. If a porch is big enough, you can leave overcoats, raincoats, wellingtons and umbrellas in it, away from the hall carpet. With an efficient doormat, a porch can help to keep that carpet unsoiled. A glass pane in the outer door gives you good advance warning of the identity and

This extension to a bungalow in Barnham, Sussex (the part of the house projecting on the left in the photograph) provides a fourth bedroom, in addition to increased space in the hall behind the door, and a new porch in front of it. Integration with the existing building is perfect, and the appeal and value of the bungalow are both enhanced by the improvement (*Drawing and picture by courtesy of Norman R. Harrison, Dip Arch, Dist (Btn), RIBA*)

character of callers, before they are face to face with you. Some of these benefits may not matter to you, but you may still want a warm place for plants, or one where the postman can leave parcels when you are out, the inner door being securely locked.

The entrance is a natural focus for attention at the approach to a building; consequently, the size and style of the porch make an important statement about a house's character and pretensions. To clap an outsize, ornate and pompous entrance porch on to a clean-lined modern semi-detached frontage is on a par with putting aitches where there shouldn't be any to impress the children's headmaster: it is a waste of time, and it does not work. Additions like that say all too obviously that the owners really wanted to move to a manor, but could not afford it.

Specialist firms can offer you beautifully hand-crafted, hardwood and glass Victorian porches and verandahs, and a range of other

The TRADA timber roof structure chosen for the Herefordshire cottage because it lends itself to self-build construction (*Drawings and photographs by courtesy of Christopher Morton, M Arch, ARIBA*)

styles. Whether or not the individual householder knows or cares about the age-old concept of unity of style — every part harmoniously fitting in with the whole — many people do, so if care is not taken to keep additions in style and proportion, the number of prospective buyers when the house is put on the market is reduced by the incongruity, and the value is reduced.

This point about unity needs to be made early on in this book; also, porches are one of the simplest parts of a house to build, or to enclose, but, because of their prominent position, easy to build badly from the visual standpoint. Of course, the principle of unity applies equally to all parts of a building, yet it is widely disregarded when extensions are built.

15

GARAGES

Relatively few pre-war houses built for the middle and lower income groups had garages attached to them, and it was quite a few years after the war that having a car became the rule rather than the exception. A garage is for this reason a first priority for many people when they decide to extend their house. In common with stables, garages are classed for planning purposes as extensions, even when totally separate from the house, if they are put up less than 5m (just short of 16½ft) away from it.

Since many families nowadays have two cars, a double garage may well enhance the saleability and value of a house in a prosperous area. In most cases, finances and space restrictions will rule out this option, but it is certainly worth making a single garage long and wide enough to take a large car, even if you have only a small one. Extra room is invaluable for storage shelves, DIY servicing, permanent chest-freezers and water-softener installations. Extra height, as well as length and width, may enable the garage to house a motor caravan or a high roof-rack. If you have a boat and boat trailer, or a caravan, your ideal may be a very long garage, or one with big doors at either end to give you a drive-through facility, enabling the trailed units to live at the back of the house. For some people, a garage is far too useful as a workshop to be wasted on sheltering a car, which can perfectly well be kept outside. If you were to go any further than this, however, and decide to make living quarters out of a garage, you could be in trouble with the planners.

Garage doors have improved vastly in recent

Before alteration, this house in Eastergate, Sussex, used to stop where you see the gutter of the main roof, above the ridge of the extension roof in the photograph. The living room was very small and there was no garage — just a tiny store enclosure projecting from the house front. There being plenty of room at the front of the house and no building line problem, the architect has had part of the existing store demolished, so that the space could be incorporated in the new garage, alongside which he has placed the new extension to the living room, and a new porch and lobby — all neatly covered by a new roof, partly flat but pitched at the front and hips. At the same time, the bedroom upstairs has been slightly enlarged by the addition of a second dormer window (*Norman R. Harrison*)

years, the deservedly popular up-and-over types being available without the cumbersome and obtrusive horizontal rail slides, their complete suspension housed in vertical channels at the sides. Builders like these systems as much as their customers do, because they are so simple to fit, bolting on to the frame sides at four points. There is a considerable variety of door-front designs, and several firms now market bolt-on door-opening units, which can be remote controlled and can be fitted to almost any existing up-and-over door.

If you do much of your own servicing — particularly if you look after an older car, spending more time under it than in it — and you are planning a new garage from scratch, it may be worth investigating having it built with an inspection pit in the floor. These pits have their problems, chiefly that they collect dirt which has to be swept out, and have to be kept carefully covered when not in use, if you have young children around.

A steel Georgian-style double up-and-over garage door by Westland Engineers, who also make 'Garamatic' automatic operating gear which can be fitted to any up-and-over door (*Westland Engineers Ltd*)

In bad weather, the usefulness of a garage is doubled when it is attached to the house and has a communicating door which allows you to walk into the house straight from the garaged car, without getting wet. You need not even get wet opening the garage's large door to drive in if you have a remote control fitted.

Foundations for a garage can be lighter, and therefore cheaper, than those for walls which might have to support two or three storeys. But if your garage is to be attached to ('contiguous with') your house, your architect and builder will probably advise you to have the foundations thick and strong enough for later additions to be built on over the garage without the necessity for any costly and difficult underpinning (post-building foundation

A modest back extension to a cottage in Eastergate, Sussex. Fitting snugly against the existing garage (to the left in the photograph), the addition provides a completely new dining area with direct access to the patio and a pleasant view on to the garden. A smaller projection (to the right of the picture) almost doubles the size of the previously minuscule kitchen, the extended part fitted out as a working area, leaving the former kitchen as a useful storage space, complete with refrigerator. The walls of the dining extension are hung with asbestos-cement 'Thrutone' slates to match those on the roof (*Norman R. Harrison*)

strengthening). The fact that the foundations are strong enough to take further building is a good selling point, even if you do not use the facility yourself.

PATIOS

A patio at the bottom of the garden is irrevocably part of the garden, whereas a patio starting directly outside a living room is in more ways than one an extension of the house. Even in the wettest and coldest parts of Britain, on a fair number of days in the year it can be very pleasant to open a door or French window on to a hard-surfaced area, especially if it has trees, shrubs and flowers planted in strategic places. With a modern sliding patio door, double glazed, easy to work and secure when closed, retreat from rain showers is quick and trouble free. Fitting patio doors — in aluminium, wood or uPVC (unplasticised polyvinyl chloride) — is the only alteration to the house itself you need to make to get this extra outdoor room; and you can make it attractive to look at, even in the rain or when the weather is too cold for sitting outside.

Amongst the facilities you can consider including in a patio designed as an extension to your living room are a flower-filled greenhouse, aviary, barbecue, and a fountain or other water display, such as a lily pool, cascade or waterfall. Moving-water installations cost very little to run, as the water is pumped round and round, and they can be very attractive lit up at night. One perennial problem — the most serious drawback to patio life in the summer — is that the indigenous insect population finds coloured lights in the darkness, not to mention eating outdoors, quite as enjoyable as we do. As with a growing number of twentieth-century difficulties, an electronic solution has been developed, in the form of a simple but ingenious insect trap. This is essentially the same as those used in fresh food shops, consisting of a high-intensity 'black light' tube (actually modified ultraviolet) mounted inside an electrified, self-cleaning grid. There is another grid outside this, so that only the pests get through and pets and wildlife cannot. Midges, flies and mosquitoes are irresistibly attracted to the black-light lure and fly through the outer grid to a quick death on the inner one. The units are weatherproof, so can be installed permanently outdoors, and come in different wattages, according to the area you need to keep insect free, from 15 watts, capable of covering about 2,000sq m (½ acre), up to 90 watts covering 8,000sq m (2 acres). They work indoors as well, but cover a much smaller area than when used outside.

Patio paving stones or blocks can be laid on a bed of sand or crushed clinker, since they carry only the weight of people and maybe the odd wheelbarrow. They are simply tamped into position with feet, or mallets and wood blocks, for pedestrian use, but if you have them laid in a drive for cars to run over, the job

The Flowtron electronic insect killer, which can be used either outdoors or indoors (*Picture by courtesy of Electronic Hygiene Ltd*)

will be longer and more expensive, because you then need a 150mm (6in) concrete base, on which they are bedded in mortar. Exceptions to this rule are the deeper, interlocking blocks. These still need the concrete, but are laid on sand and vibrated into place using a powered plate vibrator.

CONSERVATORIES

Conservatories are extensions consisting mostly of glass, set in a framework of wood, aluminium or steel as a rule, though latterly uPVC may form at least part of the structure. They may vary from small, modest units that are little more than lean-to greenhouses to large and imposing, even palatial, ones able to accommodate a swimming pool. They have the considerable advantage over patios of being weatherproof, keeping out rain, wind and snow; however, to be comfortable in sunny seasons they need either heat-reflecting glass or shading blinds, and of course they

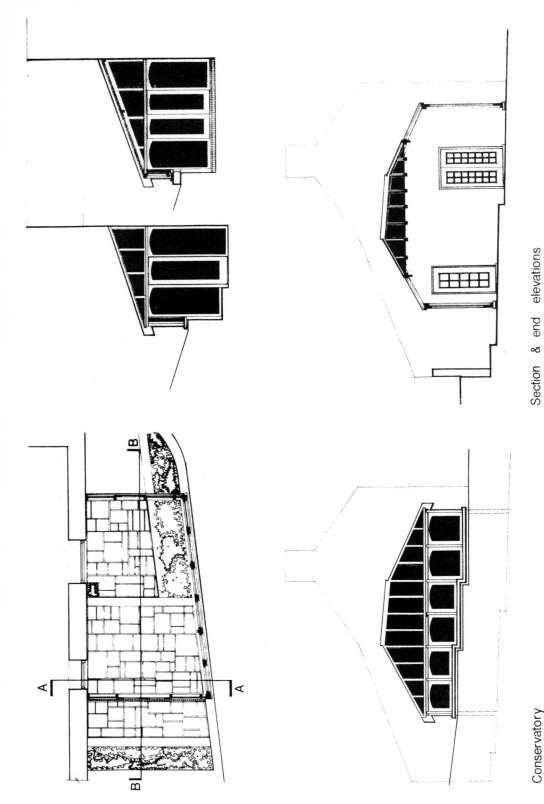

Section & end elevations

Conservatory
Ground floor plan & front elevation

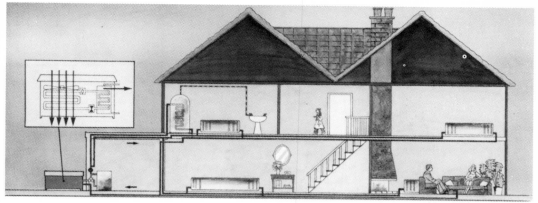

should have efficient ventilation.

Far from being just a revival of an old-time fad of the well-to-do, conservatories make good sense today from the energy-conservation viewpoint. Even in overcast conditions, they pick up and trap a fair amount of heat from the sun, which can be used in cold weather to supplement your fuel-burning system. The warm air in the conservatory can be tempted into the house naturally, by leaving open the door leading from it into the adjoining room. A more sophisticated method, adopted widely in American designs, uses fans and controlled high-level wall ventilators to direct warmed air to the interior. More advanced still are systems using heat pumps sited in a conservatory to extract heat from the air and feed it into a general or domestic water heating circuit. Heat pumps

Figs 4 & 5 This conservatory forms an extension to a cottage built in simple, vernacular style at Great Asby in Cumbria. It provides an extension to the indoor living space, as all conservatories do, but in this case the glazed area was conceived not as an indoor room but as an outdoor sitting space with protection from the elements. A slightly unusual roof shape has resulted from alignment with the existing retaining wall which, in common with the existing paved terrace, has been incorporated into the conservatory's design. Simple and robust painted timber windows and glazing bars are in sympathy with the style of the cottage, which had been already refurbished by the same architects. Both cottage and extension received a Civic Trust commendation in 1982, and also an award in the Trust's north-east 'House and Cottage' section (*Wm Binney Associates*)

Fig 6 This drawing shows how a heat pump can be used to boost the heat input into a standard wet central heating system. If the pump is powerful enough, it can be used instead of a boiler, but in either case its 'free' heat output is usually two or three times as great as the input represented by the electricity used to work its pumps. Figures quoted by manufacturers are normally based on the pump being used for two-thirds of the time on day-rate electricity and the remaining third on the more economic off-peak power (*Eastwood Heat Pumps*)

work similarly to refrigerators, taking heat from one place and giving it out in another. They need not be in a conservatory, but can extract heat from the air outside, or from coils buried deep in the ground or immersed in water that can be relied on not to freeze in winter, such as mill races. These ingenious units can transform low-temperature heat into warmth of a temperature suitable for heating systems. Although they run on electricity, they produce about two-thirds more heat from free sources than the amount of electricity they consume could provide. Some of the electricity can be bought at off-peak, 'white meter' rates, but even at normal tariff charges, running costs are economical.

Planning permission for a conservatory of the lean-to kind — which means most of the standard designs you can buy — is unnecessary, so long as its volume (not floor area) does not add more than 15 per cent to the volume of the original house. The absolute maximum volume for a conservatory put up without permission is 70cu m (slightly under 2,500cu ft).

(*above & right*) These photographs of prefabricated glazed extensions clearly demonstrate the wide range of possibilities of this type of structure. A really large glazed extension may accommodate a swimming pool, a jacuzzi whirlpool (plate 10) or a sun-lounge. Plate 9 shows the Aston 'Curve' — a small, relatively inexpensive conservatory providing a pleasant outdoor-view sitting room usable for most of the year. There is also a straight-eaved version of this conservatory — the 'Classic'. Both are made in a wide range of sizes (*Aston Home Extensions*)

(*opposite top*) The Marley sun-lounge. All the glass in this unit is toughened

(*bottom*) The Marley Celebrity conservatory, featuring white-painted, chip-resistant aluminium framework and bronze-tinted toughened glass, a permanently vented ridge section and louvre vents in the flanks

Fig 7 This drawing well illustrates how much more spacious a well-designed conservatory appears than a normal interior room of similar dimensions would, and underlines the degree of rain protection afforded by the overhanging roof

(pages 25–6)
Figs 8–11 This conservatory is designed to harmonise with the large Victorian house in Cumbria on to which it is built. Proportions, styling and materials had to be in keeping with the high quality of the main house — which is constructed largely in local limestone, with sawn sandstone surrounds to the windows and doors and has a steeply pitched slate roof. The architect had to make the conservatory serve several purposes: as an extension of the existing drawing room; as winter quarters for part of the owner's collection of exotic birds; and as a sheltered viewing point for the gardens and for

the outdoor aviaries in the gardens. An enclosed space within the conservatory has been provided for the indoor winter aviary, with provision for fine environmental control. Since the conservatory fits into the angle formed by the main part of the house and one of the wings, and receives much direct sunlight, a partially rather than fully glazed roof was decided on to reduce the problems of solar heat gain in summer and loss of heat in winter. This presented the opportunity of creating an open-air breakfast area on the flat roof outside the main bedroom. A separate thermostat for each part of the conservatory is incorporated into the heating/cooling system. The extract ventilation is linked to a heat pump, which transfers the surplus energy to the domestic hot water system, some gains being possible even during winter. Heat pump and extract fans are located in a small box at the edge of the flat roofed part of the conservatory, where the enclosure forms a useful seat (*Wm Binney Associates*)

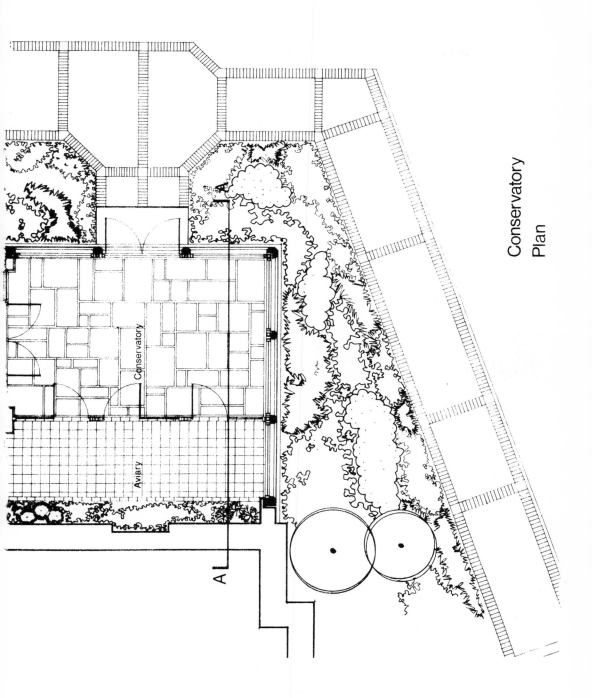

Conservatory
Plan

Conservatory

Aviary

A

Conservatory
Front elevation

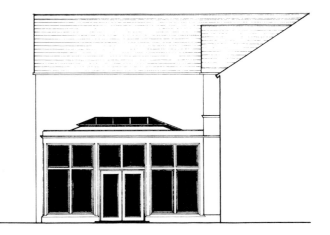

Conservatory
Side elevation

26

Conservatory
Section

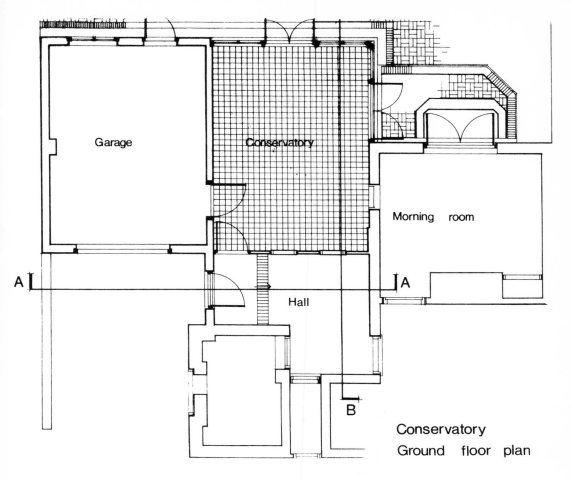

Garage

Conservatory

Morning room

A | | A

Hall

B

Conservatory
Ground floor plan

There is no compulsion, of course, to have living greenery growing in a conservatory. If you like the softening look of plants, but lack green fingers, have little time to cultivate growing things, or if you happen to be allergic to them in some way, you can always take a leaf out of the book of the business world, where silk-polyester artificial plants and flowers are widely used, both in foyers and in offices. Extremely lifelike, if unchanging, in appearance and texture, they do demand a bit of maintenance, in the form of an occasional wipe with soapy water. Otherwise, they are virtually everlasting, and trouble free.

(above and overleaf)
Figs 12–15 This conservatory forms an integral part of a larger extension, which includes a garage, new rear entrance and morning room. The whole construction is designed to be sympathetic to the existing house, which is built in the style of the turn-of-the-century arts and crafts movement. The house's steep roof and the limited depth available for the extension gave rise to problems in design, and the architects also had to ensure that the extension formed a positive and secure barrier between the accessible front garden and the private rear part of it. Steep roof pitches parallel to those of the existing house are used in the extension structures, the glazed conservatory section linking the slated garage roof and the main house, with a small lead-covered flat roof above the new rear entrance. Details are carefully designed to harmonise with those of the original house. Tiling, brickwork and glazing match completely. Simple industrial double-glazing units are used for the conservatory roof, which incorporates three opening rooflights with automatic control *(Wm Binney & Associates)*

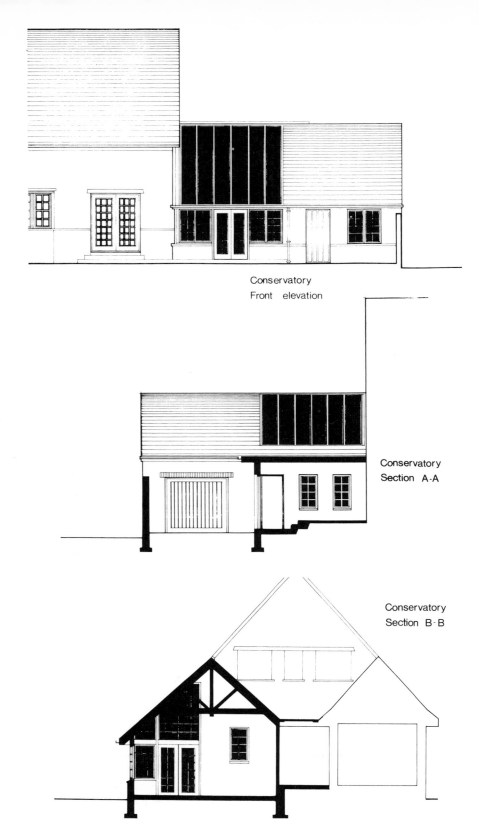

Conservatory
Front elevation

Conservatory
Section A-A

Conservatory
Section B-B

People living in glass houses can only throw stones if their conservatories are glazed with safety glass — be it toughened, tempered or laminated, or with a clear polycarbonate glazing sheet material, such as Makrolon. Makrolon is available in single, double and triple skin forms, for higher thermal insulation — produced as in double and triple glass panes, by trapping air between the sheets, except that the separation is effected by connecting webs of polycarbonate, instead of sealing strips. Whether you or the manufacturer specifies safety glass throughout the structure or not, it has to be used in parts under rules specified in British Standard 6262, which also lays down ratios between pane size and glass thickness where untempered glass can be used.

Factory-made conservatories, marketed in a vast range of designs, sizes and specifications by firms such as Aston Home Extensions, Banbury Homes & Gardens and Marley Buildings, offer a good deal of extra room for the outlay involved, whether you choose a small and simple one costing a few hundred pounds, or a more elaborate construction which might cost a few thousand. Their relatively low price level, compared to that of a similar sized extension put up by normal building methods, is easily explained: they are light structures, having only themselves to support, not needing expensively heavy foundations to stand on; and they are prefabricated, simple and quick to put together without big labour costs. You are buying an off-the-peg item, but looking down the row of your neighbours' houses you would be most unlikely to see one just like it. In any case, as with an off-the-peg suit or coat, if the fit is good, who is going to notice?

Conservatories, rather more matter-of-factly called greenhouses in the USA where some of the current designs originated, or in some brochures called sun-lounges, do not have to be standard at all. Architects love designing them to order. One designed and built as a one-off special can scarcely fail to blend in with your existing home as if it had been part of it from the outset — and that, in

Fig 16 The Solairal rooflight consists of two very rigid tubular sections, one for the fixed frame and one for the opening light, two hinges and a special remote opening system. Quick to assemble and highly reliable, the Solairal rooflight is the key part in conservatory ventilation, which it both regulates and checks. It also offers the most efficient way of fighting condensation. A 1cm opening is enough to eliminate this disadvantage and to maintain ventilation even when the occupier is away (*Technal*)

a nutshell, is the main advantage of an architect-designed extension. That is not to imply that architects have had nothing to do with designing the standard units on the market, but their job is to design a standard, ready-to-build item which gives excellent value for money.

REARRANGING AND ENLARGING EXISTING ROOMS

In general, rearranging the shape and division of existing rooms in your house or flat is less expensive than extending outwards. In the case of a flat on an intermediate level, of course, this is your only option. In a top flat, you may possibly be able to expand upwards, if you have rights over the roof space, and in a ground-floor flat you may be able to extend outwards, as if it were a house. It is when you start digging out new foundations, moving pipes, manholes and cables around, that costs rise higher.

If reorganising your interior space can solve your problems, there are few alterations that are technically impossible, though there are some that are more troublesome, and therefore more expensive, to carry out than others.

All the garages in this street of modern houses at Barnham in Sussex project forward from the fronts of the main houses. The architect has here taken advantage of the advanced building line resulting from this feature to fit in a substantial and excellently integrated extension to the dining room, taking the new roof right over the previously flat-roofed garage to achieve the valuable 'been there for ever' look to the finished job (*Norman R. Harrison*)

Dividing large rooms into smaller ones is in principle easier than taking out dividing walls to make two or more rooms into one, because walls added in can be very light in construction, putting little strain on existing parts of the structure — possibly even strengthening it. At the same time, modern cladding and insulating materials can give them all the sound-deadening, impact-resistant and decorative qualities needed.

Once you start taking walls away, however, the problem of providing support in some other way for whatever they were holding up, or together, arises, unless they happen to be 'dummy' or non-load-bearing walls. This means careful calculation of the section and type of beam or arch to be substituted for the wall to be removed, very skilled work getting it into place — as it has to be built in and doing its job before the original wall is taken away —

and equally skilled making-good of the inevitable scars of the operation. With a timber-frame structure, both original structure and difficulties are lighter, but most of the small-rooms-into-big-ones alterations occur in brick- or stone-built property, where the substitute support has to be a heavy RSJ (rolled steel joist) and the cutting in and out work entails a lot of noise and dust.

Failing the availability of enough existing space for internal room enlargement, you will have to consider extending outwards, building on new wall and roof sections to acquire the extra space you need. At the front of a house, this is generally difficult or impossible because of the restrictions imposed by planning authorities' insistence on maintaining the building line of the street, so unless you have an isolated property you will almost certainly need to think in terms of spreading out to the sides or back. Assuming no boundary or planning permission prohibitions, your least costly option is to extend ground-floor rooms, using flat-roof constructions rather than pitched. If you need more room higher up, it is more economical to build extra storeys at the same time as the ground-floor one than to add them on later in a separate operation. In the event of your either not wanting or not being allowed to extend at ground level, yet needing to extend upstairs rooms, it is technically possible to have upper stages sticking out, but as this involves cantilevering the support beams, it tends to be an expensive job. One reason for doing it may be to leave an open walkway down the side of the building where it adjoins the boundary, rather than creating a covered (and probably heated) but largely under-utilised passage.

Balconies can be cantilevered out at first- or higher-floor levels, using rather lighter constructions than covered extensions. If you are considering upper-floor balconies, you could perhaps support them on pillars to give yourself a verandah underneath, possibly doing away with the cantilevering problem in the process.

For a relatively small outlay, adding on a bay window can make a significant difference to the amount of space available in a room and a world of difference to its character. Originally designed to allow a panoramic view, bay windows fell into some disrepute due to the tendency of older types to let warm air out and cold air in. Modern frames and weather sealing, however, coupled with insulation glazing, overcome the cold-radiator and draught problems completely, so you can have all the benefits of a bay window without the traditional penalties.

One extremely useful and popular form of bay window is the large, rectangular kind that is effectively a small, outshot extra room, usable as a kitchen, dining section or sitting area. These bays are unfortunately all too easy to put up with minimal attention to their looks from outside, so that they are unnecessarily ugly and obtrusive. A modern conservatory would serve much the same purpose in many cases for equivalent cost of construction, possibly lower.

CONVERTING EXISTING ATTICS INTO HABITABLE ROOMS

A vast number of older houses have commodious roof spaces which, either at the time they were built or afterwards, have been pressed into service as attics. Building regulations have not always been as stringent as they are now, so there are probably many attics being used as normal rooms quite illegally. To make a room in the roof legally habitable, it has to conform to building regulation requirements — as interpreted by your local authority's building inspectorate — concerning overall space, minimum headroom over a prescribed area, ventilation, window positioning and fire precautions. You may not use it as a bedroom, for example, unless it satisfies the inspector in all these matters and has a permanent staircase. A loft-ladder is not enough.

Not only must the attic itself conform to these demands, but, since you are putting on an extra storey from the official viewpoint, you may also find that the fire resistance of lower-floor doors and passageways may have to be upgraded, usually to 'half-hour' standard. If the staircase you put in is enclosed, fire-resistant materials will have to be used in the construction, because under fire conditions an enclosed stairway acts as a chimney, funnelling smoke and flames upwards.

Complying with fire regulation requirements is not necessarily expensive, but it does mean forethought in choosing and using materials. Professional builders and carpenters take this as a matter of course, knowing their work is bound to be inspected, but a DIY constructor may fail to do so unless warned. Emphasis is laid on the regulation at this point, because converting roof spaces is not too difficult for non-professionals, who can do a lot to their own houses without drawing the inspectorate's attention.

Fire-resistant materials abound in the building trade, mostly looking not at all out of the ordinary. So if you do or have something done to your attic, you will not have to put up with slabs of sheet steel and rough-textured industrial-looking boards. Most boards, insulating slabs, batts, rolls and tiles are officially tested and given ratings under British Standard (BS) 476 for fire resistance (how long to burn through on the test rig), ignitability, fire propagation (contribution to fire growth) and surface spread of flame. For the last mentioned, Class 0 is extremely good, Class 3 pretty miserable — though remember that spread-of-flame ratings are often affected, for better or worse, by decorative treatment. Paint a board with a good rating with gloss paint and you make it worse. Conversely, a board with a medium rating can acquire a better one if you paint it with emulsion.

Roof constructions are tested as complete units — wood, waterproof (sarking) felt, battens, tiles and all. Specimens 838mm (33 in) square are blasted with flame under controlled conditions and given separate class ratings (A to D) for fire resistance and spread of flame. Under BS 476 Part 3, a roof system may get a rating Class BA EXT F X. From that you know it will resist penetration under fire conditions for half an hour (first letter), that it shows no tendency at all to spread flame (second letter), that it was tested flat (EXT F) as opposed to inclined (EXT S) and that it either developed a hole during the test or began to drip (suffix X). A most unlikely combination, but it demonstrates the principles behind the coding.

BS 476 Part 4 specifies a non-combustibility test. Products and materials passing this are 'classed as non-combustible under BS 476 Part 4'. Part 5 of this standard is an ignitability test, an X rating signifying easy to set alight, and a P rating, not easy.

Part 7 sets out the test under which boards and similar products are given surface spread-of-flame ratings, and Part 8 specifies test methods and criteria for establishing the fire resistance of construction elements under different load-bearing conditions.

This is a simplified account of the tests and standards involved, some of which are quite complex; but they are simple in intent, being designed to ensure that where there is a fire risk, materials and methods suited to the situation will be used. In terms of finding out what you can and cannot do, complexities are enormously reduced by the very tightness of the regulations. It is almost a case of what is not forbidden being compulsory. The golden rule is, whether building yourself or having the work done, hire competent design services and have the plans approved before you start.

EXTENDING INTO THE ROOF SPACE FROM SCRATCH

Expanding into virgin roof space has much to be said for it. In most pitched-roof houses there is a great deal more rectangular space available for exploitation than you think, and even more room to be taken advantage of if you are prepared to tolerate some sloping sections of wall and/or ceiling in your reclaimed rooms. As you are not extending the area of ground covered by your house, planning and neighbour objections are less likely than with side or back extensions. Heavy reconstruction and 'wet trade' work is usually unnecessary; delays in conversion work due to bad weather are limited to waiting for a dry day to put the windows in, except where the vertical clearance in your roof is so limited that it is essential to raise the whole cover. This makes the house walls higher, but the extra need not be masonry. It can be constructed in timber, with suitable cladding, in many cases.

Loft rooms in some houses can be enormous, and they need not be bedrooms, utility rooms or playrooms. Bathrooms, sitting rooms, music rooms, studios, offices — even saunas and steam rooms — are feasible. There is a subtle charm about roof rooms, which can give the feeling of the artist's tucked-away garret, the eagle's eyrie or the plutocrat's penthouse. Treetops at eye level, greater than usual distance from everyday sound sources outside and inside the house, dramatic lighting effects from sloping windows and a general feeling of being suspended timelessly in space all contribute to their fascination.

There are practical problems to be overcome in making living space in an area designed to house spiders, water cisterns, pipework and junk. To start with, upper-floor ceilings are hung as a rule on very light joists — maybe only half the size and strength of those used for intermediate floors — so new, strong beams have to be introduced to make it possible to lay a proper floor. Almost certainly the plumbing and electric wiring dotted about at random will have to be re-planned and re-routed. Some methods of roof construction use rafter support struts that are disposed in a V-formation, resting on a massive central joist. They have to be cut out, once the roof has been strengthened by other means, because they interfere with the rectangular space that you want. Older houses, otherwise classically suitable for loft conversions, often have support battens for tiles or slates nailed straight on to the rafters, so that there is no waterproof sarking felt to stop any leaks. In the northern counties of England and in Scotland, the slates or tiles will probably have been 'torched' (backfilled with mortar) to stop them blowing away in high winds. However, when there is going to be nothing but outside roof between you and the elements, you want that roof to be absolutely watertight, so sarking may have to be inserted. As the felt or other waterproof membrane goes between rafters and tile battens, these have to be taken off and replaced over it.

Thermal insulation is another consideration to be taken into account. However cold, damp and generally badly built your original house may be, any new work done on it has to be carried out to present-day building regulations, unless there are very special reasons for them to be relaxed — as they occasionally are in the case of listed buildings. To meet current standards (dealt with in detail in the section on building materials in Chapter 7), a pitched-roof section will need a somewhat greater thickness or higher quality of insulation material than is needed over ceiling joists to produce a given performance. Since the greatest proportion of the heat lost, or gained from the sun, in your house passes through the roof, it needs to be thermally efficient, passing the minimum of heat in either direction. Unless the insulating material used is a closed-cell product — rigid urethane foam, for example — it is usual to leave an air space of abot 25mm (1in) between insulation and sarking, as an insurance against moisture condensation. So it may be necessary to build up the thickness of the rafters to obtain the required thickness without compressing the insulation and so reducing its effect.

A rough idea of the extent of usable room in the roof of your house can be obtained by climbing up there and balancing your way carefully round on the joists. Take a measured stick or a tape rule with you and mark the rafters with chalk to show where a 6ft-tall person could stand upright. Mark where the feet would be on the joists. When you have done this on all the sides where the roof slopes, you can measure the approximate floor area which will count as 2.3m (7½ft) high living space, though vertical walls are allowed to be as low as 1.5m (a little under 5ft) where they meet the sloping ceiling.

The proportion of extensions in Britain which are loft conversions is relatively small, though in terms of absolute numbers plenty of such conversions are carried out. However, a loft conversion is a type of extension far less familiar to the average local builder than are garage, side and back projects. A number of national and local contractors specialise in loft conversion work and its peculiar problems, and consequently have more direct experience of them than a general builder can normally obtain. Some of the specialist firms are very large, the largest in the UK, Crescourt Loft Conversions, having not only its own architectural department for producing designs and drawing plans, but also manufacturing facilities for staircases and windows, a steelwork fabrication department and structural engineering services. Whilst bearing in mind the firm's size, Crescourt's total of 15,000 loft conversions in the sixteen years up to 1983 serves to emphasise the breadth of experience to be expected from a contractor working exclusively in roof-space conversion.

A typical train of events in getting a conversion done by a large loft contractor, once you have made an enquiry to its head office or to a representative, might start with a visit from the company's local surveyor. He will look over your roof and house, listen to your requirements and go away for a day or two to prepare a scheme, which will come to you with a written quotation for the work specified. Normally this price will exclude decoration. At 1983–4 prices, a loft conversion might cost you anywhere from £3,000 to £25,000, with the average somewhere between £6,000 and £8,000 — low by comparison with the figure for a side or back extension.

If the specification and price appeal to you, the next step is to have a look at a conversion or two previously carried out in your area by the company. Assuming you want to go ahead after that, you will sign a contract and probably pay a deposit which will be in the region of 10 per cent of the estimated cost — this usually being the last payment you will asked

to make until the job is complete.

There should then be a very detailed structural survey, not affecting the price, for the purpose of drafting plans and making applications for planning consent if necessary and building regulations approval in any case. The company should make these for you. The wait for planning consent will probably be the longest one involved — from a few weeks to three months, depending on the way your local authority works. Once the plans are approved, materials will most likely arrive within two or three weeks, the job will be started seven or ten days later and, unless your conversion is extraordinarily big or complex, may be finished in another two or three weeks. Most loft conversion firms offer a guarantee. Make sure that your firm does — it is reasonable to expect them to underwrite their quality for three to five years.

In smaller houses, one of the most delicate problems is usually where to site the staircase. Many semi-detached houses have upstairs landings far too restricted to accommodate a permanent flight of stairs, so some space will probably have to be taken off one of the larger bedrooms for the purpose. Where a straight staircase, with or without a turn, does not fit neatly into the situation, it may be worth investigating the possibility of a spiral one. Models exist with overall diameters as small as 1,420mm (4ft 8in). Particularly bulky items of furniture — a piano, for example — may be hoisted through the hole before the stair is installed, or even through window apertures during construction. Spiral staircases can in many instances take up less floor space in a loft room than standard straight ones, and make visually attractive features into the bargain.

Unless normal windows can be built into vertical gables, roof-room windows have to be either dormers, which have vertical panes and flat, curved or sloping rooflines interrupting those of the main roof pitch, or roof windows of the Velux type, lying flush with the original roof in most cases, though occasionally slightly raised at the top for roof pitches between 10° and 20°. A roof's pitch is the angle between the

The casing of this small dormer is moulded in grp (glass-reinforced plastic) and its window is a sliding aluminium unit. The roof around it is covered with Cascade profiled metal panels, which look convincingly like individually fixed, scalloped tiles. Being very light, and fixed by a special clip system, they are particularly suitable for steep pitches. Here newly laid and therefore still bright, these copper 'tiles' will soon acquire the characteristic soft green patina of the metal. Cascade roofing panels can equally well be used for vertical cladding and are made in colour coated steel as well as in copper (*IMI Broderick Structures*)

A Roto roof window fitted with exterior awning blind (*W. H. Colt [London] Ltd*)

slope of its rafters and the horizontal plane.

Dormer windows may be built up on site or factory made and fitted into prepared openings. Some of the smaller types are moulded in GRP (glass-reinforced plastic) with uPVC or aluminium window frames. Loft-conversion specialists tend to favour dormers of very generous dimensions, because they present a valuable method of creating the maximum of rectangular space in a steeply slooping roof void. With careful matching in, such windows can be used without making the house look too top heavy, but badly executed dormers can be real eyesores — you can see plenty of them on an urban bus or train journey.

Light comes through a dormer window with very much the same effect as in normal rooms, where the height and width of the unit are fairly large. Narrower dormers funnel their light intriguingly into the room, often having no panes at the sides, so that shafts of sunlight, shadows and reflections play on the side walls. Older dormers with uninsulated sides and roofs and single glazing tend to make a roof room very cold, though with remedial additions of insulation and double sealed units you can avoid this problem.

Traditionally, dormer windows have been regarded as superior to 'skylights' or roof windows set flush with the tiles because they were far less likely to leak in wet weather, a habit for which the skylight was notorious. Present-day roof windows, however, are a very different proposition. Flashing — the formed metal strip which surrounds the frame outside, tucking under the tiles to keep water out at top and sides, and over them at the bottom to let it run off — can now be relied on to do the job indefinitely. Double-glazed opening frames, though they can be traditionally top-hung, are normally pivoting types, reversible for cleaning. Some of these can be swung open sideways if need be, to provide an emergency escape facility. Above all, modern roof windows — at least, those worth the name — are clad outside in non-corroding metal, so you never have to bother painting them.

A roof window should be of such a size, and

35

so positioned in the roof slope, that people can see clearly out whether they are sitting or standing. Size for size, a roof window will let more light in than a dormer, because it is set at an angle. Since this virtue can also become a vice, in the sense that a pane catching more light can equally well admit heat and glare from the sun, some form of shading is needed. Manufacturers provide several options. If you are prepared to accept a reduced amount of light from the window, it can be fitted with a heat- and light-reflecting outer pane, which typically cuts both by something over 40 per cent. Internal, foil-coated blinds not only keep out glare, but efficiently darken the room when you want to sleep, watch TV or project films or slides. Decorated fabric roller blinds, however, should be good enough for normal shading. Provided your roof pitch is 30° or over, you can have venetian blinds incorporated in the specification. The most effective sun shields are PVC exterior awning blinds, which keep the sun off the glass altogether. More practical than they sound, these are operated from the inside, rolling neatly up inside the window's top cover when not required.

Not all roof windows are used in roof rooms. Some downstairs extensions have sloping roofs, and they can perfectly well be mounted in these. In such situations they will most likely need remote controls — cords, rods, hand winding or electrical gear — to open and close them. Here, they will be supplementing vertical windows in the wall, so heat- and light-reflecting glass probably makes more sense than blinds.

Apart from the special models already mentioned for inclusion in 10° pitch roofs (technically classed as 'flat'), roof windows are suitable for roof pitches from 15° to 85°.

BUILDING ON COMPLETE NEW ROOMS

Building on a completely new room brings you a problem that you miss when simply enlarging an existing one — that of access. If the only way you can walk into an added-on living or dining room is through a previously existing room, there is no undue inconvenience. Where a bedroom, on the other hand, can be reached only from another bedroom, the value of the extra room is greatly reduced in practical terms and it does not increase the number of bedrooms you can label your house as having if and when you want to sell it. Consequently, a bedroom without independent access to a hall or landing will not increase the value of your house by as much as a truly private room.

Ideally, larders should be accessed from kitchens, storerooms from hallways, landings or garages, and cloakrooms, bathrooms and kitchens from hallways or landings. It is advantageous for a ground-floor kitchen to have a door to the outside as well, preferably one that keeps clear of pantry, larder or storeroom doors sited nearby. Designers and builders ought to avoid this kind of door-opening clash, but in smaller kitchens it often happens. Sometimes it is impossible to move either of the mutually incompatible doorways through sheer lack of space, but even then, the one that does not have to cope with weather can be a bi-fold type (hinged in the middle as well as at the side, so that it folds to half its width on opening). Alternatively, there are excellent plastic, pleated folding doors on the market which can seal an interior opening quite as effectively as a solid door, and need no painting. These hang from a track, rather as a curtain does, usually on nylon T-supports, and the better ones have a trellis metal frame on top for greater control over the folding action.

Fig 18 Greatly increased accommodation has been achieved in what was originally a two-bedroom bungalow near Denbigh by adding a carefully designed extra storey at the garage end. Downstairs, a covered way in front of the garage has been created, together with a new breakfast room next to the kitchen. At the same time, the bathroom has been converted into a toilet, since the new upper storey contains a new bathroom. Bedrooms 1 and 2 downstairs became bedrooms 2 and 3, as the master bedroom was moved upstairs into the new extension, which also features a walk-in wardrobe and capacious storeroom (*G. Parry Davies & Associates*)

36

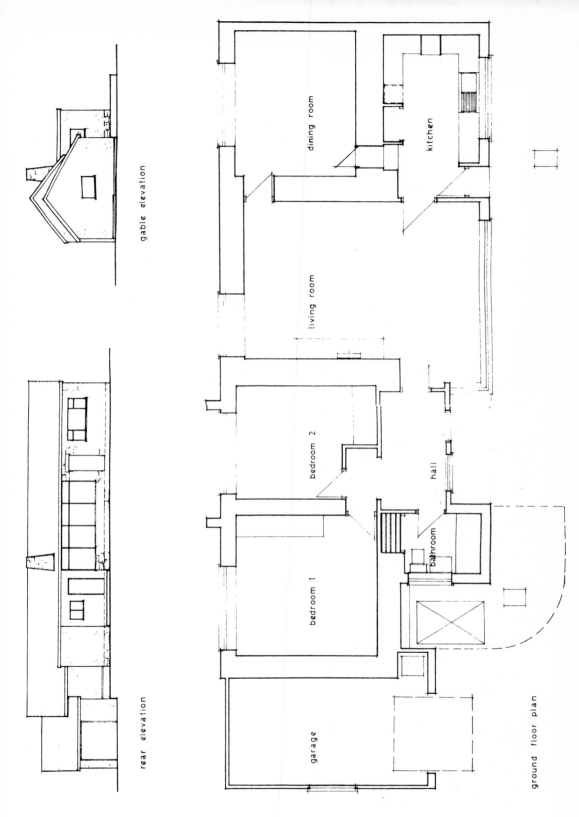

gable elevation

dining room

kitchen

living room

bedroom 2

hall

bedroom 1

bathroom

garage

rear elevation

ground floor plan

A rare case, where there was virtually no restriction on space, so the architect was able to more than double the size of this lodge in Adsdean, Sussex, adding downstairs a porch, split-level hall, lobby, cloakroom and large conservatory and upstairs a new master bedroom and gallery, beyond which the conservatory reaches to full roof height. Extensive alterations to the existing part of the lodge were made to extend and rearrange kitchen, living and bedrooms. Much careful work was required to preserve the essential character of the original lodge, leaded lights being repositioned in new frames and salvaged tiles being re-used. The new building is on the right (*Norman R. Harrison*)

(*top right*) Modern laminates used to produce a light and airy effect in the English Rose 'Kensington' kitchen (*Ideal Timber Products*)

(*right*) The 'Warwick' natural hardwood kitchen in the English Rose range

Maximum utilisation of corner cupboard under-counter space in the Glendale 'Culture' kitchen (*Glendale Furniture*)

Formica 'Antique Cork' laminate looks and feels like real cork, but does not have the same tendencies to flake or fade with the passage of time.

Bi-fold and concertina folding doors are also convenient for cloakrooms and storerooms, as they take up little or no space on restricted landings or in narrow hallways. As bi-fold systems use rigid, narrow door panels, these can be the louvred type, which afford a certain amount of ventilation for a cloakroom or store.

In addition to considering entrances to new rooms, you should also think about the services they need and where these will come from and go to. A bathroom — or even a bedroom with a shower enclosure and/or a pedestal sink or vanitory unit — has to have piped hot and cold water and a convenient drain to connect with its waste pipes. Waste pipes in particular need to be kept fairly short to work at their best. Unthoughtful planning can lead to long horizontal runs inside or to over-long pipes on the outside wall — much more vulnerable to freezing weather than short runs which empty quickly. You can move or extend existing drains, but this is an expensive job which can often be avoided by siting a new washing or bathing facility close to the existing units.

Drain access can be especially problematical when you need an extra toilet in a particular place and it turns out to be difficult or impossible to bring the standard 100mm (4in) soil pipe to it. In these situations, you can install a special type of toilet unit, which works absolutely normally as far as the user is concerned, but which requires only a standard 19mm

(¾in) plumbing pipe for the waste. It incorporates a waste-macerating unit similar to an under-sink waste grinder and an automatic pump. The narrow pipe is easy to route along long and awkward paths to connect with the main large soil pipe, which can be up to 65ft away.

Add-on extensions are not necessarily individual rooms. Where there is plenty of ground space to build on, they can be quite large, even incorporating separate suites of rooms — with or without their own means of access and services. Quite a number of firms now offer what can broadly be described as package-deal extensions, some based on prefabricated components, others designed or modified for your particular needs. The Marleywing is a good example, using steel-reinforced, precast concrete wall sections, with polystyrene slab insulation and plasterboard lining, flat roofs with polyisocyanurate insulation and double-glazed aluminium doors and windows. As the components are standard, they can be produced in a factory at economical cost, so that extensions built with them can be attractively priced. Precast panels are quicker to put up than walls built brick by brick, so there is also a time-saving benefit. Standard components can be fitted together in a number of different combinations to produce a required overall size, with doors and windows where required, so the systems are quite flexible. Exact matching of their finish to that of the rest of your house depends, however, on how close that is to one of the wide range of standard panel finishes.

Aston Home Extensions have a different approach to the package-deal extension, using specialised building methods, centralising and systematising the organisation of all services, from surveying and planning to site supervision, to achieve speed and consistency of performance. This company has a patented process by which it claims not only to be able to match existing finishes — including brick, stone, mortars and renders — but to 'age' and weather new walls into the bargain. Windows are again standard, but available options

include wood, aluminium and plastic in a variety of styles.

Amongst the advantages of dealing with a firm that operates on a large — in some cases national — scale are that you have a clear if somewhat Hobson's-choice contract with an organisation whose profits are adversely affected by delays in construction. Having a corporate identity, they are more sensitive to adverse public comment than the small, private builder. This fact works for you if there does happen to be some cause for dissatisfaction, and makes such cause less likely to arise.

Their salesmanship is as professional as their other services as a rule. Your enquiry will be dealt with in a businesslike manner, with written answers to your questions if you want them. So long as a sales representative or executive is on a firm's payroll, you are unlikely to be plied with claims that cannot be substantiated; there is not the overriding need to make a sale regardless of all ethical considerations that can sometimes drive the commission-only salesperson to make exaggerated statements.

CREATING SELF-CONTAINED SUITES OF ROOMS

Although a package-deal company may design a scheme for producing separate sets of rooms, an architect working exclusively for you will certainly achieve a more satisfactory arrangement, from both the aesthetic and property-value points of view. Even if the extra accommodation is obtained by adding rooms on, as opposed to splitting off a set in a house large enough to allow it, the process of making two homes out of one is one of the most difficult to carry out, and not one which an extension firm is likely to have done very often.

A suite of rooms can be self-contained without going to the extent of providing separate access. This would give, say, an older relative effective privacy when there is no need for totally separate quarters. Once you make a completely independent dwelling, with its own lock and key, planning application fees and ultimately rates are both going to be higher than they are in respect of simply altering a house.

DESIGNING AND BUILDING FOR PEOPLE WITH A DISABILITY

It may be that the accommodation to be produced by extending your house is intended for the use, exclusive or shared, of a person with some form of disability. There are special problems associated with designing and building for handicapped people, but there is an enormous amount of advice, specialist knowledge and help available in the business of adapting living space to their needs, so that they can lead independent lives. In a short chapter, space allows only an outline of the kind of assistance procurable. Architects have to give a lot of thought to catering for disabled people when designing public buildings, so most of them will have a good deal of practical experience on the subject, in addition to having read, in the course of their career, several highly detailed books on it.

Specialist organisations — of which the Royal national institutes for the Blind and for the Deaf and the Spastics Society are only three of many — are well able to offer advice and help in connection with the specific disabilities they were founded to assist, but in the UK the single most comprehensive source of detailed information on all aspects of catering for people with handicaps is the Disabled Living Foundation. This registered charity maintains a showroom at its London headquarters in Harrow Road, crammed with displays of equipment and ordered stocks of manufacturers' literature. It also keeps a library of books, periodicals and official publications relevant to disability, and runs a continually updated information manual service on a subscription basis for architects, local authorities and other practitioners and organisations. Visits to the showroom are always made by appointment, and a small fee (waived in the case of disabled visitors) is charged for the facility, but this also includes the services of an information officer. There are many other aspects of the foundation's work, those outlined being the ones most useful in relation to fitting out living accommodation for the disabled.

The Department of the Environment has published an information pack entitled *Housing for the Elderly*, giving a great deal of hard fact in straightforward terms. There is also a British Standard, BS 5619 *Design of Housing for the Convenience of Disabled People*. Building adaptations and many items of special equipment which help handicapped people to lead independent lives qualify for grants covering some or all of the cost involved. The occupational therapist from your local Department of Health and Social Security office is in the best position to advise you as to the help available.

Security equipment

Life is not really independent if you have to leave your front door in the control of other people, so that they can drop in to check your state of well-being. Door-phone and electric remote-control lock systems, as used in blocks of flats, can solve this problem for a person with mobility limitations, combining good security with a convenient communication facility.

Another invaluable means of providing effective emergency arrangements with day-to-day privacy is an electronic personal alarm system, such as the Answercall. This uses a rechargeable, hand-held transmitter, with a light or buzzer warning that tells you when the battery is low. This transmitter activates a central control box via receiver units installed in every room — and in garage, garden or greenhouse if you use these. The circuit control box is connected to an automatic dialling unit (approved by British Telecom), programmed when the alarm button is pressed to call a preset series of numbers one after the other in a preset sequence for up to ten minutes, delivering a recorded request for help on getting through.

Heating and general arrangements

Heating systems should be powerful in relation to the thermal insulation qualities of the structure, and should ideally provide for individual temperature control in each room. Windows should allow a clear view outside from a chair or bed, and should be easy to open and shut, manually or electrically, as appropriate to the disability involved. Power points should be plentiful and set — as should switches for lights — at door-handle height. The Elektrak socket system may have advantages over the standard type for some people, as the plugs are less fiddly to locate and intrinsically safer to use. Meters and fuse boxes should be accessible, and have easy-to-read labels, dials or digits. All carpets and other floor coverings should be non-slip types. TV and telephone sockets should be planned in at an early stage, and early thought also given to the provision of rubbish-disposal facilities. A chute may well be more practical than the usual bin system.

Mobility

For people whose disability allows them to move about reasonably well on foot, normal staircases are fine, but they should have easy-grip handrails, preferably on both sides, fitted at a height convenient to the person concerned and extending a minimum of 300mm (1ft) beyond top and bottom step nosings. Stair treads should not exceed 175mm (7in) in height and their 'going' (length from nosing to next riser) should be at least 265mm (10½in) for easy negotiation. People who walk only with difficulty, or not at all, will need mechanical assistance to move from one floor to another — where, for example, the rooms they have are not all on the same level, or if they are not on the ground floor.

A lift in an enclosed shaft is one solution to the difficulty, but it is very expensive and unlikely to be necessary. Several specialist firms make simpler but no less effective devices costing much less to install. One of these is a personal — one-person — lift which runs on vertical rails fixed to a wall. The user sits in an enclosed and topless box, rather like a church pew but infinitely more comfortable. The box is lifted straight up on to the upper floor through a hatchway, which is completely closed by an anti-draught device once the lift is at rest.

Where there is a staircase available, a stair-climber could be the answer to the problem of mobility between floors, particularly when the stairs are shared with people able to walk. Mounted on metal tube or channel guides neatly and unobtrusively at one side of the stair, the carriage may be a folding or non-folding chair, a standing platform with support rails or a platform designed to takes its passenger in a wheelchair. Different models are made to cope with different stair configurations and gradients. All types start and stop well clear of top and bottom steps, and have efficient fail-safe devices.

Driveways and the entrances to car ports and garages for disabled people's vehicles should be at least 3m (10ft) wide, and access to the house from the parked vehicle should always be under cover. Wheelchairs need paths no narrower than 1m (3ft 3in), with firm, hard, rain-shedding surfaces free from loose gravel or other material — and this goes also for garden paths. All wheelchair paths need to be level, as far as possible, the steepest incline they can happily negotiate being 1 in 12. If because of the lie of the land a ramp as steep as this is necessary at the approach to an entrance door, there should be a level platform at its head 1.2m (4ft) long to allow secure parking whilst the door is unlocked and opened.

High thresholds are out, and all draught- and weather-sealing flanges or other projections should be mounted on the bottom of the door so that the hump for the chair to roll over is not more than 25mm (1in) high. Most standard door manufacturers market patterns which cater for this requirement. So long as the run in from the entrance door is straight, a doorway width of 750mm (2½ft) is adequate, but if the chair has to negotiate a right-angle turn immediately inside it, the doorway should be 850mm (2¾ft) wide. Doormats need to be

The Gimson Personal lift (*Gimson & Co [Leicester]*)

sunk in mat wells, and should be hard ones. The absolute minimum width for internal passageways is 900mm (3ft), ideally wider for wheelchairs — and it is no use measuring from wall to wall if there is a radiator mounted on one of them which reduces clearance.

Interior doors should afford a clear gap of 770mm (2ft 7in) when open, and should be hinged in the corners of rooms for easy chair entry. Where not hinged on a corner, the handle-side doorpost must be 300mm (1ft) from the nearest wall. Thresholds are banned altogether, and furniture and fittings must not

be placed so as to necessitate 90° turns as the chair enters. Except in very small toilets and bathrooms, side-hung doors, if properly positioned, are just as easy for a person in a wheelchair to operate as sliding ones.

Toilet aids
Toilet doors may open inwards or outwards, or slide, though inward opening is unlikely to be feasible where a small toilet room has to take a wheelchair, in which event it has to be wider than for a walking person. Privacy locks should have provision for emergency opening from outside, just as many patterns do for normal household use. A walking handi-

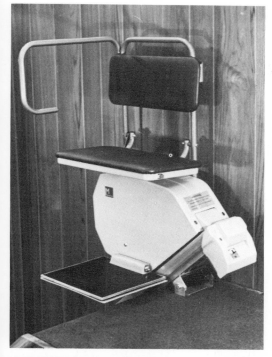

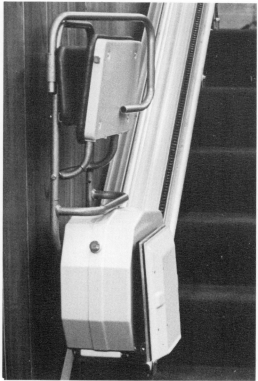

capped person may need very little in the way of special equipment, a little careful consideration on the choice of fittings making a lot of difference to ease of use. A minimum bowl rim height of 400mm to 425mm (16in to 17in) and a seat height of 425mm to 450mm (17in to 18in) is recommended.

Substantial grab handles (which walls must be strong enough to support) should have epoxy or nylon non-slip coatings and be positioned to suit the particular nature of the user's disability. Washbasins should be placed where they will not knock against a wheelchair, but should be reachable from a position seated on the toilet.

Standard toilet units can be fitted with a variety of accessories, from simple cushioned seats and backrests to micro-switch controls and supplementary seats incorporating automatic washing and drying facilities. Complete units with the washing and drying equipment built in are also available, both these and the accessory kits requiring an electric supply as well as the normal plumbing connections.

Bathing aids

In bathrooms, door and wheelchair access requirements are the same as those for toilets. If possible, a bathroom should have enough room for a wheelchair to turn round, to avoid the necessity of backing out. Showers are often preferred to baths, and should be provided either instead of baths or, where funds allow, in addition. Non-wheelchair people may be able to use a normal shower enclosure, fitted with a shower seat and perhaps a knee-operated control for the water flow. There are larger enclosures which will accommodate portable shower chairs or walking frames.

Baths for handicapped people should be a bit shorter than normal, between 1.6m and

Minivator Ambassador stairlift with seat down and footplate level with top step. With seat up, this lift can be used to transport a standing passenger (*Minivator*)

The Ambassador stairlift folds when not in use, so as to take up the minimum stair width and present no obstruction to normal traffic (*Minivator Sales Ltd*)

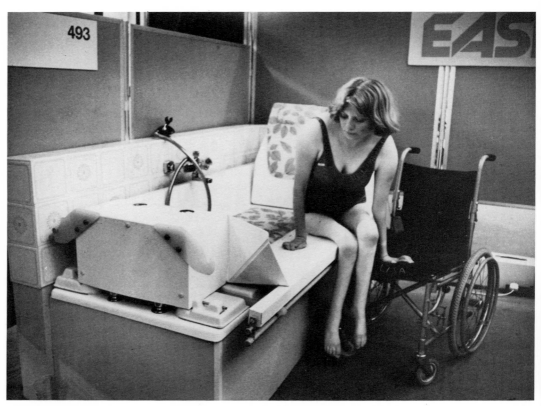

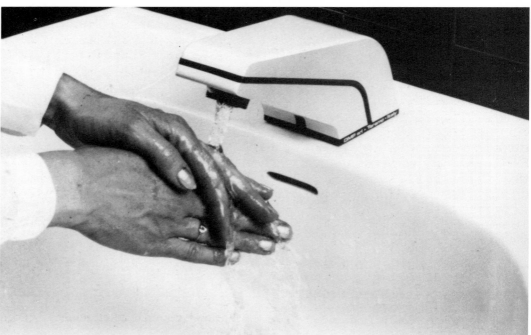

1.7m (5ft 3in and 5ft 7in), with flat bottoms and rims about 500mm (1ft 7in) off the floor. Unless there is some mechanical device for getting into and out of the bath, it should have a 400mm (1ft 4in) platform at the end opposite the taps to form a seat. The ultra-short Sitz bath does not need this, having a moulded-in shelf to sit on within its overall length of only 1.09m (3ft 7in). One highly developed version of the Sitz bath has a side-opening door, so that you can get in over its very low threshold. Once the door is closed, the bath can be filled up normally. This is Medic-Bath's XP model. Thermostatic control of all bath and shower water is well-nigh essential.

Quite a wide choice exists of aids enabling a disabled person to lift him or herself into and out of a normal bath. One is a swing seat, mounted on a heavy plate screwed to the floor next to the bath. Provided the user is able to turn a short handle on top of the upright pillar supporting the seat, it can be smoothly wound upwards and swung gently over the bath before being lowered in by reversing the handle rotation. An otherwise very similar device takes all the work out of the process by raising its pillar hydraulically, using the mains water supply to provide the power. This unit is controlled by a simple up/down lever at the side of the bath, carries up to 159kg (25st) and has a five-year guarantee. A similar guarantee is given with the third example — a polypropylene, watertight box which sits securely on top of the standard bath. Either side of it can be effortlessly folded down to make a strong shelf-seat able to carry 127kg (20st). Even a wheelchair user can slide on to this wheelchair-height seat, swing round to sit on the base of the unit and fold up the side again so that the box can be filled up for bathing. Thermostatically controlled tap and hand-shower units are available as extras for fitting

The Easibath (*Kingcraft*)

An automatic tap for bathroom sink fitting. Automatic taps are obviously ideal for people who have difficulty in turning ordinary taps on and off (*Clos-O-Mat [Great Britain] Ltd*)

either to the foot of the superimposed bath or to the wall above it.

The handle-wind device is the Autolift, made by Mecanaids, the hydraulic type is the ABC by Glideshaw and the polypropylene box-bath (which you empty before letting the side down to slide out again) is the Easibath by Kingcraft.

Washbasins' installed height should be 850mm (2¾ft) and taps should be of the single-lever type, which are easier for most disabled people to work than knob or press models. Single-lever mixer taps, whose control is moved in one direction for flow and the other for temperature, are widely available, intended primarily for the luxury bathroom market. Some kinds now have ceramic discs instead of the normal washers, to give them an almost limitless working life without the usual washer problems. A recent development, albeit a fairly expensive one, is the automatic mixer tap, which has its own built-in thermostatic control and turns itself on or off as you put your hands under it and take them away.

Kitchen aids

Whilst on the subject of taps, the single-lever, thermostatic and auto-operation types mentioned in connection with bathrooms are all made in kitchen-sink versions as well. Not all of them, however, have the swing-over kind of arm that will position the tap nozzle over a draining board at the side of the sink, so that a kettle or saucepan can be rested on it whilst filling, not hand-held.

Sinks, worktops and cooker hobs always need to be level with each other, arranged ideally in a continuous sequence: worktop – sink–worktop – cooker–worktop. The height of all these from the floor, however, may need to be lower than the usual 900mm (3ft) to suit individual people. For wheelchair users, the recommended height for worktops is normally 800mm (2ft 8in), with a knee clearance of 650mm (2ft 2in). Pull-out chopping boards are useful. Storage may only be reachable from just below worktop height to about 1.5m (5ft) off the floor.

Niagara electronic kitchen tap, turned on and off by means of an optical sensing device when hands or objects are placed underneath it or removed (*Clos-O-Mat [Great Britain] Ltd*)

Gas cooking for disabled people: a kitchen designed to be used by someone in a wheelchair. Appliances are Cannon 'Cuisine' oven, Cannon SP2 hotplate and Cannon RG1S Mark II rotisserie/grill. Kitchen furniture is by G. Moore Ltd (*British Gas*)

Cooker tap handles for disabled people: these four types of tap handles have been specially designed by British Gas to meet the needs of people with various hand disabilities. They fit a wide range of cookers (both current and non-current models) and customers can choose the design of handle which suits them best. From left to right: A, for people with arthritis; B, to help people with a general weakness of the arm and hand; C, for people with poor muscular co-ordination or tremor; D, this tap handle has a detachable lever and is especially suited to cookers where controls are very close together. The handles are available in a choice of black or brown *(British Gas)*

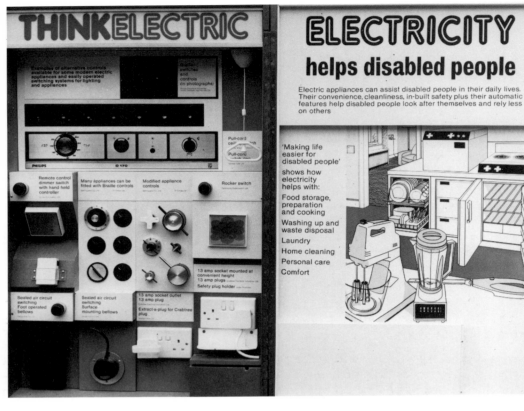

A display panel showing some of the many special controls developed to help people with disabilities to use electric appliances (*Electricity Council*)

Kitchen units are available wall mounted on adjustable-height brackets, and there are sinks which can be raised or lowered at any time, using flexible plumbing connections so that they can be worked at with equal convenience by a disabled or a non-disabled person.

Oven and hob controls can be modified by most manufacturers to suit specific disabilities, and the gas and electricity showrooms usually have on their staff home-service advisers to help with equipment choice and modification questions. Both utilities have developed ranges of modified knobs and other cooker and appliance controls.

As for non-disabled people, kitchens are far safer and pleasanter places to work in with adequate lighting where it is needed — over the work stations, not throwing shadows on them from a central fitting.

2
Preliminary Considerations — Assessing Feasibility

LEASE OR FREEHOLD DEED RESTRICTIONS

Although it is unlikely that any clause in the original documents conveying ownership or building rights of the land on which your property stands could prevent you from putting up an extension, or limit size or type, it is just possible. A solicitor can very quickly check any doubts for you on this score.

EFFECT OF AN EXTENSION ON YOUR PROPERTY'S VALUE

Having checked that you are perfectly free to extend, it makes good long-term sense to establish what your house or flat is likely to be worth with various kinds and sizes of extension added to it, to make sure that the money you put into new building work is recoverable when you come to sell the altered property. You may think you are never going to move, but remembering that the average mortgage contract runs for only seven years, the possibility that you may have to sell should be recognised, and steps taken to avoid losing money if you do. Even if you stay put your property remains an asset — probably your biggest one — and is universally acceptable security for borrowing money if you need to, once any mortgage debt is paid off.

To obtain an accurate assessment of your home's present and 'extended' market values, you need the services of a person who has qualifications both as a surveyor and as a valuer. To be absolutely sure, cast an eye down the Yellow Pages under 'Surveyors — Building' and look for the letters FSVA or ASVA after the names. These indicate that the surveyor concerned is a member of the Incorporated Society of Valuers and Auctioneers. Failing such an entry, a letter or phone call to the society's London headquarters asking for names and addresses of building surveyors and valuers in your area will put you in touch with a suitable person. ('Incorporated' in front of the name of a council, guild or society's name, simply means that legally it is a limited-liability company.)

As regards charges for surveying and valuation services, there is no set system. You make your own deal with the surveyor/valuer before commissioning him or her to do the work for you. The exercise will be of greater benefit if you have a pretty clear idea of the extra accommodation you want, and of the way or ways in which you think it can be achieved. A surveyor/valuer can be expected to know about all the factors affecting property values — number and size of rooms, building quality and soundness, state of repair and decoration, type of surrounding area and proximity to shops, schools and public transport facilities, for example. It may be that you can gain exactly the same amount of extra room by extending to the side or back of the house, or by having the loft converted. Your valuer should be able to estimate its value complete with one or the other type of extension, so that when you have investigated how much each would cost, you can see which represents the best investment in your particular case.

EFFECT OF AN EXTENSION ON RATEABLE VALUE

A house or flat has several values, each worked out for a different purpose. In addition to its

51

market value, it has three others — all notional, though not without potential impact on your cost of living. Firstly, in the event of your property being valued by a building society for the purpose of calculating what it can lend you on it by way of a mortgage, is its mortgage value. This is considerably lower than the market price, as the society has to envisage the most pessimistic circumstances under which it could find itself obliged to get its money back. Secondly, there is the rateable value, the basis for local authority rate

The front view of the extended Hare Hall in the Lake District illustrates how even a large extension can blend happily with existing houses. The new part of the Hall is obviously at the end without a chimney, but — as with Warriner's Cottage — weathering will soon tone down the newness of the roof covering. The photographs were taken before the soil vent pipes were resited and the chimneypots altered, giving appearances more like those shown in the relevant drawings (*Speakman Architects*)

demands. This is typically around 10 per cent or less of the market value. Thirdly, domestic property is given a 'gross value', which is the weekly rent that it could reasonably be expected to produce if it were vacant and to let.

Your local authority levies and collects rates, but does not carry out the official assessment of your property on which they are calculated. This is done by a district valuer, who works for the Inland Revenue. When you want to build an extension, even one too small to require planning permission, you still have to submit the plans to your local authority's building control officer to make sure that it conforms to current standards of construction. In addition to vetting plans and inspecting the work at various key stages, this officer also sends a form through to tell the district valuer that change is afoot.

When your extension is finished, you will receive a visit from the valuer, who has to establish whether or not your property is now

Hart Hall : Extension.   PETER Speakman

Fig 19 The rear view of Hare Hall (*Speakman Architects*)

worth sufficiently more than before the extension to warrant putting up its rateable value. Systems of calculation vary from one area to another, but generally an extension which enlarges the floor area of your home by less than 10 per cent — in other words, which is too small to require planning permission — does not increase the rateable value. Even a large conservatory probably will not increase it by very much, the district valuer being mainly concerned about additions with 'solid', slated, tiled, felted or metal-clad roofs. A garage may not put up the RV very greatly, and possibly not at all where its individual gross value is no more than £30.

An idea of how your rateable value is likely to be affected can be obtained in advance of building your extension by contacting the district valuer's office for advice on the subject. Your local authority is allocated a specific district valuation officer as a rule, whose telephone number is listed in your local directory under 'Inland Revenue'.

ARCHITECTURAL GOOD MANNERS

Blending in your extension with the general style, appearance and character of your house is not only architectural good manners; it is a sensible thing to do from the point of view of obtaining planning permission at the first attempt. Also it widens the spectrum of prospective buyers when you put your home on the market, thereby increasing its market price — without putting up the rateable value any more than would a non-matching extension of the same overall size.

OBTAINING PLANNING PERMISSION

The look and character of your house affect not only its own value, but also those of other houses in the same street and general district. Conversely, the appearance and style of neighbouring houses have an influence on yours. When you buy a house, you buy more than a pile of bricks and mortar. You pay for a home base in a given area whose general character makes the property worth more if that character is appealing, and less if not. What you do to your house may impinge on

Warriner's Cottage at Beckfoot in Cumbria with the work nearly completed (see plan on pp 56–7) (*Speakman Architects*)

the lives and property of your neighbours, and consequently you cannot be allowed to do exactly what you want. Having paid good money for a house in a quiet, residential area, you do not want to wake up one morning to find yourself in the middle of an industrial estate. It may be quite difficult to imagine that happening, but nothing would stop unlooked-for changes without public control over property development and use.

Not everyone likes the existing system — administered by local authority planning departments — but no one can deny the need for one. Most districts contain examples of extensions and alterations apparently carried out without the slightest regard for architectural good taste. There are probably extensions all over the area very similar to what you have in mind, yet your own plans may encounter objections. However galling this

may be, your local planning department is entitled to apply its current policy — which may have changed since the precedents you are not allowed to follow were put up.

The criteria applied to planning applications by local authorities are mostly designed to preserve the character of the district. If this is historically determined by a preponderance of semi-detached houses with integral garages, the planners may take a dim view of proposals for building additional rooms over the garages, since if everyone did it you would have a series of terraces. Applications to make the garages into habitable rooms may be given the cold shoulder, and attempts to turn garages into earnings-related workshops an even colder one. Above all, requests to be allowed an extension which is disproportionately large in relation to the house's present size are almost certainly doomed to failure, a 60 per cent increase in total floor space being the most likely upper limit imposed.

All this does not mean you have to work totally in the dark, as the planning officers have nothing to gain by creating a situation that brings them a constant flood of hopeless applications. Many planning departments make available guides to the policies they adopt with regard to planning permission, either free or at a small charge. Plans drawn up by an architect, surveyor, architectural technician or builder who has had a good deal of experience of designing buildings in the borough or county, and consequently a thorough grounding as to what is and is not acceptable, have a good chance of gaining acceptance. This is especially so if the department is one with a big throughput, where each officer might be processing 200 or more applications a year.

On average, a busy planning department can take anything from eight to twelve weeks to give you a yea or nay to your application, working through the inevitable committee system — which at least means that success or failure does not depend on the prejudices of any individual. If you are refused permission and feel that the refusal is not fair and just, or that any stipulations — for example, as to window sizes or positions or how near the property boundary you are allowed to build — are unreasonably made, you have six months in which to make an appeal to the Department of the Environment to have the decision overruled. You can equally appeal to the DoE over the planning department's head if they take more than eight weeks to give you a verdict, but if you know the planners normally turn applications round in about three months, you may not gain very much time this way. Planning decision appeals for England are dealt with by the DoE's Bristol office, for Northern Ireland by the Planning Appeals Commission in Belfast, for Scotland by the Scottish Office in Edinburgh and for Wales by the Welsh Office in Cardiff. The response to your appeal may be no more than a brief visit of inspection followed by a letter saying whether or not you have been successful. This does not mean the procedure is being skimped, as the inspector may have to check only a single technical point, and in any case

the appeal costs you nothing, the DoE acting as a kind of ombudsman for a citizen with a grievance.

In the event of a DoE appeal being turned down, you can change the design to remove the objected-to factors, give up the idea of extending completely, or take the authority to court. You have to sue at your own expense, however, and this can be considerable, particularly if you lose the case and the authority is awarded costs against you.

Making a planning consent application costs both time and money. You have to pay someone to create a design for your extension and to draw the plans in the first place, pay an application fee and, if the worst comes to the worst, you may have legal fees and expenses to find. This is one good reason for obtaining the best designer you can afford, one familiar with the relevant authority's policies, and for listening to his or her advice concerning the kind of alteration or extension plan likely to receive approval. You can apply for 'outline planning permission' for the basic scheme before any detailed work is done on developing the idea. This needs little more than a small drawing showing the exact location of the property and a letter describing the kind of extension proposed. In this way, early agreement on the principle of what you want to do can be obtained, but final permission is withheld until detailed plans are drawn up and approved. Approval in these circumstances is almost certain to be forthcoming without difficulty, as long as the basic idea first put forward has been adhered to.

The designer should be briefed at the outset about costs involved so that work can be kept to an agreed budget and not result in a scheme you cannot afford. Assuming that you need to borrow, the building society criterion for what is affordable is perhaps the most realistic, their basic rule being to limit loans to two and a half times the annual gross income of the borrower or borrowers. The societies usually expect you to find some of the money yourself, and cash will be needed for valuations, surveys and design services.

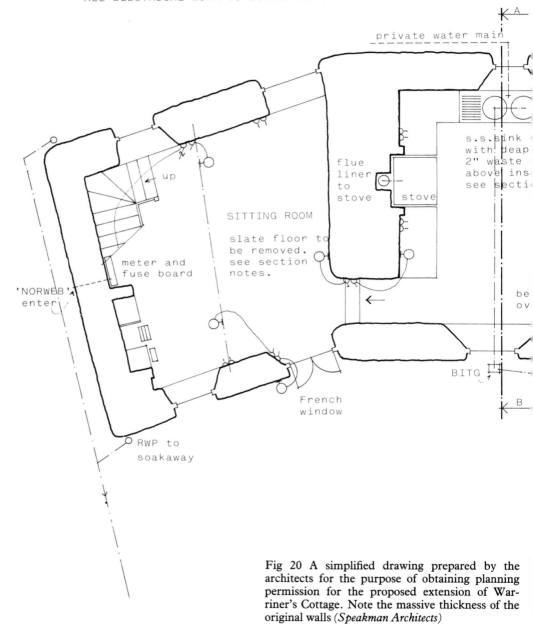

ALL DRAINAGE WORK TO BE TO THE
SATISFACTION OF 'BUILDING CONTROL'
INSPECTOR.
NEW PVC GUTTERS AND RWP's TO BE
FITTED THROUGHOUT.

ALL ELECTRICAL WORK TO COMPLY I.E.E. REGS.

private water main

flue
liner
to
stove

stove

s.s. sink
with deap
2" waste
above ins
see secti

SITTING ROOM

slate floor to
be removed.
see section
notes.

up

meter and
fuse board

'NORWEB'
enter

be
ov

BITG

French
window

RWP to
soakaway

Fig 20 A simplified drawing prepared by the architects for the purpose of obtaining planning permission for the proposed extension of Warriner's Cottage. Note the massive thickness of the original walls (*Speakman Architects*)

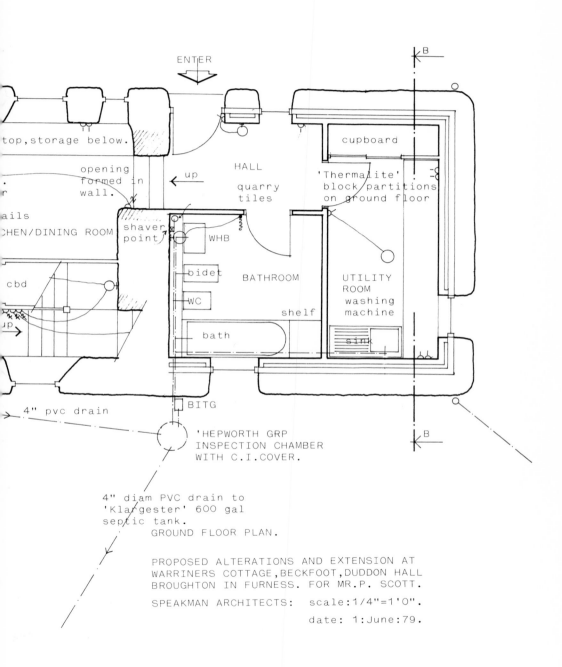

ENTER

top,storage below.

opening
formed in
wall.

ails

CHEN/DINING ROOM

cbd

up

4" pvc drain

up

HALL

quarry
tiles

shaver
point

WHB

bidet

WC

bath

BITG

cupboard

'Thermalite'
block partitions
on ground floor

BATHROOM

shelf

UTILITY
ROOM

washing
machine

sink

B

B

'HEPWORTH GRP
INSPECTION CHAMBER
WITH C.I.COVER.

4" diam PVC drain to
'Klargester' 600 gal
septic tank.
        GROUND FLOOR PLAN.

PROPOSED ALTERATIONS AND EXTENSION AT
WARRINERS COTTAGE,BECKFOOT,DUDDON HALL
BROUGHTON IN FURNESS. FOR MR.P. SCOTT.

SPEAKMAN ARCHITECTS: scale:1/4"=1'0".

                       date: 1:June:79.

PERMISSION TO EXTEND OR ALTER LISTED BUILDINGS

Certain buildings, including private houses, are listed by the DoE as being of special architectural or historical interest, the lists being supplied to local authorities so that their planning departments are aware of those in their area. The buildings are selected according to criteria devised by the Historic Buildings and Monuments Commission and fall into four groups: all pre-1700 buildings retaining anything approaching their original form and condition; most of the buildings surviving from 1700 to 1840; buildings selected as being 'of definite quality and character' from 1840 to 1914; and 'high quality' buildings dating from 1914 to 1939. This last group has not yet been completely listed and the first three groups are in the process of being re-surveyed.

A listed building is special in that it enjoys statutory — meaning legal — protection against unauthorised demolition, alteration or extension. This means that application to the local planning authority for 'listed building consent' is necessary before anything can be done to a protected house, the object of the exercise being to make sure that whatever is done will not alter or spoil the building's essential character. Even changing the door-knobs without asking can result in a fine, and there are bigger fines for more serious transgressions, with no upper limit and the possible ultimate penalty of twelve months in gaol — imposed instead of, or in addition to, a fine.

The pity is that similar protection cannot be given to listed buildings against natural dilapidation through neglect, though authorities can take powers to effect compulsory purchase to stop this going too far. You are not absolutely entitled to a loan or grant covering all or part of the preservation work just because you have a listed house, but there are government and local authority funds available for discretionary contributions towards remedial work costs — but not towards regular maintenance or decoration. Your planning department will tell you about these.

Value Added Tax was initially imposed in 1984 on all building alteration and extension work, but following effective protests, listed buildings escape the tax in respect of extensions and alterations which amount to 'substantial reconstruction' and which have received 'listed building consent'. It is important to remember that 'listed building consent' can be given in relation to buildings which are *not* listed, but which are in a conservation area. In that case, the work is standard rated. There are two more vital points. Although the building work and materials relating to listed building plans which have listed building consent are zero-rated, any professional advisory or consultancy services, such as those supplied by architects or surveyors, are always standard rated. Also standard rated is work on listed buildings which has *not* received listed building consent, as this counts as mere running repair and maintenance expense. The law becomes vastly more complex when you sell or lease or grant another person an interest in a listed building, but is straightforward, as described, if all you are doing is extending it with proper consent.

It is impossible to own a listed building and not know about it, as the DoE has a statutory obligation to notify owners when a building is listed. The listing is recorded on the Land Charges Register, so will come to your attention during the conveyancing process automatically. However, the process of listing is a continuing one. Where you have an old house that might conceivably have attracted the selectors' attention, you need to be sure it will not be listed between commissioning designs and starting work. In these circumstances, you can apply to the Secretary of State for the Environment for a certificate stating that there is no intention to list the house for which extension or other planning permission is being sought. This certificate conveys immunity from listing or having your house put under a preservation notice — a six-month provisional listing in effect — for five years. If the Secretary of State does not issue the certificate, your house will immediately be listed. Either way, you find out exactly where you are.

Hafryn Cottage received a Civic Trust Award in 1980 (*G. Parry Davies & Associates*)

(*pages 60–1*)
Figs 21 & 22 Originally a stable/coach-house/cottage complex serving the nearby Hafryn House, Hafryn Cottage was left inside some 1½ acres of garden, orchard and paddock when the house was sold off with the remaining ½ acre of formal garden. The alterations had to provide drawing- and dining-room, kitchen, den, three bedrooms, two bathrooms and circulation space on one floor level, utilising the ground floor of the original cottage and outbuildings to accommodate a study, drawing office, boiler house, fuel store and general storage, plus a double garage with workshop, store and laundry *en suite*, the owner being an architect. For ease of access to the main living floor and to the garage suite and cloakroom, the entrance hall was made a split level. Although the cottage character of the complex has been largely retained, some of the William Morris detailing of Hafryn House has been echoed in Hafryn Cottage to acknowledge and to emphasise its close association with the major building. The original buildings forming Hafryn Cottage were part stone and part brick, pebbledashed and had slated roofs. Additions have been built in reclaimed Jacobean brick and second-hand slates, the bricks being laid uneven face out to enhance the texture. Dry-laid matching brick pavings, screen and dwarf walling are featured on the forecourt setting, and blue slate paving is used on the south and west terraces (*G. Parry Davies & Associates*)

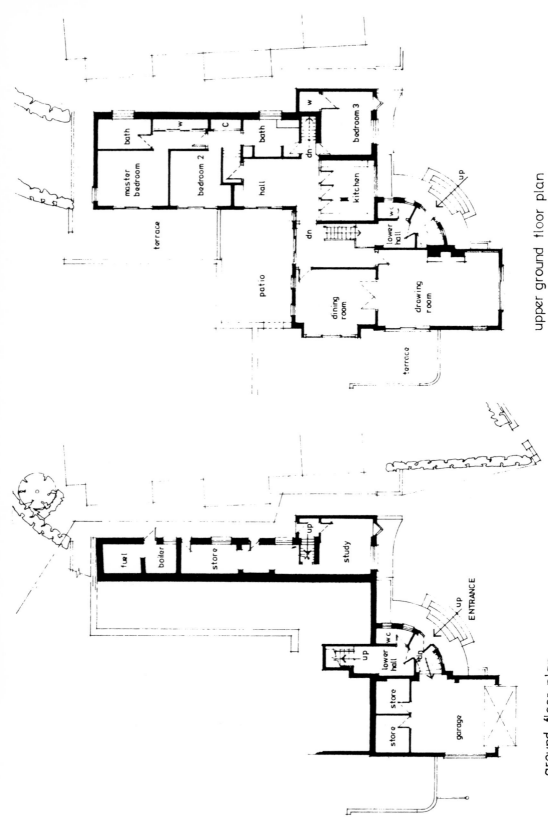

upper ground floor plan

master bedroom

bath

bedroom 2

w

c

bath

w

bedroom 3

terrace

hall

kitchen

dn

dn

lower hall

wc

up

patio

dining room

drawing room

terrace

ground floor plan

fuel

boiler

store

up

study

up

ENTRANCE

wc

lower hall

up

store

store

garage

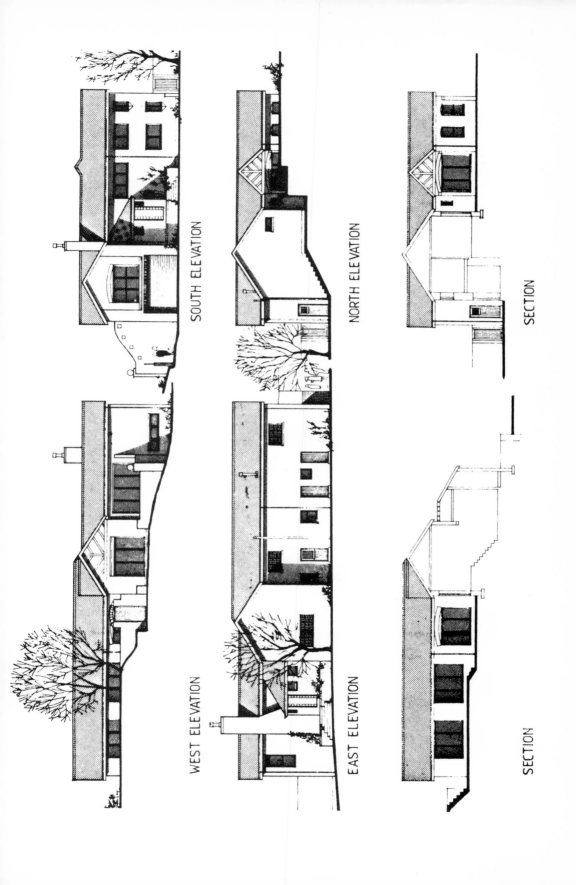

SOUTH ELEVATION

NORTH ELEVATION

SECTION

WEST ELEVATION

EAST ELEVATION

SECTION

If application for listed building consent to extend is refused by the planning authority, you have a right of appeal to the Secretary of State. If either the local authority or you ask for one, the appeal procedure can and normally will include a local inquiry, at which you can argue against the justification for listing the house.

BUILDINGS OF PARTICULAR LOCAL INTEREST

A local authority planning department probably has its own list of buildings important to the area. If your house happens to be on this list, you will not discover the fact from the conveyancing documents in the same way as you would if it was DoE listed, but you will certainly be made aware of it when you apply for planning permission, in the unlikely event of the authority having failed to advise you before. You cannot be fined or flung into gaol for interfering with a building of special local interest, but the planners will obviously take a somewhat more pernickety attitude towards granting planning permission than they would for a run-of-the-mill building. On the positive side, you are likely to find them especially helpful with regard to advice — and possibly grants if they want special remedial work carried out as a condition of planning consent. A house is unlikely to be designated as of local importance arbitrarily, since planning officers are mostly people with degrees in town planning and well aware of the effects of their decisions, which they are constantly liable to have to justify. With a good architect you should not need a good lawyer.

3
Building Design Services

ARCHITECTS

Buildings, alterations and extensions can legally be designed by any one of a number of professional people, some of them with technical qualifications and plan-drawing abilities equal to those an architect possesses. An architect, however, is trained in all the aspects of building design, including the technical, health, town planning, stylistic and aesthetic ones, so has a unique blend of skills to offer. This is recognised in law, under which no one can describe him or herself as an architect unless registered by the Architects' Registration Council of the United Kingdom.

Having achieved registration, an architect is in a position to apply for membership of one or more of the different professional bodies, of which the Royal Institute of British Architects is the largest and perhaps most widely known, but he or she has no obligation whatsoever to join such an organisation. The letters ARIBA are not in themselves a degree designation, but simply an indication that the person after whose name they appear has been accepted by the RIBA as an associate member, though registration is a prerequisite for membership.

In alphabetical order, here are the principal UK professional organisations which architects join — at least, the principal bodies with a practical architectural character. All the following, with the single exception of the Architectural Association, run client advisory services of some kind, so can be useful in finding architects interested and experienced in extension work. This is important, as architects can specialise in industrial buildings or any other sphere of construction work, and many architectural practices do not undertake extension commissions.

Architectural Association

This is a learned society which runs a highly respected school of architecture. Its membership consists largely of architects who are ex-students of its school, but other professional people, including surveyors and art critics, may join. The association does not run any form of client advisory service, but is mentioned because its diplomas have the status of degrees, qualifying an architect for registration with the Architects' Registration Council. Different diplomas are granted, but the graduate diploma taken by architects at the end of their five-year course allows them to add the letters AA Dipl to their name.

Faculty of Architects and Surveyors

The Faculty of Architects and Surveyors is closely associated with the Institute of Registered Architects Ltd, a body founded by Sir Edwin Lutyens to provide services to architects in private practice. The two organisations merged in 1974, since when the faculty has acted as the representative professional body, the institute specialising in the distribution and marketing of professional documents published by the faculty. As its name suggests, the Faculty of Architects and Surveyors has members who are not architects. Surveyors probably do as much extension and conservatory designing as architects do (more on that topic later on). You will find the letters AFAS or FFAS after the names of associates and fellows of the faculty if they are architects, the surveyors having AFS or FFS instead.

Being a good deal smaller than the RIBA, the FAS has no regional offices, running its client advisory service from its headquarters in

Chippenham, Wiltshire, a letter or phone call to which will bring you the names of architects or surveyors in your area.

Incorporated Association of Architects and Surveyors

In most respects, this is an organisation very similar to the FAS. Since it is an incorporated body, its members can describe themselves as 'corporate architects' or 'corporate surveyors', according to their particular qualification. As in the case of all the architectural bodies, registration with the Architects' Registration Council is necessary for architects before they are eligible to join. Both architect and surveyor members have the same letters after their names when they belong to the association: MIAS or FIAS.

Enquiries from the public relating to architectural or surveying services are welcomed. Letters and phone calls should be directed or made to the IAAS headquarters in Northampton.

Royal Incorporation of Architects in Scotland

The letters ARAIS or FRAIS indicate an architect's membership of this body, which is separate and distinct from the RIBA, though similar in character. Members are registered architects working either for themselves or in practices or partnerships mostly restricted to architects, as compared to mixed practices which might include civil engineers or surveyors with building or town-planning qualifications. As it possesses its own royal charter, the RIAS confers on its members the right to call themselves 'chartered architects'. It is a big organisation, so you will almost certainly find an RIAS enquiry number under 'Architects' in Scottish Yellow Pages directories which will lead you to its client advisory service. It publishes a comprehensive *Directory of Architectural Practices*, which includes notes on the types of service offered, the practices being arranged in alphabetical order for each district — Aberdeen, City of Dundee, North of the Tay and so on. If you would rather comb

(By courtesy of Larry and of the Royal Incorporation of Architects in Scotland)

through the directory for practices interested in extension work than enquire locally, you can either buy a copy from the RIAS headquarters in Edinburgh, or consult it in one of the larger reference libraries.

Advice offered to clients by the RIAS is educational, without being patronising, directed towards establishing a clear understanding of the way a building contract works. Like the RIBA, the incorporation publishes both an explanatory leaflet about the architect's function and a booklet setting out contractual conditions and recommended scales of fees and expenses. For 'small works' — which most if not all extensions are — members are not bound by fixed scales or percentages, but can make arrangements appropriate to the project.

While all professional bodies have codes of conduct for members to follow, the RIAS also has an investigation committee, set up specifically to look into complaints against architects concerning code-of-conduct infringement allegations. This committee does not deal with questions of professional competence, which usually involve legal proceedings. Most of its work consists of conciliation, but it can adjudicate on the sizes of fees charged, or nominate an arbitrator — in Scotland called an 'arbiter' — where necessary.

Royal Institute of Architects of Ireland

Despite the fact that the Republic of Ireland owes no allegiance to Her Majesty the Queen, Ireland's institute has firmly retained its royal title. Its architect members have the letters ARIAI, MRIAI or FRIAI after their name, and a fourth designation, RIAI (Tech), indicates a technician member — equivalent of an architectural technician in Great Britain, where there is a separate society, which will be described later.

Not being so densely populated as the UK mainland, the Republic does not have enough architects to maintain an organisation of RIAS or RIBA size. Its client advisory service is run from its Dublin headquarters, along similar lines to those provided by the British FAS and IAAS.

Royal Institute of British Architects

This, the largest of the architects' professional organisations, is directed from its impressive Portland Place headquarters in London, but maintains eight regional offices outside the capital, including one in Cardiff. The names and addresses of the regional secretaries running these offices are published in Yellow Pages directories. Enquiries relating to architects' services in response to Yellow Pages advertising make up nine-tenths of the thousand or so that the RIBA client advisory service deals with each month in England and Wales. So many of its members work outside the country that it has to publish two directories — one for England and Wales and another for overseas; enquiries for services abroad are received mainly through British consulates. The RIBA has close links with the RIAS and the Royal Society of Ulster Architects, directing enquiries for Scotland and Northern Ireland to their offices. Many RIAS and RSUA members are also members

of the RIBA. Long-standing Fellows and Associates may still use FRIBA or ARIBA after their name, as appropriate, but for some time now, the Institute has standardised on simply RIBA for all entrants.

In addition to running the full gamut of advisory, introduction and arbitration services for the public, the RIBA supplies both member and non-member architects, on a subscription basis, with a vitally important service — the RIBA product data manual, a highly detailed multi-product 'catalogue' in categorised, looseleaf form. Manufacturers pay, more or less cheerfully, to publicise their products in it to architects and other building industry subscribers, to whom the constantly updated publication is an invaluable source of reference.

Royal Society of Ulster Architects

This Society, in addition to working independently under its own Royal Charter, also acts as a RIBA regional office. Its members, for the most part, opt to use RIBA, FRIBA or ARIBA after their names but could, of course, use RSUA if they preferred.

BUILDING CENTRES

If you live in or near Bristol, Durham, Glasgow, London or Manchester, you may have noticed or even visited exhibitions at a Building Centre. Originally set up some fifty-odd years ago to display building products and provide information to major users and specifiers of them, these have gradually developed into a multi-faceted international organisation with services to offer to everyone concerned with buildings — including those who live in them. One of the Building Centre services which may be useful when you are considering an extension is expert counselling. If you feel it might be helpful to talk about your general ideas with a specialist building or design consultant, you can ask any of the centres to try to arrange an appointment for you. The service is charged for on a time basis, between £10 and £17 an hour at 1984 rates, plus VAT. If you

(By courtesy of Larry and of the Royal Incorporation of Architects in Scotland)

happen to live in or near London, or are paying the city a visit, you could combine the consultation with a look round the permanent building products display at the Building Centre in Store Street — or at least part of it, as there are products and services on show from more than 400 different manufacturers, trade associations and bodies such as the Electricity Council and British Gas. Other facilities at the centre include stocks of manufacturers' literature and a bookshop carrying over 1,000 titles on building construction, home improvement and DIY subjects.

ARCHITECTURAL TECHNICIANS

The letters MSAAT after a name show that a person is a fully qualified member of the Society of Architectural and Associated Technicians and legally entitled to practise as an architectural technician. The term 'architect' is protected by law from being used at all loosely, but the word 'architectural' is not; so 'architectural designers' or others offering you 'architectural plans' are quite possibly not averse to giving you the impression that you are getting the services of an architect when you are not. This is no reason to suspect an architectural technician, however.

Before about 1965, there was no recognised system for obtaining qualifications in the technical aspects of architectural practice without becoming an architect, so that architects had to find and train their own technical staff. The need for a proper qualification was recognised at an architects' conference on education in 1958, and a few years later the RIBA succeeded in founding the SAAT, which quickly built up a comprehensive and demanding course and qualification structure. Prior to 1970, you could become an MSAAT by proving that you had ten years' relevant experience and getting a detailed reference, but since 1970 all SAAT members qualify through a combination of examinations such as the Higher National Certificate or Diploma in Building and carefully monitored practice under an architect or qualified SAAT member.

All SAAT associates and members have technical drawing qualifications and MSAATs have completed at least 240 hours of design studies, mostly under architects in polytechnics or colleges of technology. Whilst lacking an architect's historical and aesthetic training, an MSAAT is thoroughly equipped to design a sound extension for the great majority of unlisted houses. An MSAAT, by the way, is an architectural technician, but an ASAAT is not, until he becomes an MSAAT.

You will probably find MSAATs advertising design and building work supervision services in local newspapers and in the Yellow Pages, but the society's London headquarters will put you in touch with members in the event of your having any trouble locating one. MSAATs have to abide by a code of conduct laid down by the society, just as architects belonging to one of their professional bodies do, and the society publishes a conditions of engagement guide for its members and their prospective clients.

SURVEYORS

The profession of surveying covers a multitude of specialities, each involving detailed and accurate study of a different aspect of the earth or of the structures built on it. Some kinds of surveyor are not primarily concerned with buildings — land, agricultural and minerals surveyors, for example. On the building and construction side, planning and development surveyors deal with schemes and environments rather than with individual buildings, and quantity surveyors work on large and complex constructions. The two surveyors most relevant to smaller building works — in addition to bigger ones — are the general practice surveyor, whose basic expertise lies in valuation of property, and the building surveyor, whose technical knowledge is on a par with that possessed by an architect. This is why there is such a high number of people able to qualify in both professions and call themselves 'architect and surveyor'. If they had to take two completely different sets of examinations, there would be hardly any with dual qualifications.

Surveyors lack the legal protection of their professional description that architects enjoy, there being no surveying equivalent of the Architects' Registration Council. Consequently, the professional bodies have to take on the policing required to stop people posing as surveyors when unqualified. Many surveyors qualify by recognised degree examinations at universities and polytechnics, but the IAAS and the RICS, for example, can and do conduct examinations of equivalent standard, which confer full professional status on successful candidates who may not have chosen or been able to study full time.

General practice surveyors (or, as the Yellow Pages put it, 'Surveyors — Building') advertise their services well in most areas, though in the event of any difficulty tracking one down, any of the relevant bodies listed in Appendix 1 will give you suitable names. The RICS has branch offices in Edinburgh and in Dublin.

A direct equivalent now exists in the surveying field for the architectural technician. The Society of Surveying Technicians was founded by the RICS to enable and encourage people lacking the educational requirements for the shorter academic courses to obtain experience and qualifications in longer stages, ideally taking RICS Direct Membership examinations at the age of thirty to become full associates. If a surveying technician does not take these examinations, or fails to pass them, he or she remains an MSST, but could not, under the Society's rules, set up in practice in the same way as an MSAAT prior to 1984. This is now possible, with specific permission from the Society.

PRIVATE BUILDERS

Private builders have to be able to read drawings, and a great number will have technical drawing qualifications at least as good as those of an architectural or surveying technician. So you may find one both competent and willing to draw up plans for the extension you want. If you find a builder with the letters MCIOB or FCIOB after his name, you have a chartered builder who has passed the final examinations of the Chartered Institute of Building, equivalent in standard to a first degree in building. Such a builder will also have a minimum of three years' experience in building production. As the CIOB membership directory does not list the firms its 28,000 members work for, the institute cannot easily say which members or members' firms are interested in dealing with extensions, but it will try to help with such information if asked to.

Builders' training and experience are biased towards the practical rather than the aesthetic, but that does not necessarily mean that a builder's design will not be reasonably good looking. The chief drawback to asking a builder to design your extension is that he is unlikely to design something he is not going to build; so he might take a dim view of your hawking his plans round two or three other builders for the purpose of inviting competitive quotations, as you can with architects', surveyors', or surveying or architectural technicians' plans.

SPECIALIST EXTENSION OR LOFT-CONVERSION CONTRACTORS

Specialist contractors generally link their design services firmly to a comprehensive contract for the complete extension or conversion. However, at least one — the London-based Argos Group — will create a design for your extension, tender for the building work as a separate job and simply charge for the design work on its own if you obtain a lower quotation than theirs for the building operation.

CHOOSING BETWEEN DESIGNERS

From the cost point of view, the higher your designer's formal qualifications, the higher his charges may be, but there are no fixed scales for small works, so if you can make your mind up as to what you want at an early stage and give the designer a straightforward assign-

68

In this large and complex extension to an eight-bedroomed house at Climping in Sussex, the original part stopped at the chimney a little to the right of the roof centre, except for a flat-roofed ground-floor extension out to where the end of the house is now. The architect's two-storey new extension covers the previous one, which has a completely redesigned front wall arrangement, replacing the former glazed screen and double glass doors (*Norman R. Harrison*)

ment, he or she should be in a position to give you a very reasonable quotation. Just as you are paying for a highly skilled person's time when you confer with a Building Centre consultant, so you are when you employ a designer. If you can streamline the consultation process so that your design can be produced in a minimum of time, the cost can be lower than if you have a lot of afterthoughts once the process has started.

No one is going to charge you for a preliminary visit and consultation. You are entitled to have a look at a number of possible designers, describe what kind of extension or alteration you have in mind, let them have a good look round the existing property and put forward rough ideas as to what they might plan for you. At this stage, each should be able to

say within reasonable limits what his or her work will cost.

Ask for names and addresses of people for whom the designer has already planned extensions near to your own in size and type. Even if it is impossible to go to look at them, the owners will almost certainly be happy to tell you over the phone whether or not the design work pleased them.

4
Contracts and Communications

LEGAL ADVICE

Apart from the help that might be needed in double-checking that there are no legal restrictions on your freedom to put an extension on your property, you are unlikely to need the services of a solicitor. However, bear in mind that, if the worst comes to the worst, you just possibly could have to take the designer or builder to court. Suppose the building work were to be abandoned at an inconvenient stage of progress, or that your extension was inefficiently constructed and developed cracks or leaks or rising damp; or suppose you were charged extra for work or fittings you thought were part of the original contract. In such circumstances, written evidence as to who asked whom to do what, and when, can be invaluable. However cordial personal relationships may have been with designer or builder up to the dispute arising, when it comes to the crunch and money is at stake, hard evidence is the only thing that counts.

Confirm major decisions and arrangements in writing, and ask the designer and builder to do the same for you. You are not saying to them, 'I want it in writing because I don't trust you blighters as far as I can throw you'; but, 'Let's keep the record straight, so that we all know exactly where we are.' Open a file — an indexed wallet with seven compartments or a few more can be labelled, say, 'architect', 'plans', 'council', 'builder', 'building society', 'bank' and 'insurance'. All letters and handwritten notes you receive should go into the file, as should copies of all letters that you write about any aspect of the extension, to anybody — just in case. Keep copies also of any forms you fill in. If there is no provision for slipping

a carbon in, ask for two copies of the form in the first place, so that you can make a copy for yourself, or have a photocopy done. Put dates on everything.

Remember the existence and popularity of telephone-answering machines. Many professional offices and businesses have them installed. When they are switched on, conversations resulting from incoming calls are automatically recorded when you pick up the handset to cut in on the answering sequence, and they can be set to record any two-way conversation. A recorded phone conversation can be used as hard evidence, so be careful what you say.

Extension specialist firms usually insist on everything being properly put in writing, to the extent of asking you to sign separate orders for any work or fittings outside the initial contract. A small private builder is unlikely to be so admin-minded, but that is no reason for you not to be.

YOUR CONTRACT WITH A DESIGNER

Whether you employ an architect, a surveyor or an architectural or surveying technician to design your extension or alteration, the range of services you can commission is variable. All four professionals are well equipped to help you with all three major stages of extension work: drawing up plans, obtaining approval by the local authority, and getting the extension built. If you want to deal with the planning application yourself — and of course with the submission of the plans for building control approval — you can contract purely and simply for the necessary detailed surveys and the production of plans suitable for a planning application.

Unless you have a particular bent for form filling, however, let the designer take on the planning and building control application work, which he or she will be thoroughly used to. The forms are quite detailed, and it is much less trouble to sign a little one giving the designer authority to act as your agent in the matter.

When approvals have been obtained, you can either take on the entire job of finding builders and obtaining quotations yourself, or contract the designer to do it for you. Having suggested firms to approach, the designer would send them copies of working drawings with enough detailed information on them to enable the builders to produce quotations for the materials and labour involved. Make sure they call them 'quotations' and not 'estimates', which do not have the same legal significance. An estimate is just a guess at the probable cost of something, whereas a quotation is a firm statement of the amount for which a firm or person is prepared to provide goods or services. A quotation can provide for cost variations caused by inflation, but except for stated variable costs it should indicate a firm price for the job, valid for a specified period of time, typically twenty-eight days. Very likely the building firm will want to send someone to look at the existing property to see if there are special difficulties — perhaps restricted access for digging or other machinery, or an unusually steep site.

Your designer will go through the tenders with you and advise which one to accept, though you can also ask for names and addresses of previous extension clients of any or all of the builders, so that you can try to see them before making up your mind. At this point, you can decide whether to take on responsibility for approving the building work yourself, or contract the designer to inspect it for you at various stages of construction. The contract is between you and the builder, but if the designer is to supervise the work it will have to contain clauses providing for this. What these clauses mean to the builder is that, when sending his invoices for stage payments as each part of the operation is completed, he has to submit a certificate from the designer stating that the work so far has been done to his or her satisfaction. The stages agreed may be (i) completion of foundations up to damp-proof course (DPC) level, (ii) completion of roof covering and (iii) completion of contract.

Assuming that you want the designer to give you an overall service, your contract with him or her should cover the following points:

(i) That the designer has your authority to act as your agent in carrying out the services that he is contracting to provide for you. This enables the designer to make applications or representations on your behalf — for example, to the planning authority — and to give instructions to your builder.

(ii) That the designer will carry out inspections of the building work. This clause may specify the frequency with which the site visits are to be made, or the stages of construction at which they are to be scheduled, but in most of the contract forms recommended to designers by their professional bodies (whose main job is to look after the designer) the clause will leave the frequency and timing up to the designer, obliging him to make enough inspections to be satisfied that the builder is carrying out the work in a reasonably efficient manner.

(iii) If the designer intends to involve specialist or indeed any other consultants in the design work, there should be a clause stating that they will be selected with your knowledge and approval, and specifying their fees. An undertaking on the designer's part should be included to co-ordinate and integrate the work of the specialist or other consultant into the overall design, but the designer will want to be indemnified against claims resulting from any slack or non-performance from the second consultant, so that in extremis you would have to sue them separately.

(iv) The total amount of what you are agreeing to pay the designer for the services specified in the contract should be spelled out, together with the dates or construction stages at which instalments are due if payment is to be phased over the period the contract is to run. Note whether the amounts stated include VAT, to make sure you do not forget to allow for it and receive a nasty 15 per cent surprise. This

71

clause will also state how often expenses relevant to the work are to be charged.

(v) A designer quotes for the work originally on the assumption that the job can be carried out on a normal and reasonable basis, with no exceptional unforeseen difficulties, such as changes in your instructions, long delays in construction or changes of building contractor partway through the job. This kind of problem may well be no fault of yours, but neither is it the designer's, so you will probably have to agree to a clause allowing him or her to charge for any extra work resulting from the problems, on a time basis.

(vi) Having perhaps gone through the process of talking to a number of designers, and having picked the one you are contracting to design your extension because you like his or her work, you will not want to find another person or firm doing the work as a subcontractor to your designer. The professional bodies' recommended contract forms usually have a clause stipulating that the designer will not assign either the whole job or any part of it without your written approval being gained in advance.

(vii) Although a design is commissioned by you and relates exclusively to work to be carried out on your property, plans, drawings and specifications connected with it embody the designer's ideas and expertise, which can quite legitimately be used for other clients' projects later on. You will be expected to agree to a clause stating that copyright in all these documents relating to the project remains the designer's, or the property of the contracted firm or partnership.

(viii) One clause in the contract should specify the amount of notice at which either party to the contract can withdraw from it. This clause will also provide for payment to the designer in respect of work carried out up to the time of termination.

(ix) Provision should always be made for any dispute arising out of the contract to be referred to an arbitrator in the event of an impasse being reached. Most professional bodies' standard forms have a clause stating that the arbitrator is to be appointed by the president of the Chartered Institute of Arbitrators, or in Scotland that an arbiter shall be nominated by the Dean of the Faculty of Advocates. Where the dispute concerns a question of copyright, the RIBA's standard clause insists that the arbitrator or arbiter shall be an architect, unless the parties agree otherwise.

A contract is a basic memorandum of agreement, a backstop document. Underlying and supporting the clauses saying what the designer is to do for you is the professional code of conduct, which itself forms most of the general assumptions that a court might make as to the kind and scope of service to be reasonably expected. It may say nothing in your contract about possible government or local authority grants to help with certain kinds of alteration, adaptation or extension work, but an architect, surveyor or architectural technician could be criticised for not drawing them to your attention and telling you how to apply.

CONTRACTS WITH BUILDERS

Forms of building contract vary to suit the kind of project concerned. The Building Employers' Federation (formerly the National Federation of Building Trades Employers), for example, has three different contract versions to suggest for 'minor building works' — meaning up to about £50,000 in total cost. One is for use where a lump-sum tender has been made, based on drawings and specifications and where the building work is going to be supervised on your behalf. Alternative versions are published to cover cases where grants may be involved, one providing for supervision and the other for the work to be carried out unsupervised. There are separate versions for contracts carried out in Scotland.

The basis of the generally accepted core of all these contracts is a series of provisions worked out by the Joint Contracts Tribunal, made up of a number of interested bodies. Neither you nor the building contractor need accept any clause just because it appears in a standard form, both being at liberty to say to each other, 'I'd like to delete that clause and substitute another'. The point is to reach between you an agreed *modus operandi*. You do not have to have a formal contract at all. An exchange of letters is possible, or you could simply shake hands on the deal and take each other's word for everything.

Even a small extension, however, can cost a

fair amount of money, so it is certainly not sensible to set up an open-ended agreement amounting to a blank cheque on one side and a licence to print money on the other. There are provisions in the standard contract clauses to protect both the contractor's interests and yours, the following forming the substance of the normal agreement.

(i) A 'recital' of the work the contract is about, the plans on which it is based and of the identity of the person or firm appointed to supervise the job. There should be a provision in this part allowing you to change the contract supervisor, in case you fall out with him or he falls ill, for example, whilst the contract is still in force. The builder will need a proviso written in to allow him protection from subsequent supervisors overturning decisions made by an earlier one. He will also want an arbitration option, in case the supervisor and he fall into dispute.

(ii) Few builders will accept a fixed-price contract, because materials and labour are financed almost entirely out of the interim payments that you make as the work progresses. You may think that he should rush out and buy everything he needs for the job as soon as the ink is dry on the contract, to pre-empt any price increases. He is unlikely to have enough storage space of his own to do this, however, and will not want to have a lot of materials cluttering up your site unnecessarily, however small the risk of pilferage may be. The Federation of Master Builders suggests a clause providing for materials to be charged at quotation levels, plus or minus an increase or decrease evidenced during the course of the contract by standard cost indices published in the federation's own trade journal, *Master Builder,* with the addition of a stated percentage for overheads and profit.

(iii) If the job involves demolishing part of the original structure, the building contractor's price may be based on his being able to salvage existing materials for re-use or even resale, in which event he may want a clause stating that materials removed in the course of the work specified will belong to him, and giving him indemnity against any third-party claims connected with such material. If you want to keep everything originally there, make this clear when you invite tenders, so there is no misunderstanding.

(iv) There should definitely be a clause covering the question of insurance — both yours and the contractor's. Insurance is dealt with in more detail later (Chapter 5), but as some contract clauses may make you responsible for covering 'unfixed materials, goods and plant on site', it as as well to check with your building society, insurance company or insurance broker that your shell and contents policies do cover such risks. Otherwise, change the clause or take out specific insurance.

The contractor should maintain employer's and public liability insurance and should be prepared to show you current policies and agree to a clause indemnifying you against claims for any accidents or damage for which he is legally responsible.

(v) Work can be delayed through no fault of the contractor's, and he will want to allow for an extension of the time stipulated for completion in certain specified events, such as failure of a firm subcontracted by you, maybe to install its own product or equipment, to appear or perform on time. You, on the other hand, may want to guard against the possibility of being left for weeks on end with an uncompleted extension by a builder trying to stretch his resources amongst too many jobs at one time. A penalty clause for non-completion by a stated date at a stipulated weekly rate is quite usual.

(vi) You can expect to have to indemnify the contractor against demonstrable loss, damage or expense attributable to delays he is not responsible for — such as those indicated in (v), changed or tardy instructions or any failure on your part to allow him free and uninterrupted access to your property, insofar as this is necessary to let him do the work.

(vii) A guarantee to put right any faults due to excessive shrinkages or other workmanship or material faults should be written in, and it is usual to retain up to 5 per cent of the contract total for three months or longer against the possibility of such faults arising after the contract is complete.

(viii) Prompt payment of charges due under the contract will be insisted on. If no contract supervisor has been appointed to certify that the work has been done properly at each payment stage, the payments clause will stipulate settlement of the contractor's stage payment invoices within seven or fourteen days of presentation. In a supervised contract, the builder will be obliged to present a certificate with each invoice. The payment clause will give him the right to cancel ('determine') the contract, remove his gear and all unfixed materials from the site and invoice you for all costs incurred up to stopping work, if any of the payments is later than specified without justifiable cause.

(ix) As the contract is based on the work outlined in the extension plans and the contractor's quotation, any variation from the job originally envisaged or any additional work subsequently requested will be the subject of a clause entitling the contractor to charge more. If the extra work involved can be accurately assessed, the increased charge will be the subject of a separate quotation for you to accept or reject. If no accurate assessment is possible, you may be asked to agree to being billed on the basis of daywork charges, plus materials and/or plant used at cost plus an overheads and profit percentage.

(x) There should be an undertaking by the contractor to comply with, and give any notices demanded by, statutes, rules, regulations, orders and byelaws that have a bearing on the contract, and to pay any charges and fees for which he is legally liable under them. If any instruction he receives from you or the contract supervisor goes against a regulation, he will notify you, demanding either changed instructions or an indemnity against the results of non-compliance, so he will want the right to do so written into the contract.

(xi) Specific defaults are usually stated as justification for instant 'determination' of the contract by either party to it. You are usually entitled to wind up the contract and ask someone else to finish the work if the contractor fails to progress the job properly or completely suspends work on the site before the job is finished, unless he can show that he has 'reasonable cause' to do either of these things. You may also cancel if he goes bankrupt or otherwise runs into serious financial trouble.

Your builder can cancel if you let him down on payments without just cause, obstruct the progress of the work in any way, fail to give him access to the site, stop the job going on for a month or more, or go bankrupt yourself.

(xii) An arbitration clause should go into the contract, similar to the one described for your contract with the designer/contract supervisor.

EVALUATING DESIGNERS' AND BUILDERS' PREVIOUS WORK

If you go to look at jobs that a prospective designer has planned — and possibly supervised during construction — for other people,

or to look at extensions or alterations that one of the builders tendering for your job has put up, don't just drive past. That tells you only what the work looks like from outside. You really need to talk to the owner about it. Most people who have had extensions done are proud of them, partly because the job incorporates their own ideas, and partly because they are probably pleased that the designer or builder is proud enough of it to ask them to show it to someone who is in the market for more work of a similar kind.

Provided you have phoned or written to ask to look round, and arranged a mutually convenient time — making sure you are not the umpteenth prospects to be put in touch in a short time — the owners will have no provocation to be unhelpful. Having an extension done is like having an operation — lovely to talk about it once it is all over, especially if you can show the scars without embarrassment.

Have a good look at the outside, keeping an eye open for leaning verticals, non-matching between new and old brickwork, cracks, messy pointing or shoddy carpentry. If the extension is so recent that the painting and decorating are also your prospective builder's work, don't let it worry you too much. Few builders employ a professional decorator. It would make their quotations too high, and the decorator's trouble might well be wasted, as some fine shrinkage cracks are inevitable in a recently finished building job and there is probably a lot of dust and grit still about.

List the questions to ask, bearing in mind that the cost of the design and building work may not be relevant to your plans, and is certainly none of your business. If the information is volunteered, all well and good. What you should go away with is a clear notion of the way the work was done, how the finished extension compares in looks and performance to what the owner had in mind before commissioning it, whether or not the general standard of building and finishing is what you are expecting, whether there has been any deterioration or problem with fittings or services since the job was completed, and whether it was

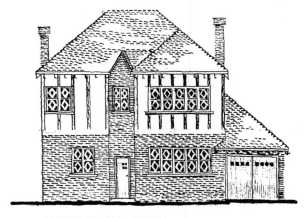

EXISTING ELEVATION

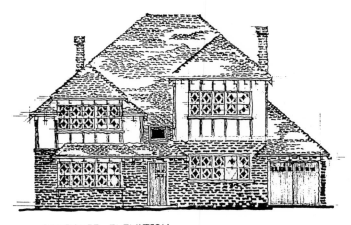

PROPOSED ELEVATION

started and finished more or less as scheduled.

If you are checking up on the designer's performance, you will want to know how well the owner's ideas were translated into reality, and how helpfully alternative suggestions, explanations of technicalities and regulations, planning applications and the management of the tender and contract process were dealt with. Where the designer contracted to supervise the building work, try to gain some idea as to the frequency with which the job was visited and of the skill with which difficulties were managed.

Just as you are within your rights in wanting to check up on designers and builders, they are equally justified in checking up on you. Their main concern will be to reassure themselves

Fig 24 The architects were asked to extend this Essex house at the back. Realising, however, that there was enough room to effect the required enlargement at the front, they made the extension more graceful and imposing by adding the extra space there (*The ATP Group Partnership, Buckhurst Hill, Essex*)

that you can and will pay their bills on time. The builder, being at risk for a greater overall amount, may well run a credit check on you if he is unsure of your standing. Builders occasionally come across clients who use minor faults to justify delay in settling substantial stage payments; your prospective contractors will probably be making their minds up as to whether or not you are in this category as they shake your hand on first acquaintance.

75

FINDING A BUILDER

If you decide to employ a specialist extension or loft-conversion firm, you avoid the problem of finding a suitable builder altogether; if you choose to leave it to your architect, surveyor or architectural technician to suggest firms, you can be sure he or she will not steer you towards a builder likely to make a pig's-ear of a good design.

Should you find yourself in the position of having to find a builder for yourself, you can comb the district looking for the name boards of firms which appear to be doing good work on local property, pick names at random from the local newspapers, or ask one or other of the leading builders' organisations to give you names of firms interested in small works.

Chartered Institute of Building

The CIOB, as already explained in Chapter 3, does not have member firms, only individual builders, but if you particularly want to explore the possibility of obtaining the services of a chartered builder — MCIOB or FCIOB — the institute is willing to search for members' firms interested in small works. This, it must be emphasised, is not one of the CIOB's standard services, so may take a little longer than your other enquiries for names. You can buy the CIOB's *Yearbook and Directory*, with the names of all 28,000-plus members, but in most cases this does not state the firm a member works for. You may well find CIOB members on the strength of building firms you trace from other sources, in which event you can be sure you have a technically advanced outfit.

Having a strong bias towards technical education rather than the more commercial side of the industry, the institute does not run any kind of guarantee scheme for small works, as the other major organisations do.

Building Employers' Confederation

This multi-faceted organisation, formerly called the National Federation of Building Trades Employers, incorporates not only the Federation of Building Specialist Contractors and the House Builders' Federation, but a number of other groups concerned with woodworking, kitchen furniture manufacture, scaffold erection, painting and decorating; so it has a capacious hat from which to produce builders' names. The confederation's 10,000 building contractors range from small local firms to multinational companies. They are obliged by the terms of membership to offer the confederation's guarantee scheme to prospective clients, but it is entirely up to you whether or not you accept the offer of a contract under the scheme, or opt for a normal arrangement.

Details of the guarantee scheme and application forms can be obtained from the BEC Building Trust Ltd in Maidstone, Kent, or through any of the Confederation's ten regional offices in England and Wales. Projects costing from £500 to £25,000 can be covered by the scheme, which is underwritten by Norwich Union. The servicing cost is 1 per cent of your total contract price, with a £20 minimum proviso.

Obviously, you cannot insure building carried out by non-members of the confederation under the scheme, but the jobs insured need not be extensions, since the cover is available for all home improvement works, including decorating, heating/ventilating, electrical, kitchen or bathroom operations. The 1 per cent premium — which is only £100, for example, to cover a £10,000 extension — buys a categorical, cast-iron assurance that if the BEC member initially contracted to carry out the work fails to finish it or to do it properly, the confederation will take responsibility for completing or putting it right. The only circumstance under which the finishing or remedial operation could cost you more than you were liable to pay under the original contract is where your first contractor becomes insolvent or goes out of business with more than £5,000 worth of work still uncompleted. Because of the conditions for obtaining membership of the confederation in the first place, however, the risk of such an occurrence is extremely small.

For the first six months following completion of the contract, all defects — even the most minor — will be put right by the contractor. Should any serious structural defects come to light during the two-year period dating from the end of the initial six months of the guarantee, they will be put right without charge. 'Serious' in this context defines a defect in foundations or any load-bearing part of a wall, floor or roof constructed under the insured contract.

These guarantees are continued even if your original contractor goes bankrupt or out of business, since they are given, not by him, but by the BEC Building Trust. Bear in mind how the £5,000 limit in these cases works. Suppose you have a £10,000 contract and your builder disappears from the scene with £6,000 worth of work to finish. A second contractor now has to quote for completing the job, and he is under no obligation to do so for the sum of £6,000. If the smallest quotation for finishing the job by a confederation member is £11,000 or under, you will still have it finished for the £6,000 you were liable to pay under the first contract, the scheme insurance taking care of the remaining £5,000. If the quotation is less than £11,000, you will still pay £6,000 and the insurance will pay the difference between £6,000 and the quoted figure. Were the quotation higher than £11,000, the insurance would pay only £5,000 and you would be liable for the entire difference between that maximum and the quoted sum. You can see from this example that the limit set is not unreasonably low.

Consequential losses resulting from breach of contract due to insolvency or liquidation are not covered under the scheme. If the catastrophe struck at a point during construction when your house was not habitable, your claim for hotel or other alternative accommodation would have to be pressed with the contractor, or his trustee in bankruptcy or his liquidator.

One condition of the BEC guarantee scheme is that you deal direct with the contracted member firm; that is, you must not also have a contract supervision arrangement with an architect, surveyor, architectural technician or any person or firm outside the contract. Your quality assurance comes from the BEC Building Trust, and any other source employed to achieve it would make liability difficult to establish in the event of argument, instead of clear-cut and unequivocal. The Building Agreement and the application to register it under the scheme, both signed by the contractor and yourself, together constitute a legally binding agreement, and your acknowledgement from the trust confirming registration is evidence of that, so keep it safely.

Under the guarantee scheme, there are two alternative provisions for sorting out disagreements between client and contractor — as to whether or not a particular job has been properly carried out, for example. An independent panel of 'conciliators' is made available by the trust. This consists of architects, surveyors and other building specialists, one of whom can be appointed to mediate in a dispute. Either you or your builder can ask for the services of a conciliator, but to ensure that requests are not made frivolously or unreasonably, the party making the request has to put down a deposit of £25, which is returned when the request is seen to be justified, whatever the outcome of the dispute. If this service fails to resolve the argument, or if either party does not want the service, the scheme provides for a simple form of arbitration. Here, the complainant pays a deposit of £50. The trust appoints an arbitrator, initially paying the arbitrator's fee (usually less than £250) to secure quick action and recovering it from the party losing the argument when the decision is made. Where a request for arbitration follows a failure on either party's part to abide by a conciliator's decision, the aggrieved person or firm can apply for arbitration without paying any deposit.

In the event of a contractor failing to honour an arbitrator's decision, the trust will take over the obligation, up to a maximum liability of £5,000, as in insolvency or liquidation cases. It has discretion under the terms of the insurance cover to index-link or otherwise update the £5,000 limit to take account of changing money values or building costs as time goes on.

Neither the BEC Building Trust Guarantee Scheme nor the Federation of Master Builders' Warranty Scheme described next affects your common law or statutory rights.

Federation of Master Builders

Whereas the Building Employers' Federation by and large represents the larger building firm, the preponderance of FMB members is in the small- and medium-size range, 'small' being generally taken to mean a firm employing fewer than 20, 'medium' an employer with anything from 20 to 200 on the payroll and 'large' a firm with a workforce exceeding 200. With some 20,000 member firms — half of them having remained with the FMB since its inception as a UK national body in 1943 — this is a thriving trade association able to back its members with a full range of advisory, information and insurance services. Its respected trade journal, *Master Builder*, helps to keep its members up to date with current regulation, product and technique developments.

Builders' trade organisations for a number of years came under a barrage of criticism from the government and from the public, pressuring them to guarantee their members' work. There were many technical, financial and organisational problems to be overcome before this could be done in an unequivocal fashion. Some schemes never got off the gound, like that attempted by the now defunct National Home Enlargement Bureau. The Federation of Master Builders' warranty scheme, however, is in being, offering an impressive package — albeit at some extra cost, since it is expensive to finance and administer.

The protection a client receives from the FMB warranty scheme is based on its National Register of Warranted Builders. To get on to this register, an FMB member firm has to have three years' or more continuous trading experience before applying to be registered, have three recently completed jobs checked in detail by the FMB's registration board, supply bankers' references and details of organisational structure and turnover, and contribute

1 per cent of its turnover as a special premium to fund the insurance and administration costs of the scheme. A firm on the register can offer you a choice between building your extension on the normal terms and conditions or, by adding 1 per cent, can offer you a job specifically guaranteed under the warranty scheme. Under this scheme, your extension will be guaranteed against defects arising from faulty workmanship or materials for two years from the date of the builder's final account for the finished job. Within that period, the builder is expected to put right any such defects without further charge.

Where the builder feels the defects are not his fault, the question is decided by the Warranty Scheme Registration Board's Arbitration Committee. If the decision is in your favour, the builder will be instructed to put the defects right; should he refuse to do so, the scheme will pay to have them put right by another builder. It will also do this where defects are proved against a registered builder who has gone bankrupt or is in compulsory liquidation.

The scheme being insurance-based, there are a few limitations and exclusions to bear in mind. Only jobs with an initial tender price of under £30,000 may be warranted, and the guarantee on manufactured equipment with moving parts is restricted to that given by its manufacturer. You have to pay the final account within twenty-one days of presentation to preserve the warranty, which could be well worth having.

CONTRACTING TO DO PART OF THE WORK YOURSELF

Where you have the skill, will and experience to do part of the work on the extension yourself, it is quite possible to write an arrangement into the contract to that effect, but you need to think the proposition through realistically. Amongst the considerations to bear in mind are these:

(i) If you do it yourself, you have to do it to a standard that satisfies building regulations, just as if you were a tradesman doing it for someone else. You will almost certainly find the local authority building control officer helpful, however, in advising you on methods and technology.

(ii) Unless your stint is carried out right at the end of the operation, when the regular tradesmen have finished the rest of the extension, you will have to finish it to schedule, to avoid holding up the building programme. Delay on your part could cost the builder money, and he will have to pass such a loss on to you. If your time is limited to evenings and weekends or a week or two's leave, it is not advisable to take on work that can be slowed or stopped by bad weather.

A wealth of information is available from practical magazines, partwork publications and books on particular trades and skills — concreting, bricklaying, plumbing, electrics, roofing and so on — and on the general process of building your own extension. Many people have successfully built extensions, and some have even built complete houses, by acquiring the necessary skills at colleges of further education, or from a combination of books and practice.

Building an extension yourself is no soft option, though it is undoubtedly the least expensive and at the same time the most rewarding, in terms of both value added in relation to outlay and personal satisfaction and pride. If you are fit, strong, generally skilled and methodical enough to take on your own building operation, you may still have doubts about some aspects of it. Maybe you are an excellent carpenter, plumber and electrician but are not too happy at the prospect of laying a few thousand bricks. This need not stop you, as you can subcontract the brickwork and do the rest yourself.

An architect, surveyor or architectural or surveying technician will cheerfully design an extension specifically for you to build yourself, taking all the factors into account and advising you as to which jobs to farm out and how to cope with the building regulation requirements. With a realistically planned and costed blueprint for the job, you are at least half-way to success.

One of the most useful DIY extension building books is *Extension Manual* by Rodney Bird, published by Construction Guidelines of Hitchin in Hertfordshire. Mr Bird has spent all his working life in the construction industry, is a licentiate of the Chartered Institute of Building and is managing director of a family building firm with an annual turnover in the region of £1 million. To readers of his book who decide to attempt their own extensions he makes available an advisory service — including personal visits on request, these being charged at an hourly rate plus car mileage. He will also supply complete lists giving types and quantities of materials needed for your extension, based on its total internal floor area, charging by the square foot for these. For those who want to organise the building, hiring specialist tradesmen as necessary, he advises on the buying in of materials and on the process of hiring skilled help. For people who intend doing some or all of the work themselves, Construction Guidelines publishes basic guides to individual crafts.

Many of the smaller sun-lounges and conservatories on the market are designed to make DIY assembly possible. This is also the case with some prefabricated-component extensions such as the Marleywing, in respect of which Marley Buildings are prepared to make purchase deals involving as much or as little DIY input as you may wish.

UNDERSTANDING BUILDERS AND MAKING YOURSELF UNDERSTOOD

If you have had a few problems to thrash out in getting your extension plans through the design and planning permission stages, you could be forgiven for looking on the builder as the final obstacle standing between you and what you want built. In fact, your contractor is simply the chap at the end of the line, who has to put the whole thing together for you. He has several bosses — most likely a designer, the building control officer and you — all sure they know his job better than he does. Consequently he feels at times like the 'poor bloody infantry' of the construction army.

Your relationship with the building contractor and the various tradesmen working on your extension needs to be as good as possible, for the sake both of minimising the strain of upheaval in your living patterns and of achieving the best possible job. So long as you treat him with civility, on equal terms, pay him on time and don't try to change the basis of the contract by asking him to do or supply things not originally specified — unless you undertake to pay the extra cost involved — he will class you as a first-rate client and work for you accordingly. This does not mean to say he wants you simply to sign his contract, give him his plans and leave him to get on with it. He likes you to take an interest. There are many little considerations difficult to include in the tightest specification, and he would much rather you care about details from day to day than wait until he has done something you don't want and then complain, so he has to do the work twice.

Building contractors and tradesmen are intensely practical people, not over-fond of office work, so remember that bits of paper are necessary evils to them, not the most effective channels of communication ever invented. By all means confirm requests and instructions in writing for your own protection as you must, but talk about them first, and if it is merely a question of stating which power points, controls, switches or items of equipment you want installed in particular places, write and draw the information on the walls and ceilings concerned. This is much more practical than writing a long screed. Words can mean different things to different people: 'insulation', for example, may mean to a plumber a thin pipe sleeve designed to stop the water in the pipe from freezing in cold weather. If he is burying a heating pipe in a concrete floor, however, that is not enough to stop significant heat loss to the concrete — so you could end up with a warm floor and cool radiators.

One of the most difficult communication situations arises when you have appointed a contract supervisor — an architect, surveyor or architectural technician in most cases — to check the builder's work and the two disagree on a major point. Rather than stop the job and provoke arbitration, the contractor will probably prefer to make you the arbitrator, arguing that the supervisor is not the boss. You are, so you are in a position to override the questioned instruction. If you do override it, you will be paying the supervisor for a service you are not using. On the other hand, the builder may be at least partly in the right, so you need to talk to the supervisor about it tactfully. Where you let the builder go against the supervisor's wishes, you cannot then hold the supervisor responsible for the results. Always try to find out what is really behind the fuss. Quite often it is a case of the supervisor picking up something he considers wrong at what may be for the builder a late stage, when he has built other parts on top of the offending structure or components. It may be that he has used a standard lintel, for example, over a door or window, when the supervising designer had gone to endless trouble to find and specify a specially slim one to maintain a roof line. If the builder already has the roof on top of it by the time the inspection visit takes place, he is obviously going to be happier leaving things as they are. Nothing is going to fall down, he will argue, and if he has to change it, the job will be delayed.

By and large, it is better to back your designer/supervisor to the hilt, because if you don't you finish up with what might have been, say, an 'architect-designed extension', but is in fact full of unauthorised modifications. What you have to say to the builder if you decide to back the designer is, very reasonably, that you have paid good money for the design, that you would really be happier if it were carried out to the letter, and that if he builds it to the designer's signed satisfaction, you will obviously hold the designer responsible if he or she is ultimately demonstrated to have made a mistake. After all, the builder quoted for the work on the basis of the designer's drawings and specification, and should not complain at being asked to adhere to the details on them. This is where you may be glad to have a contract which provides for some quick and inexpensive conciliation service by a building expert, such as that devised by the Federation of Master Builders for supervised contracts.

Notwithstanding the fact that much of their work comes to them from architects', surveyors' or architectural technicians' recommendation, many builders are deeply and instinctively prejudiced against them in their role as supervisors. It was not possible to effect a nationwide survey for this book, but even the small sample of builders interviewed on this subject showed up a remarkable strength of feeling. Architects, surveyors and architectural technicians are all lumped together as a professional class looking down on and talking down to a more practical one. The degree of responsibility accepted for their work is held to bear no relation to the size of the fees they charge. They are seen as arty, preoccupied with appearance, yet with scant regard for unity. Wanting their work to be noticed, they design it to stand out from the rest of the street, rather than blend in. Above all, they are felt to lack practical on-the-ground experience — and therefore common sense. Yet whereas a builder may well make a reasonable living putting up nothing more complex than a house, a designer may well have to plan a small extension today and a block of flats or a civic centre tomorrow. He or she does not feel too impractical, despite a lesser degree of involvement with trenches, bricks and mortar.

Builders in general also have a none-too-high opinion of local authority building control inspectors, largely because of the discretionary powers they have with regard to the interpretation of building regulations. It can be exasperating to find different inspectors apparently making their own rules, so that you are never quite sure what is going to be allowed or objected to, however sound the principles behind the system may be. Building regulations are complex sets of rules designed to ensure that nothing is built that is going to fall down, blow up, blow away, shed bits from a great height on to passers-by, leak, become damp or otherwise unhealthy to live in, or catch fire too easily. There is one set of BRs for England and Wales and a separate set each for Greater London, Scotland and Ulster. Although local authority inspectorates can make concessions or extra stipulations to take account of particular local conditions, they would have to account for their actions in bending the rules if the broad aims of the BRs at any time proved not to have been met. It is often impossible to apply current regulations to the letter when dealing with older buildings, especially listed ones, so the discretionary power has to be there, though it is not hard to see the builder's point of view.

You may imagine the average small building firm to consist of a single owner, or perhaps a husband and wife, father and son or two brothers in partnership, plus a more or less permanent set of employee tradesmen. Often, however, the owner or owners operate the business — quoting, contracting, buying materials, hiring plant and keeping books — whilst using self-employed tradesmen to do the actual building work. This system benefits the contractor by restricting the outgoings for labour to periods when there are funds due to pay for it and by saving him national insurance charges. The tradesmen can sell their skill to whichever contractors have a need for it, and you benefit from competitive quotations based on *ad hoc* labour costs. A builder working in this way will normally use the same tradesmen time and time again, because he knows the quality and speed of their work, and they will work for him willingly because he has always paid them on the nail. This is important to them, firstly because they are paid only when they work and secondly because they are not in a good position to sue for payment of a bad debt.

A small builder will almost certainly finance your building operation out of the cash flow produced by your stage payments, buying materials from the nearest builder's merchant as and when they are needed. Having to quote for new business, organise maybe two or three contracts at a time, make out invoices and keep his accountant and VAT man happy, he may not have enough time to comb his trade journals for information on new products. Consequently, you may well be better informed in some areas of equipment than he is. If there is any item he is expected to buy and fit of a particular make, type or specification not listed on the plans, he will be entitled to class it as a 'variation' and charge extra. If no specific details appear on the original specification for kitchen units, for example, his quotation will probably contain a nominal value for them, relating to standard units he can buy 'off the shelf'. Be prepared to give him precise information about any special items you want, including where to go for them if possible. If you feel that the price he then quotes you for the extra quality is too high, he will cheerfully agree to your shopping around for a better price, let you buy the material direct and allow for it when totting up the bill, charging only

for fitting it. If you have not thought about them at the planning stage, you should think early on in the contract about which electrical and plumbing fittings, heating units, fireplaces, doors, windows, and door and window furniture — locks, handles and so on — you want, otherwise standard items will most probably be fitted that might well be far from your ideal choice.

Apart from his worry that non-standard special items may cost more than his budgeted amounts, your builder may also be concerned at the prospect of delays in procuring them upsetting his schedule, which one way or another will cost you money; so it pays to give him early warning about specials, and all the information you can. He is unlikely to complain too much about the bother of obtaining them if his overall profit is safe, and if the items concerned turn out to be easy to fit he may ultimately be grateful to you for drawing them to his attention.

5
Insurance — Who Insures What?

IS YOUR DESIGNER INSURED?

However unlikely it is that you may have to sue your architect, surveyor or architectural or surveying technician for professional negligence in the preparation of your design, or in the management of the building contract if supervising the work for you, there is no harm in making sure that your designer is worth suing if you have to. After all, most affordable insurance is about unlikely occurrences. Building designers are not all as rich as you may think, but they are still favourite targets for litigation in connection with building failures — mostly in the field of larger contracts.

Professional indemnity insurance is both an expensive and problematic item in a designer's overheads. The reasons for the high cost are the number and size of claims; those against architects alone, for example, became so numerous and costly in the 'seventies and early 'eighties that one insurance company which had underwritten the main RIBA insurance scheme for ten years withdrew completely from underwriting professional indemnity cover.

One of the difficulties with professional indemnity insurance in the building design field lies in the length of time which can elapse between a building being finished and a claim being made. If a designer or firm of designers has no professional indemnity policy in force when a claim is made against them, they cannot invoke a policy that *was* in force when the offending building was built. This gives building designers the peculiarly onerous obligation to keep themselves insured well into retirement, in many cases relying on their former practice to effect cover for them. Companies providing professional indemnity cover demand total honesty with regard to the information on proposal forms. Any undisclosed previous claims or withdrawals of insurance cover enables them to 'avoid' a policy — simply repudiate a claim. Remember that any insurer of anything can, and very well may, do this if facts or circumstances relevant to the risk insured are left off the original proposal, or falsified in any way.

THEFT OF OR DAMAGE TO MATERIALS AND EQUIPMENT ON YOUR SITE

Most householders owning their homes, or buying them through mortgage loans, have two separate insurance policies, one covering the building and its fixtures and another covering the contents. Unfixed building materials are not regarded as part of the building and are certainly not 'contents', so they will not normally have any automatic cover on standard home policies. Some companies will arrange special temporary cover for building materials if you pay an extra premium related to a declared adequate value, but will probably charge quite heavily for materials left in the open, as most of them have to be.

To be properly covered for theft or damage of unfixed materials, you have to be legally liable for them and buy specific cover. You cannot just assume that the contents policy will suddenly be extended for no additional premium to cover a substantially increased risk. If you are building an extension yourself, the materials are yours and you are legally liable for them. Unless you sign a contract under which you assume legal responsibility for insuring a contractor's materials, the contractor should insure them until the job is finished. From that point, you have to insure the completed extension. Remember that the sum insured under your buildings policy should be high enough to allow for both house and extension — including any alterations and fittings — to be rebuilt or replaced from scratch. This amount will very likely be bigger than the house's resale value. If you own the house, you will have your own buildings (or 'shell') policy, but if you are still paying off a loan for it, your building society or bank will have its own policy in force, so you will need to authorise increases in cover and premium.

Builders' plant and equipment can be expensive, and no company will cover it under a normal domestic policy. Your contractor should take full responsibility for covering both equipment and materials until the job is done and he is off the site. He can effect cover with less trouble and expense than you can, particularly if he belongs to a big trade association like the FMB or BEC, which can negotiate favourable rates for members. Make sure there is a clause in the contract putting liability for plant, equipment and materials firmly where it belongs — on the contractor.

COVERAGE FOR GOODS AND CHATTELS DURING BUILDING

Theft of or damage to your household goods is covered during the building operation to the same extent that it is covered normally under your standard policies. Your buildings policy covers the fittings and fixtures of the 'main building', meaning the existing house, and your contents policy covers everything else up to the amount you are insured for, though some companies do not cover money or stamps, or limit the value of these to be covered.

In the unlooked-for event of anything of yours being stolen or damaged by one of the contractor's tradesmen or labourers, your contents or buildings policy would cover the loss,

but the insurance company would probably want to counter-claim against the contractor's own insurance.

ACCIDENTS

In spite of the utmost care, there is bound to be a greater potential for accidents to people whilst building is going on than when it is not. Uneven ground, possibly with holes or trenches in it, slippery mud in wet weather and heavy materials in stacks or piles are inevitable, and can all lead to some form of personal damage. Under the standard home policies of the Commercial Union, General Accident and Guardian Royal Exchange companies, personal accidents to your family or yourself are not covered, so you should have separate personal accident cover in case the mishap is your fault, and a properly insured contractor to claim against if the fault is his. Eagle Star home policies have a death benefit provision covering accidents in the house or garden, and the Pearl contents policy covers you and your spouse for death or loss of limbs up to a maximum of £2,500, or for total disablement benefit at the rate of £10 a week. It is wise to arrange personal accident cover, whether DIY building work is envisaged or not.

Under the normal contents policies of the Commercial Union, Eagle Star, General Accident and Pearl companies, provided you have taken the property owner's liability extension where it is available, accidents to builders' staff will be covered. The same applies with Guardian Royal Exchange policies, but only if the accident is due to your negligence. If you are paying someone to help you out with a DIY building operation, you could technically be employing them, in which case they would not be covered for accidents under your home policy.

Where you make yourself legally liable for accidents to the contractor's people, not through negligence on your part in the building operation but by signing a contract that makes you liable, you will probably find that your home policy will not provide the required cover. Here again, your contractor ought to have his own insurance. If he does not, you could have claims made against you even without formally taking responsibility, since you are using an uninsured contractor.

In the context of accident insurance, 'third parties' means the general public, including the postman and the milkman. Not included are people working on your property who are employed by a public utility or who are installing equipment for a manufacturer or supplier.

If your child plays with the contractor's stack of bricks unobserved and leaves one or two on the pavement outside your house or in your driveway, you would be liable for accidents caused to people falling over them — including the contractor's staff. If the contractor's people left a similar obstruction, the contractor would be liable.

When drawing up contracts, you should not only include a clause putting responsibility on the contractor for insuring his proper liabilities, but make sure the clause also obliges him to check that subcontractors are equally well insured.

DAMAGE TO YOUR EXISTING HOUSE AND GARDEN

Some variation exists in standard buildings policy cover against accidental or careless damage to your existing house and garden during alteration or construction operations. Commercial Union holds the builder liable if he is negligent, otherwise covering such damage in an optional extension to the standard policy, provided the requisite additional premium has been paid. Eagle Star policies likewise provide accidental damage cover for buildings for an extra premium, but exclude such cover whilst building operations are in progress. General Accident accidental damage cover is limited to glass and underground services. Cover for buildings is available separately, but not for gardens or for growing plants. Where the builder was demonstrably negligent, this company would seek to recover damages from him, or his insurance company.

Accidental damage to buildings is covered by the Guardian Royal Exchange company only if you have paid for all-risks cover. Pearl policies cover damage by you to your dwelling — which is interpreted to include patios, drives and paths, but not gardens — but hold the contractor liable for any damage he causes during the job.

WHAT INSURANCE SHOULD THE CONTRACTOR HAVE?

Your contractor should carry public liability and all-risks insurance, and be prepared to show you evidence that it is in force. Under a standard JCT (Joints Contracts Tribunal) contract, he is expected to indemnify you against all accident, loss, death or expense claims caused by his or subcontracting firms throughout the works envisaged. He is also supposed to cover himself for damage to property and to insure the extension under normal buildings cover until it is handed over to you. This form of contract does, however, seek to put responsibility for insuring unfixed materials on to you. If you cannot obtain suitable extra cover and the contractor will not accept responsibility, you must find a better deal elsewhere. The Federation of Master Builders takes the view that a builder should insure the extension and unfixed materials right up to handover point. The only builders you can rely on to have taken out full insurance, however, are those involved in the FMB warranty or BEC guarantee schemes. In all other cases, you should ask to see their policies or ask for evidence in writing of the scope of insurance cover they have.

CHECK THE FACTS OF YOUR SITUATION

The foregoing summaries can be only a general guide to insurance. You must check the extent and nature of insurances affected by your particular circumstances. The company or companies with which you have insured your normal house and contents are invaluable sources of help and advice, as are insurance brokers. Insurance companies' staff will be as sympathetic as anyone else if unfortunate things happen, but when it comes to the crunch, either an eventuality is insured for, or it is not.

Also bear in mind that insuring something for a specific amount does not necessarily mean you will be paid that figure in compensation. Where the loss takes place some time after the original insurance was taken out, what you are entitled to may be a lower value, adjusted to allow for depreciation. Some companies will insure on a 'new for old' replacement basis, for appropriately higher premiums, but for possessions which appreciate in value with time — houses and some antiques, for instance — you need to have them periodically revalued, and adjust the insurance's declared value and the relevant premium.

6
House Construction Systems in the UK

FOUNDATIONS

Since the earth does not provide a stable-enough base for supporting buildings, they have to stand on various types of foundation, according to the nature of the soil. Occasionally, soils are so loose and unstable in texture that the concrete ground beams or rafts almost invariably used for wall support have to be suspended between piles — long shafts of steel-reinforced concrete buried vertically in the ground. Most houses, however, are based on deep, narrow concrete slabs made either by simply filling precisely cut trenches with concrete, or by pouring concrete into prepared wooden moulds — though the boards giving the concrete its shape are called by the generic name of 'shuttering' in most building contexts.

Both the dimensions and the quality of foundations have to be suited to the stresses likely to be put on them by the structure they are intended to carry. If the ground lies over old or current mine workings, or the site is particularly steep, foundations may need to be reinforced to guard against walls moving relative to each other as the ground shifts. Clay soils may be thought of as pretty solid, but they have their own movement problems, brought about by shrinkage as they dry out in summer drought conditions and expand again when wet. During the expansion phase, the clay soil pushes upwards — and also outwards if it is boxed in by foundation slabs. The concrete can be forced out of place by the expanding earth's pressure, a condition known as 'clayheave'.

Heavier foundations resist clayheave better than the lightly reinforced slabs and beams often used to carry light building structures nowadays, but even the more massively built older property suffered millions of pounds' worth of structural damage through the phenomenon during the hot, dry summer of 1976. Clayheave can occur in most clay areas, and also in carboniferous shales and certain glacial deposits. Its cause may lie simply in natural climatic changes, but the alteration of subsoil water content which creates the problem may equally be due to changes made in land drainage arrangements or to the removal of trees. A fair-sized tree might have been 'drinking' 40 gallons of water or more before being pulled out of the ground, which then has suddenly to cope with the extra moisture.

The solution to the clayheave problem is to allow for it when making the foundations. Voids are formed under and alongside foundations at the casting stage, so that when the clay expands it has somewhere to expand into. This can be done by using factory-made, pre-stressed concrete slabs, suspended on piles or beams to leave a space for subsoil expansion. A less expensive method is to use for some of the shuttering a 'board' which can be relied on to collapse after the concrete has set, so forming the necessary voids. Expanded polystyrene is sometimes used for this purpose, but a more recently developed product is Clayboard. This is a fabricated panel comprising two thin outer boards separated and connected by thin webs, rather like those inside a modern flush internal door or building panel. It is only strong when dry, so has to be protected by polythene sheet during construction, but when it becomes wet — as it does when wet clay expands — it collapses, leaving the desired space.

The first steps in building — starting to cut a foundation trench in line with site markers (*John Wickersham*)

SOLID MASONRY WALLS

Prior to the general introduction of walls with an air gap in the middle around 1924, walls had been built in solid masonry throughout their thickness for thousands of years. There were cavity walls before them, but they were rare. Any wall built badly can be weak and any wall built well can be strong, but given comparable construction quality, solid walls are significantly stronger than cavity ones of equivalent thickness.

When built of stone, they vary widely in thickness and quality, from the random, almost boulder-and-rubble style of old country cottages — often as much as 1m (over 3ft) thick — to the cut-and-dressed classic regularity of sophisticated town houses, whose walls may be only a third of that thickness. Natural stone has been too expensive for

general building for quite a long time. Most of the stone-built houses (or stone-fronted ones) put up since World War II use reconstituted stone, made from ground stone and cement. This material not only looks attractive, but is probably stronger than much natural stone, whose blocks may hide internal cracks and fissures.

Solid walls can also be made from precast concrete sections designed to slot together, as used in Airey, Woolaway, Unity and Orlit system-built housing, or cast *in situ* like the 'no-fines' open-textured concrete structures widely used in Scotland.

Although they are strong, solid walls have several disadvantages, the principal ones being that they tend to allow water penetration — especially in driving rain — and they let out a lot of heat. More correctly, they let heat out

Chapel Cottage, Ulpha, with the gable wall partly cut away during the extension work. The original 3ft 6in thick stone and clay walls date back to 1650 (*Speakman Architects*)

and in quickly, so that a solid-walled house is expensive to heat, except where it is a really thick-walled one, which is slower to let heat through simply because there is so much material in the way.

There are about five million solid-walled houses in Great Britain, the vast majority of them built in brick, with or without a 'rendering' on the outside of cement, sand and possibly gravel to improve water resistance. If you can see the bricks in a house wall, you can tell at a glance whether or not the walls are of solid construction. In a cavity wall, all the bricks are laid sideways-on in the outer leaf, but in a solid brick wall there are some called 'bonders' that are laid end-on to add strength. Bricks are twice as long as they are thick, so the thickness of a solid brick wall is usually the length of one brick, plus the thickness of any render coat.

You can have solid walls that have good insulation properties, if they are built in modern insulating, lightweight, load-bearing blocks. Both these and older solid walls can have their water resistance improved markedly by treatment with a silicone water-repellent solution, which prevents rain getting in but does not stop the wall breathing to let existing moisture out.

CAVITY WALLS

Cavity walls came in long before silicones were heard of. Having an air gap of a nominal 50mm (2in) to 75mm (3in) in the middle, they keep heat in much better than the older type of solid wall, but the cavity was not originally designed to prevent heat loss. Its primary purpose was to stop water from penetrating the wall: any water getting through to the inside of the outer leaf will run downwards instead of carrying on through the inner leaf, which will therefore remain dry. Cavities used to be, and sometimes still are, ventilated by inserting airbricks at intervals, so as to help any trapped water to evaporate.

If two one-brick-thick walls were built completely out of contact with each other, they would both be pretty wobbly before any useful

height was reached. To enable them to hold each other up effectively, 'ties' are put in at regular intervals. These may be butterfly-shaped wire loops, metal or plastic strips spanning the cavity and embedded firmly at either end in the horizontal mortar joints between brick or block courses. Ties always have a loop or a twist or a projection in the centre to induce any water that happens to run across the first half to drip harmlessly down the cavity. However, if ties are bent or put in slanting downwards towards the inner leaf, or if mortar blobs (derogatorily referred to in the trade as 'snots') are allowed to dry on them, they can help water across the cavity and defeat the purpose of the construction system.

Another device often used for preventing water from reaching the inner leaf or 'skin' is the cavity tray, which may be a metal pressing or plastic moulding. As the name indicates, these are essentially thin, flat shelves, profiled in various ways to catch water in a cavity or to

A Catnic cavity wall tie. Note the mortar-gripping sprags and central drip profiling (*Catnic Components Ltd*)

This tie is for anchoring a brick 'skin' wall to a timber frame. The spragged horizontal tongue goes into the mortar and the upright flange is nailed into the timber studding (*Catnic Components*)

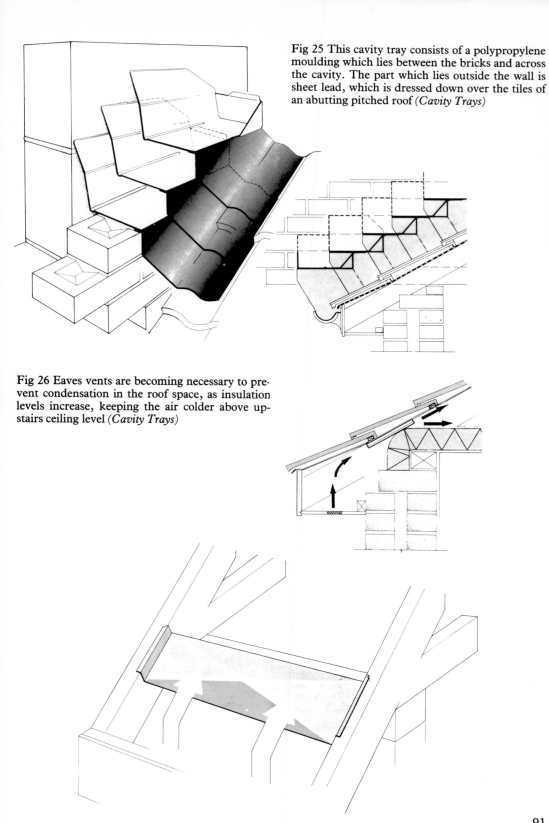

Fig 25 This cavity tray consists of a polypropylene moulding which lies between the bricks and across the cavity. The part which lies outside the wall is sheet lead, which is dressed down over the tiles of an abutting pitched roof (*Cavity Trays*)

Fig 26 Eaves vents are becoming necessary to prevent condensation in the roof space, as insulation levels increase, keeping the air colder above upstairs ceiling level (*Cavity Trays*)

stop it entering at the tops of door and window openings, or where roofs butt up to walls. They are not substitutes for ties. In fact, often they are not embedded in the inner-leaf mortar joints; in most applications, their job is to catch water and deflect it downwards away from the inner leaf towards the outer one. At the base of a cavity, they can direct penetrating water back to the outside via weepholes inserted in the outer skin.

Some types of cavity tray combine the functions of a damp-proof course (DPC), a cavity drain and a flashing strip, these being particularly useful where a sloping roof meets a higher vertical wall, as it might in the case of a contiguous garage or single-storey extension. Such applications require a series of trays built into the outer leaf of the wall in steps, descending — or ascending — one brick at a time. Another similar type exists for use where flat roofs meet higher walls. It is sometimes necessary to insert a damp-proof course (DPC) in an outside wall which has been turned into an inside wall because an extension has been built up against it. The new course is required not at ground level, but where the new lean-to or flat roof joins on. One system uses plastic trays, with clips to join them together at the sides so that they can be inserted one at a time. These save a good deal of time and trouble, compared to the otherwise necessary operation of cutting out about 300mm (1ft) or more depth of brickwork for the whole length of a large tray, instead of two bricks at a time to insert smaller, interlocking trays. More purpose-made trays fit over door and window openings and under window sills.

The inner leaf

Originally the inner leaves of cavity walls were made of brick — mostly of a utilitarian, plain variety, since there was no need to bother about the appearance of components that were going to be rendered and plastered. Later, breeze blocks were often substituted. These were open-textured units containing a high proportion of clinker and ash, quite a bit of air being trapped in the granular structure, so

This is the Stranlite Thermguard lightweight building block, with its full-length cavity filled with rigid insulation material (*Plasmor*)

giving the blocks better insulation qualities than brick. Although strong enough to carry vertical loads, breeze was awkward stuff to make wall fixings in, the most careful drilling, plugging and screwing being generally less effectual than the 'Manchester screwdriver' method — banging nails straight into it.

Both breeze and brick have now almost entirely given way to various forms of insulated block, most of them moulded in aerated concrete. These are light in weight, so can be made much bigger than bricks without being too heavy to lift with one hand. Many have moulded-in cavities, which in some cases are filled with foam insulation material. The reason for these measures is that a complete cavity wall has to meet a certain standard of thermal conductivity under current building regulations. This will be discussed fully later, but the immediate point is that the present insulation requirement of a cavity wall cannot be met by using inner-leaf blocks of any old specification. Unless they are very good insulators, the cavity will have to have insulating material put into it — well worth doing to achieve extra thermal performance, but uneconomical if it is being done just to meet the minimum BR requirement.

Modern load-bearing insulating blocks hold

wall fixings better than breeze, and are easier to make fixings in than brick. They can be used for outer leaves as well, but need a weatherproof facing in the form of rendering or cladding. The ease with which building materials can be cut, drilled and channelled out is a very important factor in building costs because of the traditional system of putting up a house's shell, then having services' installers — electricians, plumbers and heating engineers — one after the other to carve channels and bore holes in it until it resembles a Gorgonzola cheese. Hard-to-work materials take more time, so tradesmen charge more for working in them.

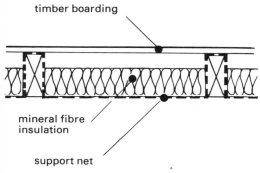

timber boarding

mineral fibre insulation

support net

Fig 27 Section through suspended timber floor, showing system of insulating with mineral fibre (*Eurisol UK*)

GROUND FLOORS — JOIST AND BOARD

The older a house, the greater the likelihood of a 'suspended' timber ground floor — so called because of the air space underneath it. In most postwar houses and in smaller prewar ones, this space is not a cellar, but a shallow void of 600mm to 1m deep (2ft to 3ft), criss-crossed by low 'sleeper' walls to support the floor joists at various points away from their ends and stop them sagging. Sleeper walls are not built solid, but with plenty of gaps to let air circulate and keep the timbers dry. At their ends, floor joists used to be let into notches in the inner leaf or face of opposing walls; a widely used alternative method of attaching them today is to use

joist hangers — steel brackets with formed shoes to fit standard joist sections and straps to fit between block courses in the mortar joints.

As natural timber becomes more expensive, the traditional tongued-and-grooved floor-boards are giving way to flooring-grade chip-board panels, which can be obtained with a variety of interlocking profiles on two opposing, or all four, edges. It is unusual for inter-locking-edge boards to be used on smaller flooring jobs, however, because the cutting and fitting involved produce a lot of square edges in any case, and square-edged boards are less likely than profiled ones to suffer site damage. Instead of allowing for shrinkage after laying as with floorboards, which are supposed to be cramped tightly together before being nailed down, chipboard has to have small gaps left round the perimeter of each room it is laid in, to allow for expansion as it absorbs moisture.

Another important difference between the two types of flooring lies in the methods which have to be adopted with regard to access to underfloor services — gas and water pipes, electric cables and junction boxes. The convention with floorboards is that, where a cable or pipe has to be run across the joists, the notches are always made in the middle of a board, so that nails never interfere with them. Within that proviso, pipes and wires can be and are run almost anywhere, but taking up the odd board or two to find them for repair or maintenance is not too much trouble. As chip-board panels are bigger units, it is rather less convenient to take them up on an experimental basis, so small service panels are inserted at strategic locations, screwed down instead of being nailed, to make removal and replacement simpler and less messy.

Suspended floors at ground level would rot or be weakened by fungal growths if they were not kept dry. Consequently the space underneath the joists needs to have plenty of air circulating round it. Currents of air are introduced artificially through air bricks in the outside walls at about joist level, so whenever an outside wall is cut into or covered up for the purpose of building on an extension, consideration has to be given to the question of maintaining the essential flow of air. Where the new sections of building also have suspended floors, the problem is easily resolved by the air bricks which have to be put into the new walls in any case, but where the extension has a solid floor, extra air bricks may have to be inserted into the existing walls to make up for those lost in the alteration process. Where a porch is added at a section of wall featuring an air brick, it is usual to bury a length of drainpipe in the porch floor to lead air from a new brick to the old one.

GROUND FLOORS — SOLID CONCRETE

Solid concrete ground floors are usually cast on the spot, but can be made up from prefabricated, reinforced slabs resting on cast plinths or pile- or plinth-supported edge beams. In either case, although there is no rot problem, the whole floor has to be kept dry, since fungus thrives in all damp conditions and a wet floor would be unhealthily cold. An equally important reason for keeping a solid floor dry is that, like a suspended floor, it is in contact with the walls and could transmit water to them via a breached DPC. Wooden joists are kept from contact with walls below damp-proof-course

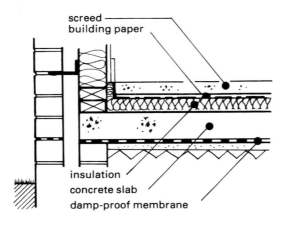

Fig 28 Solid concrete ground floor with mineral-fibre under-screed insulation (*Eurisol UK*)

level by being placed above the DPC — suspended at the appropriate height by joist hangers or supported by a timber beam called a 'soleplate' which in turn rests on the damp-proofing material.

Cast concrete floors have to be protected from rising damp in a somewhat different way. The most typical method is to put a thick plastic sheet over the hardcore, which is first levelled off with sand to stop sharp corners puncturing the sheet. If the concrete is to be thermally insulated — as it certainly should be — the insulation is laid over the plastic and the concrete poured on and levelled. The damp-proofing membrane is continued up the walls at the sides to connect with and overlap the DPC in the walls. Glass- or rock-fibre slabs are sometimes used for ground-floor insulation, compressed to make them strong and rigid. Expanded polystyrene is more often used, being cheaper, and occasionally perlite. Perlite is a white, powdery substance in appearance, but is in fact a mass of tiny bubbles of glass-like material containing the trapped air upon which all insulating materials depend for their efficiency. It behaves just like sand.

Prefabricated concrete slabs often have thermal insulation built in underneath, and may not need a continuous damp-proof membrane, as they are usually cast in the form of a wide, flat, inverted 'U'. They don't touch the ground underneath their broad span, so need protection from rising damp only at their 'feet' where they rest on plinth or beam. Some types of prefabricated floor slab have trunking (tubes or channels) cast in for electric cables, heating elements, central heating or other service pipes. The space underneath can be ventilated by air bricks in the walls and/or by ventilators cast into the 'feet' of the slabs themselves. Inspection hatches can be cast into the spans if required. By and large, prefabricated floors are used more for timber-frame housing than for masonry constructions.

Concrete ground floors are often finished with a thin, smooth screed of concrete finer

Spreading oversite concrete for a solid floored house
(*John Wickersham*)

Levelling concrete to make a solid floor (*John Wickersham*)

Taking delivery of ready-mixed concrete (*John Wickersham*)

Using a vibratory roller to tamp down oversite hardcore. The machine's vibration produces the effect of a roller many times as heavy (*John Wickersham*)

than the mix used for the thicker supporting floor, and then with decorative tiles, stuck down with adhesive. It is increasingly common, however, to put 'floating' timber floors on top of them, usually chipboard on a framework of 50mm x 50mm (2in square) wood battens. In this case, the thermal insulation layer — ideally a resilient material, such as glass-fibre quilt or wood-fibre insulating boards — is placed on top of the concrete, so that it can combine the two jobs of preventing heat loss through the floor and reducing impact sound. The insulation has to be continued at the side of the floor boarding, to isolate it from the wall, and a resilient strip has to be inserted between skirting board and floor, to make the sound reduction performance effective. It is possible to leave out the batten framework in a floating floor, laying the boards direct on to the insulation, but the batten system has the advantage that you can lay wires and pipes underneath the boards, instead of having to bury them in the concrete.

INTERMEDIATE FLOORS IN MASONRY CONSTRUCTIONS

Most masonry houses have joist and board intermediate floors, which are quick to install and convenient for the ceilings underneath them and services in between. In more modern houses, ceilings are normally built up from 10mm (3/8in) thick plasterboard with a thin skim coat of plaster, or one of the harder, usually textured or patterned finishes. In older houses, ceilings are more likely to consist of thin wooden laths about 25mm (1in) wide, nailed to the joists and covered with a sand/cement or lime-mortar layer, pressed well into the spaces between laths and plastered over.

INTERNAL NON-LOAD-BEARING WALLS

In small modern houses, internal walls not carrying essential vertical loads, but simply doing a dividing job, are mostly built in light blockwork, similar to that used for the inner

leaves of the cavity walls but without such high insulating qualities, and therefore cheaper. Older properties may have any one of a number of 'dummy wall' constructions, including single brick, breeze block, timber studding (framework) covered with laths and plaster and — right up to the mid-'twenties — occasionally cane-reinforced plaster. Since they have nothing but themselves to hold up, dummy walls need no heavy foundation. If they were built at the same time as the original house, they probably stand on a sleeper wall, but the lighter ones can simply be built on to a floor. Sometimes, when a wall is needed on an upper floor in a situation where it lacks a lower wall to stand on, it is supported by an RSJ (rolled steel joist) resting on two load-bearing walls.

TOP-FLOOR CEILINGS UNDER PITCHED ROOFS

As there is no floor to carry above it, a top-floor ceiling is supported by much lighter joists than those used for intermediate floors. In some cases these simply rest on the 'wallplates' — heavy sections of wood fixed to the tops of load-bearing walls. In older and/or larger houses, with greater spans between the available points of support, there are fairly widely spaced heavier timbers across the support points, the lighter ceiling joists being 'hung' from them, usually by downward skew-nailing. In either system, the ceiling joists will often be nailed to the rafters where they intersect with them at the outside wallplates.

PITCHED ROOFS

Although they are more expensive to construct, pitched (sloping) roofs are easier to weatherproof reliably than flat roofs, simply because water runs off instead of standing around waiting for the waterproof covering to spring a leak. The higher the pitch, the quicker the water runs off. Therefore, the lower the pitch, the better your waterproofing has to be. In Cotswold traditional housing, for example, you find exceptionally steep roof

Another Swedish ageing-resistant plastic membrane, Tenoroof, used here for roof sarking under tiling battens (*AB Celloplast*)

slopes, because the stone tiles used are not too good at shedding rain.

Pitched roofs can be simple, with two slopes forming a horizontal ridge between gable ends, or complex, featuring additional slopes. Broadly pyramidal forms — for example when there is a slope up from all four walls of a square or oblong house — are called 'hip roofs'. Where a house is L-shaped, or of any other form that requires pitched-roof sections to intersect, 'valleys' are formed as well as hips, and you have 'hip and valley' roofs. In a simple pitched roof, all the rafters can be the same size, as there is no need for the end ones to be stronger, because the gable ends support them. In hip or hip and valley roofs, however, the hip rafters at the corners and the valley rafters in the angles have to be of much larger-section timber than the common rafters in between.

The whole roof is held up by the rafters, which are notched underneath near the lower ends with an L-shaped cut called a 'bird's mouth', so that they can sit firmly on the outside angle of the wallplate, to which they are nailed. Ideally, the rafters would be so numerous and close together that no further support would be needed, but most of the timber used

in the UK has to be expensively imported, so rafters remain economically spaced out, reinforced where spans are large by horizontal auxiliary timbers connecting the main rafters in mid-slope. These extra timbers are called 'purlins', and may themselves be further supported by spars transferring some of the strain on to the load-bearing walls through the horizontal timbers at ceiling level. To stop any tendency for opposing rafters to 'do the splits', they are often connected at purlin level by horizontal spars called 'collars'.

Roofs with meeting slopes have quite complex geometry, as many of the timbers that make up their framework have to have their ends precisely cut, not only as regards length, but as regards angles — mostly compound ones, both mitred and tilted. As already mentioned in Chapter 1, older properties rarely have waterproof sarking felt over the rafters, though some may be boarded. New roof sections added to extend a house will have to have sarking felt between the rafters and the

Fig 29 A special flashing unit for abutting roofs of corrugated plastic. The vertical flange goes under the usual lead, zinc or aluminium flashing strip let into the mortar course above (*Cavity Trays*)

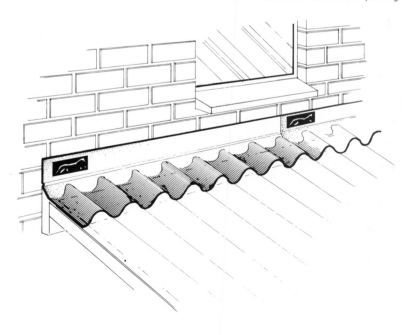

approximately 25mm (1in) square battens that are nailed horizontally on to them to support tiles or slates. It may well be worth asking the builder of your extension to quote for sarking your existing roof whilst he is on site.

Riven quarry slates and the asbestos-cement tiles which can be coloured to look very much like them are always nailed to the battens, but the heavier concrete or clay tiles have lugs underneath at the top end to hook over the battens. They also have nail holes, but except in very exposed areas are usually nailed only at strategic points — in sheltered districts probably only at ridges and eaves. Hip-roof sloping ridges and all apex ridges have ridge tiles mortared on to bridge the gap between meeting stretches of slates or tiles. Valleys, however, must have either special angled slates or tiles or, more commonly, a lead, zinc or aluminium flashing strip fitted under the slates or tiles. This is not a simple strip of metal, as it has to incorporate a fold to allow it to expand and contract with heat and cold, without tearing away from its nails or buckling upwards.

At its bottom end, the valley flashing is extended to hang over the roof's gutter, which is not horizontal but slopes gently down to a downpipe or series of downpipes disgorging rainwater into the drainage system.

LEAN-TO ROOFS

Lean-to — or 'mono-pitched' — roofs may be constructed with rafters, felt, battens and tiles or slates, or they may be simple sheet structures made in corrugated or otherwise profiled plastic or metal sheeting. The gutter drainage works similarly to that for the multi-pitched roof, but the waterproofing problem arises at the sheeting's joint with the vertical house wall. The angle between the sheet and the wall is most simply covered by one of the profiled flashing strips available — such as the Type F made for corrugated plastic lean-to roofs by Cavity Trays Ltd. This takes care of the awkward problem of folding metal into corrugations, leaving only the straightforward job of waterproofing the joint between the shaped

flashing strip's flat upstand and the vertical masonry. One of the cavity trays designed to double as a DPC can be used for the job, or a lead, zinc or aluminium flashing strip can be mortared into a groove chiselled into one of the horizontal joints and dressed over the upstand, so that the rain has nowhere to run but down the wall, over the metal, along the profiled flashing and down the sheeting into the gutter and drain. If aluminium flashing is used, it has to be treated with bituminous paint before being mortared in, to protect it from attack by the chemicals in cement. With this proviso, it is an excellent and long-lasting substitute for expensive lead.

FLAT ROOFS

Any roof with a pitch of less than 10° is regarded as 'flat', because it will not shed rain quickly enough to make surfacing with slates or tiles a practical proposition; the water would simply drip through the interstices. Even roofs that are visually flat normally have a built-in slope of 3°, to provide at least some water run-off properties, but the surface must be absolutely waterproof.

Few domestic flat roofs are made up of concrete slabs, which are difficult to insulate and need cranes for their construction. Flat roofs on garage and other extensions — usually but by no means always single-storey ones — mainly consist of joists covered with WBP (water- and boil-proof) plywood or moisture-resistant chipboard. Mastic asphalt, butyl rubber and metal surfaces are possible, amongst others, but the normal treatment is three layers of heavy-duty roofing felt, each bedded in hot bitumen, laid with the strips forming each layer running at right angles to those forming adjacent layers. Gutters are sometimes fixed beneath the overhang on flat roofs. Occasionally deep fascias clad with tiles or slates are put round the edges, to help an otherwise non-matching flat roof blend in with the rest of a house. Where the roof has a parapet, waterproofing at the edges meeting the parapet is achieved in the same way as for

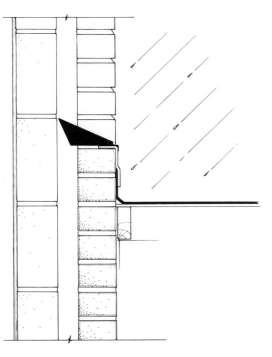

Fig 30 A cavity tray/flashing strip combination for an abutting flat roof (*Cavity Trays*)

joints with other vertical brick or blockwork.

Light-coloured stone chippings are embedded in the final coat of bitumen — not for decorative purposes, but to reflect the heat of the sun as far as possible, which can melt the bitumen whilst making the boarding underneath expand, so that joints in the waterproof skin above the roof 'deck' tend to pull apart and ultimately leak.

There are two ways of insulating a flat roof. The one favoured for industrial and commercial buildings is the 'warm-roof' system, so called because most of the mass of the roof construction — the joists and decking — is on the underside of the insulation, which is laid in the form of rigid slabs between the decking and the waterproof covering of the roof. Although the covering is subject to wide temperature fluctuations, the roof deck is not, remaining at or near the warm temperature maintained inside the building. It is easier to insulate decks constructed with profiled metal sheet or

concrete slabs by the warm-roof system, because the rigid insulation spans any irregularities or undulations in the decking, and makes a good base for the waterproof cover. Another advantage is that there is no need to ventilate the space under the roof deck to prevent condensation, since it remains warm enough not to induce condensation in the first place.

With the alternative 'cold-roof' system normally used for domestic flat roofs, one of the benefits is that the waterproof covering is bonded directly to the timber or manufactured board decking, so that the roof covering has less tendency to move relative to its base under thermal stress than it would mounted in contact with a layer of insulation. Rigid insulation costs more than the quilt, batt or loosefill insulation materials which can be used between a roof deck and plasterboard. There has to be a

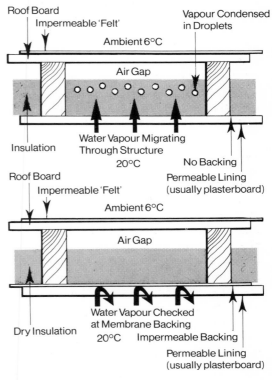

Fig 30a These drawings show why a vapour check membrane needs to be provided on the warm side of insulation material

space of 50mm (2in) or more between the insulation and the roof deck, and that space has to be ventilated by air bricks in opposing sides of the roof equivalent to continuous slots along those sides 25mm (1in) wide. The air bricks should have grilles designed to stop large insects and birds from entering the roof space. Condensation in the space above the insulation can theoretically be prevented by a vapour-check membrane under the insulation. If this membrane could be made totally continuous over the whole roof area, and also 100 per cent efficient, no water vapour could get through to condense as it passed through the roof structure to the colder levels. Nevertheless, a **vapour-check membrane should be incorporated on the warm side of the insulation**, in the form of polythene sheet 60 microns thick (250 gauge), kraft paper or plasterboard backed with polythene or aluminium foil. Mineral-fibre insulation is available faced with polythene or kraft paper, the insulation being cut to the right width for fitting between joists at standard spacings and the vapour-check facing material projecting beyond it to form convenient flanges for stapling to the joists. If the cellulose-fibre form of insulation is used, the backed plasterboard is installed first, and the material is blown in sideways before the fascia boards are fitted.

The terms 'cold roof' and 'warm roof' have no significance with regard to the insulating abilities of the type of structure concerned: a cold roof with a higher level of insulation than a warm roof will keep the space underneath it warmer. To reach the present Building Regulation requirement for thermal performance, a flat roof with a timber deck will probably need at least 100mm (4in) of cellulose- or glass-fibre insulation. The same standard of performance can be obtained by 75mm (3in) of similar insulation installed at ceiling level in a pitched roof, but to achieve it in pitched-roof structures by under-slate or tile insulation — as you have to when making rooms in a loft — would require an approximately 25 per cent greater thickness of any given insulation material, as in the case of flat-roof construction.

TIMBER-FRAME CONSTRUCTIONS

Many examples still remain of the half-timbered house style, widely imitated by the mock-Tudor frontage. In half-timbered construction, the frame — usually of oak — was not clad, but its spaces were filled in with whatever 'mortar' was available from local sources. Fire was the main reason for the almost total changeover that eventually took place to masonry construction. Most of the buildings lost in the Great Fire of London in the reign of Charles II were made of wood. Modern timber-framed buildings, however, have fire ratings as good as those for brick- or stone-built ones, thanks to present-day fire-proofing and construction techniques applicable to wood and wood-based components.

Essential differences from masonry constructions

In a timber-frame construction, the load-bearing shell consists entirely of wood. Even though a house may look brick built from the outside, it could still be a timber-frame house, with a brick 'skin' that is not in fact holding anything up. It is possible to fabricate a timber frame as building progresses, cutting and fixing studding, joists and other units as and when required, but most systems use factory-assembled panels, which can be quickly bolted down to the base or to each other on site. A typical panel would be made from 100mm x 50mm (4in x 2in) studs, forming an outer frame, which would have further similar studs standing vertically at 600mm (2ft) intervals, braced with horizontal timbers at some points — either for added strength or to make window or door openings. The whole frame would be covered with a skin of exterior-quality plywood sheathing, 13mm (½in) thick or more.

Floor construction is very similar to that used for conventional houses, but most roofs in timber-frame construction are at least partly prefabricated, rafters, ceiling joists and bracing being delivered to the site ready assembled, like large coat-hangers. These

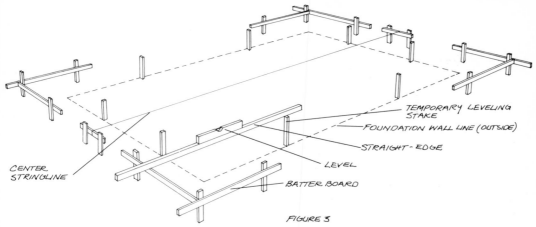

FIGURE 3

Fig 31 Site markers laid out for a timber-frame house (*American Plywood Association*)

'rafter trusses' or 'trussed rafters' are usually fixed together by multi-perforated galvanised steel connector plates called 'gang-nail plates', which are increasingly used in normal roof constructions.

Advantages of the timber-frame system

Speed of erection is one of the chief advantages of the timber-frame system, reducing overall labour costs and cutting down the risk of having to wait for the weather since, once the foundations are laid, houses can be brought quickly to the stage at which most work takes place under cover. It is not uncommon for a system-built house to have its shell completed, including the roof, in a single working day.

Most of the work involved in putting up a timber-frame house is 'dry', so there is no prolonged drying-out period, as there can be with an average brick house, whose construction requires something in the region of 4,500 litres (1,000 gallons) of water. Timber-frame structures, surprisingly, resist ground movements caused by earthquakes, mining subsidence and heavy traffic vibration better than masonry constructions, being lighter in mass and better able to withstand 'racking' (sideways-pull) loads.

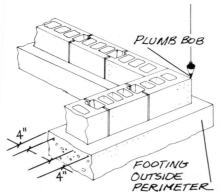

Fig 32 Corner detail of a block wall base for a timber-frame house (*American Plywood Association*)

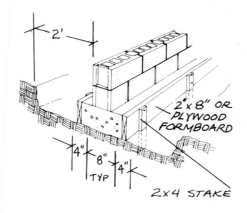

Fig 33 Perimeter wall base for a timber-frame house, showing shuttering method (*American Plywood Association*)

103

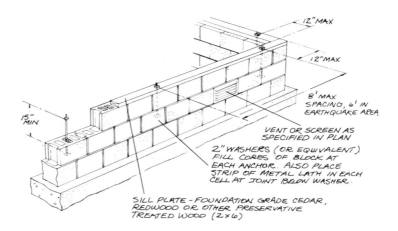

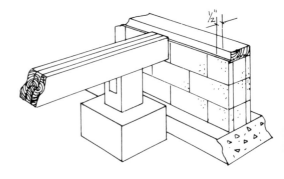

Fig 34 Masonry foundation for timber-frame house completed, up to sill-plate stage. The sill plate is timber, and is fixed to the wall with masonry anchors (*American Plywood Association*)

Fig 35 End detail of timber-frame house central-floor support girder (*American Plywood Association*)

Fig 36 Completed girder. Blocks stand on oversite concrete (*American Plywood Association*)

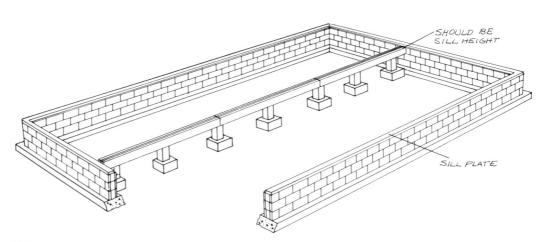

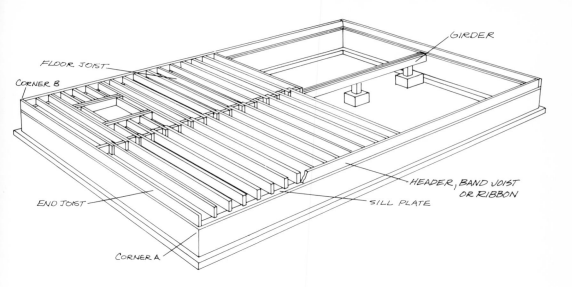

Fig 37 Partially completed floor in a timber-frame structure. Note joists overlapping on central girder, strengthening webs at overlap and access hatch (*American Plywood Association*)

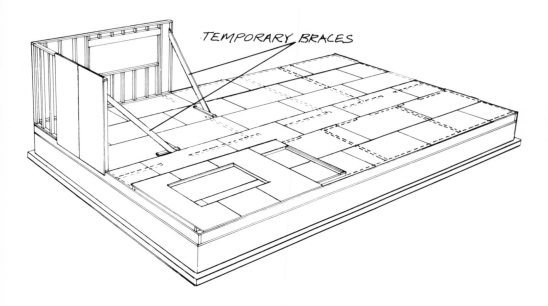

Fig 38 Temporary braces are used to support the first sections of a timber-framed house's walls, until the circuit is completed and the structure firm and true (*American Plywood Association*)

105

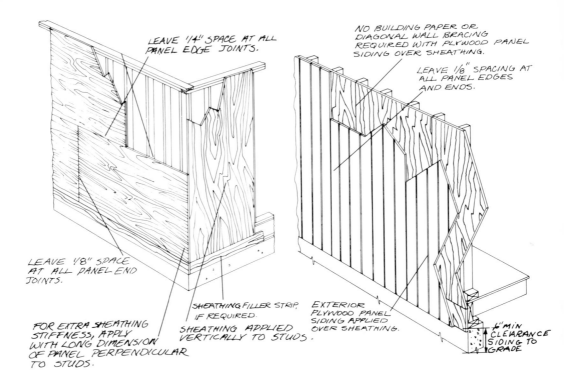

Fig 39 Two methods of cladding timber frames
(*American Plywood Association*)

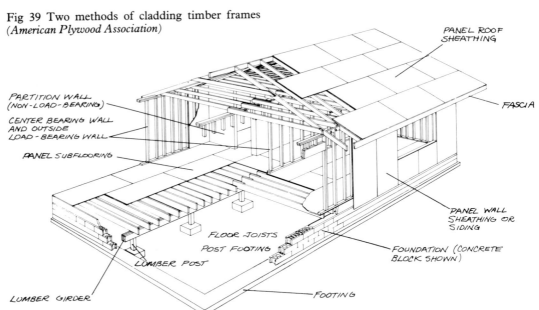

Fig 40 Cut-away drawing of a timber-frame house,
showing wall and roof sheathing system (*American
Plywood Association*)

106

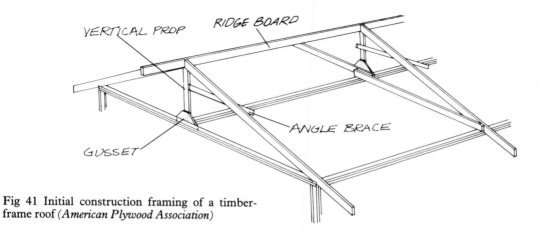

Fig 41 Initial construction framing of a timber-frame roof (*American Plywood Association*)

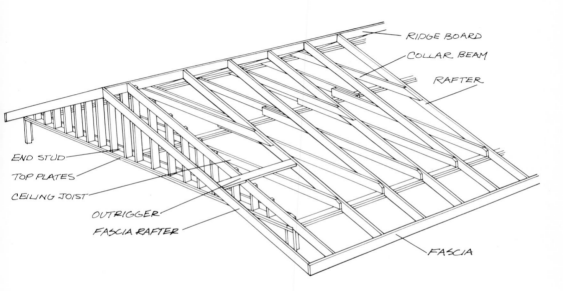

Fig 42 Complete timber-frame roof structure, to rafter stage (*American Plywood Association*)

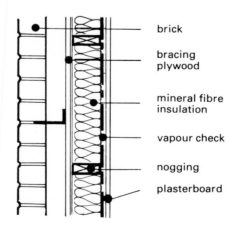

brick

bracing plywood

mineral fibre insulation

vapour check

nogging

plasterboard

Fig 43 Section through a timber-frame wall with a brick skin, insulated with mineral fibre

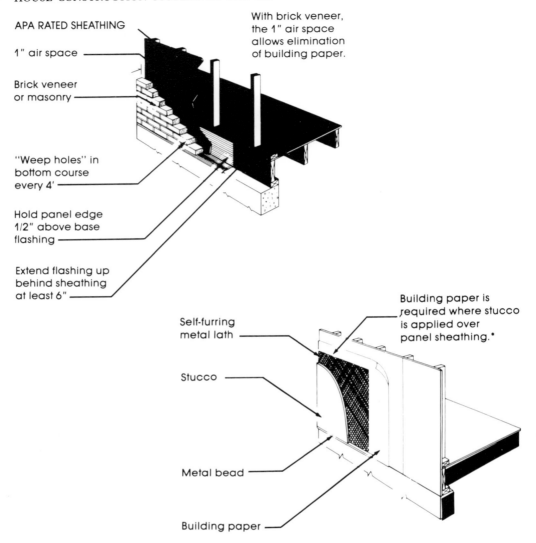

APA RATED SHEATHING

1" air space

Brick veneer
or masonry

"Weep holes" in
bottom course
every 4'

Hold panel edge
1/2" above base
flashing

Extend flashing up
behind sheathing
at least 6"

With brick veneer,
the 1" air space
allows elimination
of building paper.

Self-furring
metal lath

Stucco

Metal bead

Building paper

Building paper is
required where stucco
is applied over
panel sheathing.*

(*left*) Fig 44 A timber frame may have a brick 'skin', but the frame carries the load, not the bricks (*American Plywood Association*)

(*right*) Fig 45 Stucco may be applied to a timber frame instead of brick or other forms of cladding (*American Plywood Association*)

It is cheaper to insulate a timber-frame structure to a high standard than most masonry structures, since instead of special cavity-fill arrangements the extra insulation can be more simply provided by mineral-fibre quilt or sprayed cellulose-fibre fillings in the panels before the plasterboard goes on.

Disadvantages of timber-frame structures

Although the heat-saving characteristics of a heavily insulated timber-frame structure are extremely good, allowing it to be warmed up quickly and kept warm economically, it does not have the heat-storage capability of a masonry-walled construction, so heating arrangements should incorporate good thermostatic control and fast-response heating units. Because the insulation needs a vapour-check membrane on the warm side of it, moisture cannot pass through the walls to the outside atmosphere, so particular attention has to be paid to ventilation to prevent condensation trouble. It is not difficult to organise suitable ventilation or dehumidification, but it needs to be thought about. Modern timber-frame houses are increasingly built with 'real' fireplaces, which help the problem, using insulated, twin-wall prefabricated chimney systems, described in detail on pp 162–164.

Despite its long history of satisfactory service in the severe weather of Sweden and North America, the timber-frame building system has received a lot of undue criticism in the UK, particularly from the Association of Metropolitan Authorities. The National House Building Council has analysed the facts available in some depth, establishing that timber-frame houses have as good a reliability record as those built by other methods, the defects receiving adverse publicity being attributable in most cases to faulty workmanship, rather than to any inherent weakness in the system.

Claddings for timber-frame structures

A great variety of claddings can be attached to timber-frame shells. Natural timber boards or shingles, PVC-covered rigid foam interlocking 'boards', cast concrete or clay sections, tiles or slates, sheet metal or pressed metal panels profiled to look like scalloped tiles — such as Broderick Cascade copper or coloured steel panels — can all be used, or brick or block skins built outside the shell, attached by ties which are nailed to the shell, and inserted into mortar joints in the brick or block skin. Alternatively, it is possible to apply stucco or other renderings over expanded metal stapled to the plywood outer sheathing.

Timber-frame extensions to traditional structures

There is no technical reason against an extension to a traditional masonry-built house being of timber-frame construction, but the planning authority will probably have strong views about the finishing skin being a good match for the original house. All the advantages of quick completion and good thermal insulation exist in a timber-frame extension just as they do in a complete house, and the system lends itself very well to DIY building. Most of the building firms experienced in timber-frame work, however, are involved in building new homes rather than extensions.

7
Building Components, Materials and Service Systems

BRITISH STANDARDS AND AGRÉMENT CERTIFICATES

Ideally, a manufacturer likes to be able to claim that his product conforms to an appropriate British Standard, but British Standards have to be very painstakingly framed. Each takes a great deal of time on the part of committees largely made up of technical members drawn from relevant industrial concerns and technical education establishments. They have to decide not only what standards are to be applied, but the terms in which they are to be expressed, and each new standard is circulated in draft form to all major manufacturers and users of the type of equipment or material concerned before final approval. Care also has to be taken that there is no lack of co-ordination between British and EEC standards or 'norms'.

Where a product breaks new ground — as the Furfix wall extension profile does, for example — there can be a long time-lapse between the products coming on the market and a British Standard coming into existence for it to conform to. However utilitarian the product, a manufacturer bringing out something new can scarcely be expected to keep it on the shelf for perhaps years until the extremely thorough British Standards Institute process is completed. To cater for such situations, a government-sponsored body has been set up to test and evaluate products — in collaboration with other bodies such as the Fire Research Station and the Building Research Station where necessary — and issue interim approvals in the form of 'Agrément Certificates'. This body is the British Board of Agrément, until recently called the Agrément Board.

The British Board of Agrément — often referred to as the BBA — must, like the British Standards Institute, maintain a non-insular stance. Its EEC orientation is the reason for the French word in its title, which has the sense of 'approval' rather than 'agreement'. It has become something of a watchdog on the quality and performance of all kinds of products for the construction industry, not only issuing certificates, but withdrawing or revising them. To enable the validity of any Agrément Certificate to be checked, the board puts out a continually updated *Abstracts and Index* publication, which may be found in a large reference library. Alternatively, the board will confirm or deny the validity of any particular certificate in answer to written or telephoned enquiries.

An agrément certificate is not a carte blanche approval of a product or piece of equipment, but a qualified assessment. It is numbered and validated up to a date stated in the heading, under which appear the manufacturer's full name and address and the name of the product to which the certificate refers, noting any separate firm which markets the product if the manufacturer does not do this himself. The certificate goes on to delineate precisely the applications for which the product is intended, and gives its assessment of its suitability for them, making provisos and imposing limitations if necessary. A cladding material, for example, may be approved for use in areas of the country classed as 'sheltered' or 'moderately exposed', but not approved for areas of severe exposure. There will be a statement as to how far the product satisfies relevant Building Regulations obtaining in England and Wales, Northern Ireland, Scotland and Greater London — four different sets, as previously explained.

Technical specification, manufacturing, delivery, storage and installation information are set out, as are details of general performance, loadings, resistances and other technical data, often in tabular form. Sectional drawings are included where necessary to make points clear. Most manufacturers are only too pleased to supply copies of their agrément certificates, since these are highly valued endorsements of their product's suitability for its specified use — endorsements which can cost them a great deal of money and trouble to obtain. Without an agrément certificate a product's sales potential is not at all good. Remember that a certificate endorses a product, not a manufacturer as such. If he makes fifty building products, he needs fifty agrément certificates.

CEMENT, CONCRETE AND MORTAR

Cement is an essential ingredient in concrete mixes, concrete blocks and bricks, precast slabs and flooring units, concrete lintels, drainage goods, paving flags and blocks, roofing and cladding tiles, mortars and renderings. Contact with water turns it into a highly adhesive compound, capable of bonding to sand, gravel and other coarse aggregates, metals, all kinds of brick and stone, and existing concrete. Normally light grey in colour, it can be bought white or coloured, or in special formulations for making masonry mortar or concrete mixes for resisting sulphate attack in certain aggresive soils. The masonry mortar version is unsuitable for any other application.

It has been estimated that cement mixes increase in strength for fifty years or more, but for all practical purposes maximum strength is attained in twenty-eight days. As the cement hardening process works by chemical reaction, not by water evaporation, setting concrete is often kept artificially wet by covering it with plastic sheeting or even by spraying additional water on it to stop it drying out too soon, but

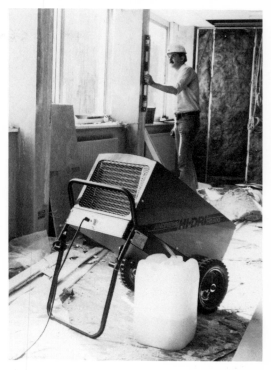

The use of an industrial dryer speeds up the building process. This one is the Andrews Hi-Dri HD 500 (*Andrews Industrial Equipment*)

the initial mix should not be too wet. In freezing conditions, the free water in the concrete mix can turn to ice crystals and cause cracking or disintegration, so frost-proofing agents such as Febspeed have to be added to the 'gauging' water to stop this happening if frost is at all likely.

Concrete for foundations mixed on site contains cement, sand and aggregate (stones/pebbles/gravel) with a maximum particle size of 20mm (¾in) and sharp or 'grit' sand in the proportions of 1:3½:2½. Where premixed sand and aggregate (usually called 'ballast') is used, the cement/ballast ratio is 1:5. When ready-mixed concrete is used for foundations, it will be mixed to a British Standard specification: C7.5P in BS 5328; ready mixes for general purposes such as steps, plinths and floors are to C20P in the same standard. A site mix for general purposes would contain cement, sand and aggregate in the ratio 1:2:3, or cement and ballast 1:4. For paving applications outside, ready-mixed concrete has the distinct advantage of entrained air, which you cannot get with a site mix and which lessens the likelihood of flaking and surface friability in cold weather, especially on drives where cars dripping road salt may stand in winter. The ready-mix concrete firms have a special formula for this job.

Mortars and sand/cement rendering mixes differ from concrete in that they have no coarse aggregate in them. Otherwise, they behave in much the same way. Texture varies according to the type of sand used, masonry mortars needing soft sand like that found on the seashore and rendering needing washed plasterer's sand — sharp, but not as sharp as concreting sand. Masonry cement used in the proportion of 1:4½ produces a more easily worked mortar, less likely to crack than one made with ordinary Portland cement. An alternative mix to achieve the same advantages consists of ordinary Portland or white Portland cement, hydrated lime and sand in the ratio 1:1:5½, and another consists of ordinary or white Portland cement and sand in the ratio 1:5½ with a mortar plasticiser added to the gauging water. Mortars often need to be coloured to tone with the bricks. Mortar made without cement, using only lime and sand, is soft and weak compared to cement types, and nowadays is used only in fireplace work, where its flexibility in changing temperatures is valuable.

FILLING AND PATCHING COMPOUNDS

The number and variety of filling and patching compounds on the market are virtually limitless, but a few special-purpose kinds may be worth mentioning, as small problems occur even in new work and it is often necessary to make good existing structures where they join on to new ones. Ordinary resin-based fillers of the car-body type and plaster-based general-purpose DIY fillers may not be good enough

for heavy-duty, permanent repairs to concrete or masonry building components.

Epoxy-resin-based putty is a highly adhesive filler, rather costly for large jobs, but extremely versatile in that it sticks firmly to almost every household and building material except flexible polythene and PVC. To give some idea of its strength, it would take a pull of about 45kg (500lb) to separate two 25mm (1in) square pieces of metal stuck together with it. Epoxy putty is not only waterproof, but resists detergents, soaps, cleaning solvents, chemicals in general and oils, and it is a non-conductor of electricity. Like most epoxy products, it is a two-part formulation, the setting action being a purely chemical one that does not start until the separately packed filler and hardener components are mixed together in equal proportions. You can sand it, but it is a very hard, ceramic-natured substance when cured, so you should smooth it at least near to the shape you want with a moist, soapy cloth as you apply it. It is difficult to press into small cracks, but it will happily roll into spaghetti-like strands for caulking operations — in which context it will tolerate a bit of dampness, but will not stick in the presence of grease or oil. You can anchor bolts, screws or hooks in it, but if you want to screw anything out of an epoxy putty plug once it is cured, the threads need to be lightly oiled or greased before they are screwed into the uncured plug.

Hydraulic cement — sold under the name of Waterplug — is a quick-setting compound for sealing gaps, joints and holes in concrete or masonry walls and floors. Its value lies in its ability to stop seeping water instantly on application, even quite fast flows, expanding as it sets. It will set under water, and will anchor bolts and other fixings. Since it does not shrink after setting, repairs made with it are permanent. Walls, floors, concrete pipes and lintels or other building components should not be oozing before treatment with this material, but they can be repaired with it whilst wet from rain or hosing, when treatment with normal patch/fill materials might not be quick enough.

BRICKS

Bricks are made from clay, from concrete or from calcium silicate. By and large, clay and concrete bricks — clay being the more widely used in most areas of the UK — are stronger than calcium silicate ones. There are, however, many more factors affecting strength and performance than the basic material bricks are made of, and there are over 2,000 different kinds of brick manufactured in the country. Within the middle quality band, there are some calcium silicate bricks which are stronger than some of the clay ones.

The fact that a clay brick has a good compressive strength rating does not always mean that it is durable, but calcium silicate bricks' durability is directly proportional to their strength rating. Clay bricks and concrete bricks are classified under BS 3921 under three broad headings: common bricks, which are anything from plain to ugly in appearance but normally of average to good strength; facing bricks manufactured for their good looks; and engineering bricks, which fall into a precisely defined compressive strength range and have particularly low water absorption characteristics. In terms of quality, meaning durability, the same BS classifies clay bricks as 'special', suitable for exposed locations subject to saturation and frost; 'ordinary', of normal durability but requiring protective design features when used in parts of exposed walls especially liable to catch the weather; and 'interior'. Common and facing bricks may fall into any of these categories, but engineering bricks — whether 'common engineering' or 'facing engineering' — are all classed as 'special'. Calcium silicate bricks have their own British Standard — BS 187.

In terms of shape and type, BS 3921 defines bricks as 'solid' (plain rectangular); 'perforated' (with small holes through them taking up to 25 per cent of their volume); and 'frog' — these being hollowed out on top to a greater or lesser extent, though the hollow must not represent more than 25 per cent of the volume, as with the perforated type. Both holes and frogs are designed to give mortar a better key on the brick, but bricks are often laid frog-down to save mortar.

The space taken up by a laid brick is nominally 225mm x 112.5mm x 75mm high (8⁷⁄₁₆in x 4⁷⁄₁₆in x 3in high), assuming that it is a British brick and that standard 10mm (³⁄₈in) wide mortar joints have been used — the brick itself measuring 10mm (³⁄₈in) less all round. Because these dimensions produce a unit whose length is twice its breadth and three times its height, it is easy to integrate bricks with one another when they are laid in different directions. Several bigger sizes are recognised by the British Standards Draft for Development DD34: 1971, but you are unlikely to come across them in the average stockyard, as the great majority of houses are built either with the BS size or with the previous imperial standard bricks which are very nearly the same size. However, the larger sizes have taken architects' fancy from time to time, so if your house does happen to be built with bigger bricks than the BS ones already described, the size you will need will probably be one of these:

> 300mm x 100mm x 100mm (11¹³⁄₁₆in x 4in x 4in);
> 200mm x 100mm x 100mm (7⁷⁄₈in x 4in x 4in);
> 300mm x 100mm x 75mm (11¹³⁄₁₆in x 4in x 3in);
> 200mm x 100mm x 75mm (7⁷⁄₈in x 4in x 3in).

Not all manufacturers make all these sizes, nor do they all make all the various types, textures and shades of facing brick. Materials, surfacing and firing techniques can all be varied to affect a brick's appearance. Whatever the complexity of the situation, it is important to match the bricks of a house very closely — allowing for the way they will weather and mature — when adding new walls. If you run into a problem finding bricks to match your existing ones, the Brick Development Association will always try to identify the original brick specification, or recommend a suitable substitute product, if you can hack a sample out for them.

Bricklaying workmanship

A brick wall is not just many bricks stuck together with a little mortar. There is a great

These are a few of the 90-odd facing brick designs produced by Butterley (*Butterley Building Materials*)

deal more mortar than you may think, and it is supposed to fill all the joints — both horizontal and vertical — to form a strong and consistent mass. If you watch your bricklayers at work with any degree of intensity, you are likely to provoke a strike, but there is nothing to stop you casting the odd interested glance as you go by, to reassure yourself you have found good ones. Here are a few of the points to look for.

Most bricklayers trowel a shallow trough in the horizontal layer of mortar before laying the next course of bricks. This is known as 'furrowing' and is frowned on by bricklaying purists, but unless the furrows are very deep, leaving next to no mortar in the centre of the joint, there is no great harm in the practice. Ideally, though, the layer of mortar should be either flat or slightly humped in the middle.

Vertical joints (technical name 'perpends') can be a nuisance to fill completely with mortar, as they should be filled. Correct filling is done by 'buttering' mortar on to the brick end before laying it. It is possible to scamp this job by simply scraping narrow strips of mortar on the front and back edges, so that a joint looks filled, but is not. Oddly enough, the non-filling of vertical joints does not affect the compressive strength of the wall too much, but it is a dangerous practice for brickwork exposed to driving rain, which can quickly turn a hollow perpend into a fissure, through which rain will be forced — perhaps with enough momentum to cross the cavity and wet the inner leaf.

Another vital factor in ensuring resistance to rain penetration is the method chosen for finishing the mortar joints on the face of the brickwork. Flush joints, in which the mortar is rubbed level with the brick surfaces, give fairly good resistance, and are the most aesthetically pleasing joints for most highly textured bricks. Weathered or 'struck' joints involve pressing the mortar into the horizontal joints, to tuck it slightly under the bottom edges of the bricks and slope it forward to come flush with the top edges. An equally resistant joint is one made by dishing both horizontal and vertical joints slightly with a round bar. This is called a 'concave', 'keyed' or 'bucket-handle' joint.

Recessed joints, made by pressing the mortar deep into the interstices so that the edges of the bricks stand out in sharp relief, are striking and decorative, but take away much of the strength of a wall compared to conventional pointing. Bricks suitable for this kind of finish need to have flat faces and clean edges to guide the raking tool evenly, and also need to be particularly frost resistant, since a great deal of rainwater can collect in the deep joints.

Damp-proof-course laying

Damp-proof courses can consist of special DPC bricks to BS 3921 set in a strong sand/cement mortar. In this case, there are two courses, so that the vertical joint staggering interrupts straight 'leakage' paths for rising damp. Alternatively, two courses of slates set in a similar mortar can be used, making a joint about 25mm (1in) thick. The more popular bitumen felt and pitch polymer flexible roll DPCs are the ones subject to most abuse. They are supposed to be laid on a bed of mortar, not direct on a brick course or concrete base where they may be punctured or torn by sharp projections. They are also supposed to stick out of the face of the brickwork, not be tucked right in and hidden by mortar.

Efflorescence on brickwork faces

White deposits on brick faces can be unsightly, but they are absolutely harmless, usually dissolving away in the rain with time. Efflorescence consists of salt crystals. Brickwork is wet when laid, so it tends to absorb any salts there may be quite readily at that stage. The salts may originally exist in the clay from which the brick was made or in the mortar sand. Absorbed into the brick in solution, they find their way out to the brick surface with the water as the drying-out process takes place, and are left on the surface as crystals when the water evaporates into the atmosphere. Unless the brick structure is so badly designed as to allow a constant flow of water through the outer leaf, dissolving and precipitating more salts on the way, the efflorescence should disappear naturally within a year or so. It is better to let the rain wash it away than to scrub at the brick surface, which might be damaged in the process, especially if it is of a type with an applied, thin facing — perhaps of coloured sand. Heavy deposits may have to be brushed off, but no wire brushes should be used, only bristle.

Naturally, the more open and porous the texture of a brick, the more susceptible it is to efflorescence of salt crystals; so harder, denser types suffer from it less than open-pored ones, and calcium silicate bricks are subject to the problem only when salts are brought into contact with them from extraneous sources, such as the ground or other building materials left stacked against the wall.

Sulphate attack

Sulphate attack is a rare but potentially dangerous phenomenon. It occurs when brickwork becomes saturated — due to faulty damp-proofing, for example — so releasing sulphates from the bricks in considerable quantity. These combine with one of the constituents of the Portland cement in the mortar, tri-calcium aluminate, making the mortar joints expand and subjecting the brickwork to the risk of frost damage. Sulphate attack is most likely to happen when faulty copings,

Furfix profiles, for anchoring new walls at right angles to existing ones, without cutting or chasing-in (*Allmat Ltd*)

flashing strips, damp-proof courses or window sills allow long-term saturation of the brickwork. Weak — meaning low in cement content — mortars also exacerbate the problem, as do the cheaper kinds of brick, which tend to have higher sulphate content than special grades. Properly protected and drained brickwork which can dry out quickly, strong mortar made with sulphate-resisting cement and bricks with a low sulphate content all make sulphate attack less likely.

Joining new walls to existing ones

If new bricks were to be simply butted up against an existing wall, the mortar joint would not remain secure or waterproof for very long. The usual techniques employed consist of cutting out a channel in the old wall, where the new one is to be built out to form a T-junction with it, and of comb-jointing old and new sections of wall, where they are to be joined end to end.

Comb-jointing is both strong and effective, and works well visually so long as the old and new bricks are a near-perfect match for each other. Channels can be time-consuming and messy to cut, however, and can weaken the old wall, at least temporarily. A recently introduced building hardware invention for avoiding these difficulties is the Furfix profile wall extension system, which consists of a metal U-section profile, fixed to the existing wall by one of the standard heavy-duty masonry anchorage devices — such as plugs and coach screws, expanding bolts or shot-fired bolts (see

DRILLING WALL   FIXING PROFILE   TYING-IN   INTERNAL WALL

p140). There are galvanised profiles for joining internal walls and stainless steel ones for external applications. Since U-section profiles always leave a strip of metal visible on an exposed wall face, single-flange L-section versions are also available. All types have small hook-tabs punched into them, so that standard butterfly-type wall ties can be clipped into them every 300mm (1ft) to hold the brick or blockwork securely.

Mastic or other vertical damp-proof-course material can be inserted between profile and existing masonry, where this is required to satisfy building regulations. Furfix profile flanges are designed to locate bricks or blocks, but cannot be expected to take lateral loads, which have to be provided for in the same way as for normally jointed extension walls. The width of profile has to be chosen to suit the width of wall or leaf to be attached.

LINTELS

Wherever door and window openings occur in brick, block or stone walls, support has to be provided across the top of the apertures for whatever is above it. One way of providing this support is to insert a beam of reinforced concrete into the masonry to span the opening. Such beams are called — in common with other types designed for the same purpose — lintels, though most architects spell it 'lintols' for some reason. Concrete lintels may be factory-made, prestressed, steel-reinforced products or actually cast in place. Some are of rectangular section and go the whole thickness of the wall, whilst another type, known as a 'boot lintel' by reason of its instepped profile, features a depth at the outer leaf of a cavity about half that which it has at the inner leaf, so that where it crosses the cavity the top surface slopes down towards the outer leaf. A flexible damp-proof course laid over it will therefore carry any water entering the cavity in the right direction.

Other types of concrete lintel are installed in pairs — one over each leaf of a cavity wall. These are sometimes one brick deep, some-times two, depending on the load they have to carry. All of them need to have a damp-proof course or cavity tray fitted above them, directing water either over the top of the lintel to the outside of the outer leaf, or to the inside of the outer leaf and down to the outside of the door or window frame.

Concrete lintels are strong and long-lived, but they have two disadvantages for house building. They are heavy to handle, especially where second- and third-storey work is involved, and they present a hard, difficult-to-drill mass over the tops of windows, just where curtain rails have to be fixed. Steel lintels overcome the weight problem by being hollow. Some kinds — most of the Catnic lintels, for example — are fabricated from steel strips welded together to form various profiles of box section, usually with a channel on the inside perforated to provide a key for a sand/cement fill on the inside vertical face. This is easier to fix curtain rails to than reinforced concrete.

Both Catnic and IG Lintels make lintels with flat flanges on the inside to allow the blockwork of the inner cavity wall leaf to continue uninterrupted, so that curtain rails can be fixed without any special measures. Both firms also make models for use in different cavity and brick/block width combinations, solid walls, timber-frame constructions, installation at eaves level and for fitting over internal doorways — heavier ones for load-bearing walls, lighter and shallower ones for partition walls.

Most of the IG range of lintels is of folded steel construction, without any welds at all, only the longer lengths needing welded reinforcement. Many of the IG cavity wall lintels are of inverted U-section, with a horizontal flange on either side. Where a key is required for plastering — on the underside of the inner of the two flanges, for example — the U-section has a preservative-treated timber insert, to which wire mesh is stapled. The mesh in contact with the inner flange is clipped to it.

Few building control officers will allow any form of lintel to be installed without a damp-proof course above it. With steel lintels, this is

A steel lintel over double doors (*Catnic Components Ltd*)

A steel lintel over a ground-floor window (*Catnic Components Ltd*)

A steel lintel over a window at eaves level (*Catnic Components Ltd*)

Another design of steel lintel over a ground-floor window (*Catnic Components Ltd*)

A steel lintel over a garage door, in a solid wall (*Catnic Components Ltd*)

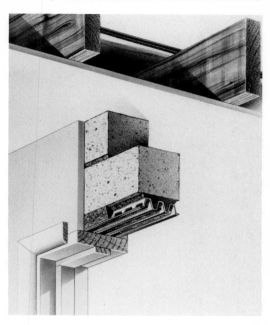

A light steel lintel in a non-load-bearing partition wall (*Catnic Components Ltd*)

A steel lintel over an opening in a timber-frame wall with a non-load-bearing brick skin (*Catnic Components Ltd*)

119

almost invariably a flexible one. Especially in Scotland, additional insulation material may have to be incorporated into lintels to give walls sufficient resistance to the passage of heat to prevent condensation occurring within the thickness of the masonry — 'interstitial condensation'. As steel lintels are galvanised, any particular rough treatment on site can damage the zinc coating which stops them rusting, as can sawing, drilling or welding operations. Contact with copper or copper-bearing materials, such as brass or bronze wall ties, must be avoided to guard against the danger of an electrolytic action being set up, and galvanised steel lintels must also be protected from any water run-off from these materials. Other common-sense precautions include the banning of mortar additives based on calcium chloride and of mortar sand of marine origin that has not been properly washed to reduce the salt content.

No matter how strong any kind of lintel may be, it can fail short of its rated load-carrying capacity if it is not given adequate support, in terms of the length of it at either end resting on solid masonry. The 'end bearing' length required is stated in the manufacturer's literature and repeated in the agrément certificate relating to the chosen lintel; it is proportional to the overall length of each lintel, typically 100mm (4in) for lintels up to 1.8m (6ft) long, 150mm (6in) for lengths up to 3m (about 10ft) and 200mm (8in) for lengths up to 3.6m (just under 12ft). Whatever is built on top of a steel lintel must be put on to it in a balanced sequence, to avoid even temporarily eccentric loading. It is not good practice to erect a substantial amount of inner leaf before starting on the outer one, for example. Both should go up more or less together.

EXPANDED METAL REINFORCEMENT

Expanded metal lath is galvanised steel sheet which has been slit through, the slits being organised in patterns which produce a regular trellis effect when the sheet is stretched out, or 'expanded'. The material is referred to as expanded metal lath because it does many of the jobs that wooden laths used to do — plus quite a few for which wooden laths would be totally unsuitable. Metal lath is thin, pliable, easy to fold and to attach to itself or to other surfaces. Its fine lattice structure makes an excellent key for sand/cement renders, mortar or plaster, so it has a multitude of applications in building.

When timber joists or beams are exposed and have to be plastered rather than given one of the standard timber finishes, expanded metal lath is usually nailed or stapled to the wood to hold and strengthen the plaster coat. Where steel box beams, lintels, steel channels or rolled steel joists are to be plastered — as they normally are, to improve both their appearance and their fire rating — it can be fixed either by clips or by tying with galvanised, soft iron wire. It is possible to use expanded metal lath nailed or stapled between joists as a base for ceiling plaster, just as the older wooden laths used to be, but this is rarely if ever done in a housing context.

Expanded metal is used extensively in conjunction with profiled angle strips to make plasterers' beads — the metal reinforcement for corners which, though only just detectable in the finished plasterwork, is an important and time-saving aid for the plasterer, adding greatly to the strength and durability of outside angles. The expanded metal is attached to the central profiled 'spine' of the bead, forming two flanges serving both as the means of fixing the bead in place, usually by nailing or plaster dabs, and as a reinforcing key for the plaster at its most vulnerable points near the corner. The beads are made in various patterns, to cope with different plaster-coat-thickness requirements. There are also variations for edging plasterboard, and/or locating it, or for forming a square, firm edge where a plaster coat is brought to a stopped end elsewhere than in a corner — at door openings without architraves, for example. A similar stop-end bead is often used to make a neat finish for outside render coatings, where they have to be terminated a brick or two above the DPC so as to prevent rising damp. It can be advantageous, when plastering I-section rolled steel joists, to fix plasterers' beads at exposed corners on top of the expanded metal lath forming the main plaster key. The beads are easily wired to the mesh, making not only a neat finished contour but also a convenient guide to plaster-coat depth.

Supplied in the form of narrow coils instead of broad sheets, expanded metal lath is used to reinforce brick and blockwork. Embedded in the mortar joints, it adds enormous tensile strength to the structure, helping it to resist stresses, vibrations, temperature variations and settlement — due, for instance, to subsidence. Short lengths of the narrow coil can be used as ties to join together walls of different construction.

BITUMINOUS FELT FLAT-ROOFING MATERIALS

Roofing felts are not all made to the same standard. Some of them are manufactured with lower-cost core reinforcement materials and bitumen coatings in order to achieve economically priced products. All are totally waterproof if they are sold for external waterproofing use and not for some specific, less demanding job such as under-slate or tile sarking. Lower performance felts give good value, but they may have a life expectancy of as little as twenty years, perhaps because they are not as resistant to movement stresses and temperature variations as the more highly priced and higher performance felts, which are designed to last the life of the building. Anderson HT350 roofing membrane is a case in point, having a high-strength core of acrylic-bonded polyester fibres, filled and coated with high-grade bitumen. Whereas a cheaper product might well fail a standard movement test, simulating repeated stretching at an average temperature of 23°C (73°F) after only a few movement cycles, a high-performance felt could stand up to 10,000 or more cycles with no structural failure at all.

Felts intended for the top layers of built-up roof coverings may be surfaced on their weather side with mineral chipping or slate flakes, but the undersides of these top-layer products are coated with fine sand — as are both sides of intermediate-layer felts, to prevent sticking in the roll. Slate-flaked products may also be interleaved with polythene for the same purpose.

A further advantage of high-performance felts is their ability to withstand compression, bending, tearing and nail-holding strains. No bitumen felt is liable to damage by birds, insects or vermin, and fungi, moss, lichen, moulds and bacteria do not grow on it. Substances which can harm it are mainly products containing naphtha, paraffin or creosote, which are based on hydrocarbon solvents.

There are two methods of hot bitumen bonding of roofing felts to roofboarding and to each other. One is to melt bitumen blocks in a propane-gas-fired bitumen boiler, transfer the molten bitumen to where you want it by bucket or pouring-can, and spread it by brush or rake. Bitumen boilers come in a variety of forms, from small 'porridge steamer' types whose bitumen container lifts out to double as a bucket to large capacity, trailer-mounted models fitted with automatic thermostat temperature controls, insulated casings and lockable lids and drain cocks. Some smaller, freestanding kinds empty by tilting their bitumen container, which pours rather like a kettle. Gas cylinders are for safety reasons connected to the boilers by longish hoses. Large cylinders often have built into their pressure-regulator valves an automatic device which senses any lack of gas-tightness in the hose, closing off the gas flow immediately this occurs. Burners are effectively wind-shielded, as the boilers usually have to be used in unsheltered locations.

A more recently developed method of achieving hot bitumen bonding is the torch-on system, using felt formulations coated with enough 'free' bitumen to effect an overall bond. The roll of felt is mounted on a holder resembling a gigantic paint-roller. As the felt

121

is unrolled on to the decking, heat is applied to its underside by means of a powerful blow-torch, to melt the bitumen and stick the felt down. Simpler holders are held with one hand whilst the operator wields the blowtorch in the other, but for bigger roof jobs there are roll holders more like lawnmowers, with auxiliary wheels and multi-jet burners to speed things up a bit, one of the better known being Euro-roof's aptly named Dragon Wagon.

For warm-roof systems, Ruberoid Building Products have developed a combined felt roll and insulation product called Rubertherm. Closely set, narrow strips of expanded polys-tyrene insulation are bonded to the felt roll's underside. As it is unrolled on the roof deck, the slats lie close together like those of a rolltop desk cover. Since hot bitumen not only tends to melt expanded polystyrene (EPS), but can produce gases in the process, Ruberoid's system has a ready-to-use bitumen adhesive called Ruberoid Vedatex, which is applied cold in strips from either a hand-operated gun or a compressed-air applicator. This adhesive has a high initial 'grab' so that newly fixed rolls do not blow away. Once the insulated first roll is laid, subsequent rolls are laid parallel to it, a felt flange at one edge overlapping the previous roll to make a seal. When the whole roof is covered, built-up layers of hot-applied or torch-on felt are laid to effect the necessary waterproof cover. As with all warm-roof con-structions, a vapour-retardant membrane should be installed between the roof deck and the EPS insulation.

INSULATING ROOFLIGHTS FOR FLAT ROOFS

In a large flat roof it may be useful to have a means of admitting some light. Windows which opened or had glass panes would entail constructional complications, but fixed GRP (glass-reinforced plastic) rooflights may be feasible. They need to be strong, long-lived and maintenance free, and to have good enough thermal insulating qualities not to bring the performance of the whole roof area

below the building regulation prescribed minimum.

One such product which is particularly simple to install and weather-seal in bitumen felt-covered flat roofs is Anderson's Dalite U Type rooflight, which consists of two sheets of glass-fibre reinforced polyester resin, separated by corrugated spacers of the same material. The lower 'pane' is extended to form a fixing flange which is screwed or bolted down to the roof deck over a mastic bead made for the purpose. If a timber fillet frame is fixed to the hatchway left in the roof for the light, strips of flashing material (also specially made) can be easily dressed over the outer edge of it to waterproof the joint. The rooflights are nominally 50mm (2in) thick, very strong, resistant to damage by impact and designed to last the life of a building. They transmit about 60 per cent of the light that falls on them, are smooth surfaced enough to be kept reasonably clean by normal rain action and are easily washable with non-abrasive soap or detergent solutions, though these should not be strong ones.

ALUMINIUM DOORS AND WINDOWS

There are now almost as many different kinds, shapes and specifications for aluminium windows as there are for wood ones, but they are basically all made in the same way — their frames fabricated from extruded, hollow aluminium alloy bars called 'sections' or 'profiles'. Extruding means pushing through a die, which can be of almost any form, so the process can produce round or oval tubes, square, L- or T-section bars or any of the complex, internal web reinforced, hollow sections used for aluminium windows and doors. In the extrusion process, the metal is highly compressed, becoming much stronger than if it were melted and allowed to set in a mould, producing cast sections.

The simplicity of the manufacturing process — for which every factory making aluminium frames uses virtually the same machinery — makes it possible to set up as a manufacturer with little experience and capital outlay, producing frames of doubtful quality. Fortunately, the UK aluminium window industry foresaw this difficulty early in the development of the business and formed a trade association, the Aluminium Window Association, to set and maintain minimum manufacturing standards and installation practice codes designed to ensure efficient product performance. By no means all the makers of aluminium windows and doors in Britain belong to the association, several non-members producing excellent doors and windows, but all member firms have to make their products conform to BS 4873: 1972, which the AWA was instrumental in drafting and bringing into being.

Well-made aluminium doors and windows, even the simplest and least expensive, have the intrinsic virtues of strength, precise overall dimensions, weather-tightness, stability and freedom from any tendency to warp, rust or rot. In the plain untreated 'mill finish', straight from the extrusion die, it is possible for a white scale to form after a period of exposure to the weather. Although this can be cleaned off, it is a nuisance, so the great majority of better-class frames are now given protective and cosmetic treatments in the forms of anodised, acrylic, polyester or stoved finishes.

Overall insulation properties depend largely on the grade of glazing chosen, but the quality of the frame is important from the heat-transmission viewpoint, not primarily for the amount of heat kept in, but for the prevention of condensation. Aluminium is a fairly good conductor of heat, so although the still air trapped inside the hollow profiles keeps the overall heat leakage down, there is enough metal in the strengthening webs and outer box of a plain profile to make the inner surface of the frame sufficiently cool to allow condensation to form on it at times. There are two main solutions to this problem adopted by manufacturers of higher quality frames. One is to bond a coating of plastic to the inside of the frame to insulate the surfaces where condensa-

tion might otherwise occur. The other is to break the continuity of all the metal webs connecting the outside of the frame to the inside by inserting a strip of insulating material in each one. This has to be done without reducing the profile's strength, so the frame components used for 'thermal-break' or 'thermally broken' units have each front-to-back web opening out into a little box section somewhere in the middle of the profile. The box is filled with an insulating resin, usually epoxy, which sets hard. A narrow strip of aluminium is then milled out from the top and bottom of each box, leaving the resin to hold the two sides together. Thermally broken profiles cost a lot more to make than straightforward ones, but they present an effective and permanent solution to the condensation problem, whilst still allowing a wide choice of finishes on the door or window's inside surface. If you don't mind a white plastic coating, the Poll Withey type of uPVC (unplasticised polyvinyl chloride) inside surface insulation, which has a low-density cellular core, prevents condensation equally well.

Because the outer dimensions of aluminium frames cannot be shaved down to fit the apertures left for them in walls, special care has to be taken to ensure that door and window openings are sized to precise limits — especially where metal frames are of the type designed to fit directly to the structure without a hardwood outer ancillary frame. If a builder has not been used to catering for metal frames, the tolerances on aperture sizes may be rather tighter than those he has been in the habit of working to for timber frames. The window manufacturer or supplier may even like him to use exact-size templates to gauge the opening dimensions. Apart from this necessary foresight, aluminium frames are as easily installed as any other kind.

Aluminium doors and windows normally leave the factory completely fitted out with all hinges, catches, latches and locks, and many are pre-glazed. Letter boxes and weather strips are also pre-fitted as a rule. Glazing is held in place by gaskets — shaped strips of

123

neoprene rubber or PVC — rather than putty or mastic. All patterns of glass can be used, including leaded-light panes. Extras which can be built in include night ventilation slots in the frame tops, draughtproof when closed and insect-proof when open, lockable limited opening hinges for windows, to stop thieves getting in and adventurous small children falling out, and security locks. Some doors — the Monarch thermal barrier entrance door, for example — have built-in electronic intruder alarms, with normal door chimes for visitors.

If you particularly want aluminium doors or windows delivered assembled but unglazed, or even in knock-down form for site assembly, you will certainly be able to find a supplier, though it may be necessary to compromise on the specification, as not all makers supply all models in all forms.

The flexible manufacturing process used to make plastic windows lends itself to a great variety in designs. This attractive bow window is a case in point (*Consort Aluminium Ltd*)

PLASTIC DOORS AND WINDOWS

Most of the plastic windows and doors on the market are made from extruded sections of unplasticised — that is, hard — polyvinyl chloride (uPVC). White is the most popular colour for profiles, so the limited range of colours available is achieved by using white uPVC sections with an integral layer of pigmented plastic on one side. As the coloured profiles are totally interchangeable with standard white ones as regards size, it is possible to have white fixed frames and coloured opening ones, or vice versa.

Plastic profiles derive their strength from their hollow, webbed — multi-box/chamber — construction, just as aluminium extrusions do, though many of the larger window units made from uPVC sections are reinforced by zinc-coated steel or sometimes plain aluminium tube, fitted inside one of the hollow chambers and screwed into place. This is done after the frame components are cut to length and before they are jointed. Cutting is done on

exactly the same kind of machinery as used for aluminium extrusions, so it is not too surprising to find that several manufacturers make both aluminium and uPVC doors and windows, or that some use both materials in the same frame — patio doors, for example, often having aluminium sills.

Corner joints in plastic frames are mitred, similarly to aluminium ones, but not mechanically clamped together. Each component is cut 5mm (just under ¼in) oversize (half that amount at either end) to compensate for the small amount of material melted during the welding process. Welding is carried out by sophisticated machines, which control temperature, heating time and weld thickness automatically and precisely, to produce a strong and hermetically sealed bond. As the hot plate which effects the end-melting is withdrawn from between the two ends being jointed and they are pushed together to fuse into one, some of the plastic 'lost' in the process is squashed outwards, forming an excrescence called a 'weld sprue'. This has to be cut off when cool, either by hand with a special knife or on a weld-cleaning machine. All-white frames usually feature a narrow channel-groove on the joint line where the sprue has been chiselled out, but in coloured frames the sprue is kept very thin and cut off flush with the frame surface to minimise the joint line width.

Since the insulating properties of uPVC are intrinsically better than those of any metal, a plastic frame will compare favourably with a metal one of equivalent section, unless the metal one has a thermal break to bring its thermal performance to a similar standard. Plastic frames can be fitted into timber subframes, but this negates their major virtue of needing little in the way of maintenance beyond the occasional cleaning with a mild domestic detergent or a general-purpose hard-surface cleaner, such as Deb's Altrans, which will also clean mill-finish aluminium and other metals. (Where aluminium windows have a factory-applied finish, however, it is essential to follow the maker's instructions on cleaning them.)

Plastic windows are extremely tough, but since uPVC is a thermoplastic material, any damage can be perfectly repaired by welding. Here a Leister hot-air gun is being applied to melt and fuse a stick of uPVC into an accidental score mark. After welding, the repaired area is smoothed back to normal with an orbital sander (*Welwyn Tool Co Ltd*)

Although uPVC frames are theoretically less secure than metal or timber ones, because they could be melted using a blowtorch, no burglar is likely in practice to attempt such an ostentatious and time-consuming entry. The thermo-plastic nature of uPVC makes it easy to repair, in the unlikely event of its being punctured or cracked accidentally. Any breaks in the surface can simply be welded together using a Leister-type industrial quality hot-air blower and a stick of uPVC. The bump resulting from the weld is sanded down with a normal power sander — preferably the Elu type of orbital sander, featuring electronic speed control and a dust-extraction system. Polishing can be done with the same machine and a fabric pad, or with a power drill, disc pad and lambswool bonnet. However, uPVC is pretty tough stuff, so this kind of expedient is unlikely to be necessary.

Glazing is invariably fixed into uPVC frames

125

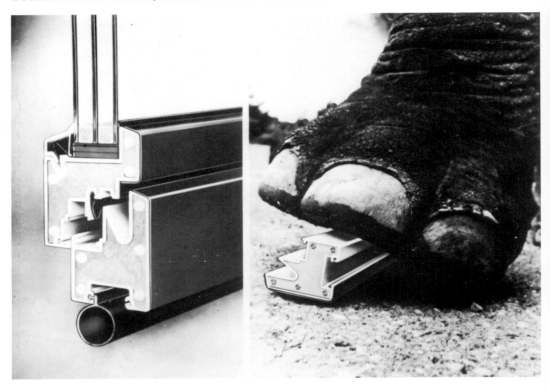

This uPVC plastic window frame is reinforced with glass-fibre rods, held in place by a filling of thermo-setting silicon spheres. The strength of the resulting frame can be judged from the second picture, showing a 'Thermassiv' profile being tested by an elephant (*Juno Roplasto*)

by gaskets of chloroprene or other synthetic rubber, in conjunction with snap-in plastic beads. Drain channels are provided for any water which might penetrate a faulty gasket. As with most aluminium frames, glazing is done from the inside. Modern weather-sealing allows inward-opening windows to match outward-opening ones in wind and water resistance, and since plastic window technology has been developed chiefly in West Germany, there are some continental-style inward-opening types on the UK market. Variety of style is one of the strong points of the uPVC window/door system. The white profiles in particular seem to lend themselves readily to the production of frames coming close to older timber

styles in appearance than metal systems can. As regards the correlation between frames and aperture sizes, it is just as important to ensure accuracy of aperture dimensions where plastic units are to be fitted direct — without a timber subframe — as it is with aluminium frames.

One of the most remarkable of the uPVC window and door systems is one called Thermassiv, made by Juno Roplasto of London. Unlike any of the others on the market, Thermassiv uPVC profiles have no metal inserts to strengthen them, but are made even stronger than metal-stiffened hollow sections by polyester-reinforced glass-fibre rods held fast in a rigid plastic binder containing air-filled silicon spheres of microscopic size. This filling not only makes the single-chamber profile exceptionally strong and stable, but gives it an extremely low thermal conductivity — only about 10 per cent of that of a normal uPVC profile with no additional insulation. Fittings can be firmly attached at any point, since the filled profile holds screws better than does hardwood. Very large glass panes, even triple glazed units, can be accommodated in Thermassiv frames, which are suitable for the most exposed locations in the UK.

Because of their welded construction, uPVC windows cannot be assembled on site from knock-down kits, as may certain aluminium systems. There is one interesting British plastic system, however; Lignum, whose manufacturer does not make factory-assembled window or door frames at all but simply markets lengths of profile, fittings and adhesives. Lignum sections are extruded from a tough, structural foam plastic material based on styrene, the extrusions being rigid, 'solid' except in the sense that there is air trapped in the foam core, and surfaced in a wide variety of plain colours and wood-grain finishes of realistic appearance. The profiles can be sawn, planed, chiselled and drilled as if they were natural timber and can be screwed, nailed, bolted or plate-jointed together, or stuck with any styrene-compatible adhesive. The only significant difference in working Lignum, as opposed to timber, is that you have to be quick rather than slow in terms of power tool speeds and feed rates to avoid blade, drill or cutter clogging. With hand tools, there is no problem at all. Thermal insulation characteristics of the material are equivalent to those of normal hollow uPVC sections of similar dimensions. Lignum profiles are combustible, but window and door frames are not usually fire sources. Some chemicals can attack styrene, acetone being one of the few. Superficial surface damage is treated by rubbing down with medium steel wool and then with a finely abrasive polish, the type used for de-oxydising motor-body finishes being suitable. The same abrasive polish treatment is used to restore the white finish, which tends to discolour slightly over a period of years — unlike the wood-grain ones, which keep their good looks indefinitely. Several sill sections are made specifically for leading makes of aluminium doors and windows, Lignum being well suited to this application, as it does not absorb moisture or warp.

STEEL WINDOWS AND DOORS

Steel is the strongest of all the materials that window and door frames are made from, its strength being not only a primary virtue but also the source of the material's ability to provide very slim, unobtrusive frames without any penalties in the way of fragility. The slimness of steel frames goes a long way towards compensating for their high thermal conductivity. Since the frame forms a smaller proportion of the total window area than is the case with other systems, the heat loss is relatively small, despite its poor insulating qualities. The area susceptible to condensation is reduced by the same token.

Many of the steel windows installed prior to 1950 gave unsatisfactory performance, especially in respect of rusting propensities and draught admission, but the modern product is a different proposition. Manufacturing standards are protected and maintained by the Steel Window Association, which represents makers responsible for some 90 per cent of British steel-window production; all the SWA member firms use the same source of supply of the solid steel sections from which doors and windows are fabricated. Since 1950, these have been rustproofed by hot-dip galvanising which, instead of simply surface-coating the steel with zinc, bonds the two metals together to form a surface alloy layer under the pure zinc coat. The resultant surface gives excellent corrosion resistance, capable of preventing rusting by electro-chemical action, even if site scratching should penetrate the alloy layer between zinc and steel.

For house installations, it is far more practical to use frames which are factory finished. The process normally used is polyester powder coating, an effective way of applying 'paint' to metal surfaces. It gives the metal an electrostatic charge, spraying it with powder colour and, whilst this is still positively attracted to every part of the surface, stoving it on. This produces a finish with strong adhesion and a tough surface which can last without further painting for 10–25 years. There are several British Standards relevant to steel

127

window and door production. The general specifications are contained in BS 990, an integral part of which is BS 729 relating to the hot-dip galvanising process. BS 3900 lays down tests for finishes — covering impact, scratch, humidity, salt spray, light and weathering resistances and also the effectiveness of paint adhesion. The Standard for installed performance of glazed frames is BS 5368, which sets out criteria for windows, fittings and fixings relating to air permeability, wind and water resistance. All units made by Steel Window Association members are tested to this Standard.

Gasket glazing is not used with steel frames, double or single panes being sealed into the rebates by metal casement putty. To avoid the necessity of painting this, it is possible to use internal glazing beads to contain the compound on the unlipped side of the frame, normally the inside.

For domestic dwelling applications, steel windows are invariably made from standard hot-rolled sections approximately 25mm (1in) from front to back, joints being welded. Standard sizes and formats are made for modern buildings in metric dimensions, older houses being catered for by frames made in imperial measurements. The metric window series is referred to as Module 100 and the imperial windows are made in three different styles: 'N', standing for normal frames having both vertical and horizontal glazing bars, 'H' standing for those with only horizontal ones, and Georgian, referring of course to frames with multiple small panes. It is not always possible in a steel frame to have double glazing in Georgian windows with very small panes.

Steel windows can be installed directly into brickwork in one of two ways — either positioned whilst the wall is partly constructed and then built in, or inserted into prepared openings. As with aluminium windows, the openings have to be precisely dimensioned — the clearance between frame and opening only 3mm (⅛in) — since too large an opening makes it difficult to seal the frame in properly. Steel frames can be used under steel or con-

crete lintels, and with steel, concrete, timber, tile or brick sills. They can be fixed within timber subframes, either the window or the subframe being put in first, and it is also possible to fix them in conjunction with plastic subframes.

Maintenance for steel frames is limited to occasional lubrication of hinges, catches and other fittings, even more occasional cleaning and — after a lengthy period if you have factory-finished frames — repainting by normal methods.

TIMBER WINDOWS AND DOORS

Natural softwood is still the cheapest material for making windows and doors. It has a high insulation value, is easily worked with commonly available tools and machinery and can be painted or stained in an infinite variety of colours and shades. Components of window and door frames for most housing styles are straight, but with timber they need not be, so if you have an opening or a fanlight that incorporates an arch or a curve, timber is probably the only material which can economically be used to make a frame for it.

Timber's two main disadvantages as a window and door material are that supplies vary enormously in quality and that it tends to warp and rot if allowed to absorb moisture. Whilst it does not itself present a surface that normally becomes cold enough to provoke condensation, water from droplets that have condensed on a cold single glazed pane can run down on to wood below the glass, become absorbed and cause trouble. Wood needs a lot of maintenance — repair and painting. It has always been a temptation to housebuilders to cut costs by using mediocre joinery units, and it is still possible to buy windows and doors which are not so much barriers to keep wind and water out as sieves to let them in.

If your house has timber windows, any extension to it should also have them, matching the originals in style as closely as you can afford. For older, especially prewar houses, you may have an unfortunate choice between

These sash windows are of an up-to-date, draught-proof design by Boulton & Paul (*Boulton & Paul Ltd*)

having special frames made to measure, replacing existing frames with ones matching the new type used in the extension but not matching the house too well, or forgetting about stylistic unity altogether because it costs too much.

Unless you take a special interest in the kind of joinery you are having in your extension, the chances are that you will get standard EJMA (English Joinery Manufacturers' Association) design, a utilitarian, primed softwood unit designed for low-cost manufacture — and often made to accept only single-glazed panes. Current building standards and rising heating costs, however, are tending to make EJMA windows compare unfavourably with an increasing number of reasonably priced alternative specifications on the market. One low-cost alternative design is Bowater Rippers' Alpha window which, although by no means a

'luxury' product, incorporates a number of features available only on higher priced units before it was introduced. Glazing rebates are deep enough to accept sealed double-glazing panes, draught stripping can be factory fitted, side-hung versions have reflex hinges to allow the opening light to be reversed for cleaning from inside and the hinges are storm-proof. Higher specification softwood windows are made from timber which is vacuum-impregnated with preservative before priming or treatment with water-repellent stains. Glazing rebates are deeper, to accommodate thicker double-glazing or triple-glazing units, and hardware is more sophisticated. Hardwood windows and doors represent a further

129

advance, being finished with a preservative stain as a rule for easy and infrequent maintenance. One Swedish window, the Svenska-Elit Alu-Wood, has a softwood frame completely clad in aluminium on the outside to minimise maintenance.

Many older houses have visually attractive, but draughty and jamming-prone, vertically sliding sash windows. These can be reasonably matched or replaced by pivoting frames or sliding/projecting sashes. But there is now a fully weather-stripped version — Boulton & Paul's double-hung sash window — which matches the older window type's charm, sliding up and down in the same old way, but with a new efficiency and smoothness. Spiral spring balances are used in place of the former weights and pulleys system.

PATIO DOORS

All the widely used window and door materials — aluminium, uPVC, steel and timber — are equally suitable for the larger patio door units, and for porch and entrance frames. The patio doors usually have heavy-duty lift-and-slide actions, based on robust rolling gear.

GLASS AND GLAZING

Ordinary glass used for small- and medium-sized panes is made by a rolling-out process, so is less optically true and flat than the thicker float glass — now almost universally displacing the more expensive plate glass. Float glass is so called because the manufacturing process involves literally floating molten glass on a bed of molten metal, leaving it flat enough to use for shop windows and mirrors.

Both rolled sheet and float glass are hard and brittle materials, breaking under impact into razor-edged, sometimes large and always potentially dangerous fragments. Horrific accidents have been caused by putting in panes of ordinary glass that were too thin in relation to their unsupported area to withstand impact, either from moving objects or from running or falling people. It is physically possible to glaze a single-pane door with glass only 3mm (⅛in) thick, yet this can be shattered by a small child running or bumping into it, with nasty results. Because of this danger, a new British Standard code of practice was brought out in 1982, BS 6262. This lays down in considerable detail recommendations of the relationship to be observed between glass thickness and type and pane size, taking into consideration the hazards of its situation. The new standard lacks the force of law; in fact many local authorities are known by the Glass & Glazing Federation to ignore the Standard's provisions because of the extra cost. Glaziers are well aware of the code of practice, which is long and complex, as it has to cover all conceivable situations. The GGF publishes it in full at £22.50, but you should be able to consult it in a public reference library. Areas of high risk include fully glazed doors, low-level panels, balustrades and bathing areas.

Glazing used in these areas and for large panes in non-hazardous locations may need to be of the thicker float glasses, wired glass or one of the types of glass treated to make them tougher. Toughened or annealed glass will withstand much greater impact force than untreated glass, and even when broken by exceptionally hard blows will shatter into small, cube-like fragments instead of long-edged, sharp slivers. Laminated safety glass consists of two separate sheets of glass held together by a layer of polyvinyl butyral (PVB). Although the outer glass layers are untreated, the PVB holds them together so firmly that they do not shatter under impact. It will craze locally in the area of the blow, but the pane as a whole will remain unbroken. There are multi-layer forms of laminated glass which will stand up to bullets and even bomb blasts; but for bodies, footballs and cricket balls and perhaps the odd tile falling off a roof on to a conservatory, architectural single-sandwich laminated glass is totally adequate. It has the additional advantage that it can be cut on site, though it has to be scored on both sides and the central PVB layer has to be sliced through with a razor blade. Toughened glass, on the other hand, has to be ordered and made exactly to the size you want it, as it would disintegrate, albeit safely, if cut by normal methods. Ordinary linseed oil or metal casement putties cannot be used for sealing laminated glass into place. Gaskets, preformed cellular strips, two-part curing sealants, non-setting glazing compounds, preformed mastic tapes or extruded solid sections are all possible alternatives.

Oddly enough, the PVB layer in the middle of a sheet of laminated glass scarcely improves its thermal performance at all, though it does cut down sound transmission quite significantly. To cut down heat transmission through glass panes, they must be double or triple glazed and sealed together at the edges to trap dry air in the gap between. It is the still air that does the insulating, but some double-glazing units use inert gases instead, such as argon or carbon dioxide. Edge-sealing strips in sealed double- and triple-glazing units normally contain a desiccant material, usually silica gel, to absorb any traces of water vapour remaining in the trapped air, or migrating through the sealing compound in the course of time.

Standard double-glazing units are flush edged, having both panes the same size, so a deeper rebate is needed in the window or door frame than for single glazing. Where it is inconvenient or impossible to obtain or make deep rebates, stepped-edge units can be made, with one pane slightly bigger than the other. The larger of the two panes sits in the rebate, sealed into place as if it were a single sheet of glass, the rest of the unit projecting inside the frame. These stepped units have two marginal disadvantages over flush-edge ones: one is that they have no more wind-pressure resistance than single panes and the other is that they may show a tendency to allow slight condensation round the edges unless additional beading is installed on the inside. Stepped units are mainly useful for replacement double glazing, but they may have an application in extension work where low-cost frames have been used, with shallow rebates.

With plain-glass components, double-glazing units let out heat at only half the rate of single panes; they let it in, however, quite freely, so can produce a considerable net heat gain which is acceptable on a bright winter's day but perhaps not so acceptable in a hot summer. There is no difficulty about making double-glazing units with the two panes of different types of glass, one of which can be of a heat-reflective kind such as Pilkington's Suncool or Kappafloat. These have thin, metallic coatings which, according to the prevailing weather conditions, reflect back a large part of the sun's radiant heat or reflect back heat into the house. Reflective units have to be sealed in with gaskets or non-setting compounds, since rigid mountings would not allow the glass to expand — which it does to a greater extent than glass that simply lets heat through.

Other special-purpose types of glass can be used to make up double units — toughened, laminated, wired or patterned. It is also possible to have panes with a mirror-action coating to provide privacy in daylight. These come in a variety of shades — gold, bronze and silver included. Heat insulation improves as the width of the air gap goes up, but there is a falling off of improvement after about 20mm (¾in) because of convection currents in the air or gas. Sound insulation is better when the panes are more widely separated, by 100mm (4in) or more, though it is not feasible to have sealed units for such installations. For extremely noisy situations, where houses are near airports, for example, additional features may have to be incorporated in the glazing system to obtain a satisfactory reduction in sound transmission. Often the edges of the space between the panes are lined with sound-absorbent material such as glass-fibre or wood-fibre acoustic tiles. Window glass is sometimes made very thick, up to 25mm (1in), and the outer and inner panes are set out of parallel with one another. To allow ventilation, both inner and outer panes can be sliding units, arranged so that the air gaps created by opening them are not opposite each other.

131

EXPOSURE ZONES AND PERFORMANCE RATINGS

Great Britain divides fairly neatly into exposure zones, classified on the basis of the Driving Rain Index produced by the Meteorological Office as 'sheltered', 'moderate' or 'severe'. Building designers and local building control officers are good sources of information as to the classification of your own site; broadly, if you live in the home counties north of the Thames, in Leicestershire, Lincolnshire, Northamptonshire, Nottinghamshire or Oxfordshire, you will probably be in a 'sheltered' zone. The 'moderate' areas are Norfolk, eastern Scotland, the rest of England except for the Plymouth and Exeter regions, Dyfed and most of Ulster. The rest of Wales, Anglesey, the Isle of Man and the whole western coastal strip from Liverpool right up to the north-western tip of Scotland, plus the Plymouth and Exeter patches in the south of England, are all rated as 'severe'.

Manufacturers rate their windows and doors as high-performance units when they are capable of passing British Standard tests relevant to 'severe' exposure zones, and agrément certificates specify which zones many different kinds of building products are or are not suitable for. High buildings, or those on high ground, may be rated as being in the next worse exposure zone to the one they are in geographically, and parts of a house subject to prevailing winds in any unsheltered location may need special attention to waterproofing, or higher grade materials.

BLINDS AND SHUTTERS FOR OUTSIDE

Solid wooden shutters might be used a great deal more in Britain if the winters were regularly as cold as they are in continental Europe, with temperatures in the region of 30°C below zero (−22°F). A solid shutter improves the insulation value of a window in four ways: by keeping wind off the glass, by keeping it dry, by maintaining a layer of relatively still air immediately next to it, and by adding the thermal resistance of the shutter material itself to that of the window unit. Standard solid shutters are almost non-existent, so small is the demand, but there is no difficulty about having them made to measure or, for the average DIY carpenter, in making them.

There are more convenient, if less graceful, ways of adding some outside shielding to windows. Metal roller shutters give almost as good weather protection and added insulation as wooden, hinged-flap types, and rather better protection against burglars. Mounted in a neat box at the window top, roller shutters are easily and quickly opened or closed, and will lock securely. There are types of Venetian blind for outside use; they have reinforced, beaded slat edges to add to the stiffness of their 80mm (3¼in) wide slats, which have a different cross-section to those designed for indoor mounting. Though designed to provide shade in the summer, they are weatherproof enough to be left in place all the year round. Naturally, they are not allowed to hang free as indoor versions normally are, their slat ends being firmly located in sturdy side guides. Able to cope with winds up to Beaufort force 10, they can be fully retracted if the weather is more severe than this, or overcast. Raising, lowering and tilting operations are all controlled by a single crank-handle if the chosen mechanism is manual, but electric motor operation is available. Electrically operated versions of these blinds can alternatively be fitted with automatic controls, triggered to open or close the slats according to the sunlight strength or wind force registered by the sensors installed.

INTERNAL BLINDS AND SHUTTERS

Internal shutters do not have to be weatherproof, so can incorporate a wide variety of insulating materials to stop heat leaking away. Their time of usefulness for insulation is limited to the hours of darkness, while they are covering the window glass, but these are also the hours during which the outside temperature is likely to be at its lowest. They are most conveniently accommodated by deepish window recesses, as otherwise some form of subframe is necessary. This itself may be obtrusive on an otherwise flat wall, and the shutters — normally of bi-fold construction — can look bulky when drawn back. Insulation values are extremely good when the shutters are in use.

Fabric or plastic roller blinds serve as decorative window, door or screen coverings, cut out sun glare, provide privacy and also have an insulating effect by reason of the air pocket they create between themselves and the window glass. There are now alternatives to the traditional spring-roller type. The newer designs are operated without springs, using an endless ball-chain control which is less nerve-racking. A very wide range of pictorial, abstract and textural designs is available, together with many plain colours, so the contribution roller blinds can make to interior décor is considerable.

Roller blinds can be made of materials with thermal insulation properties, or of polyester film coated with sun-reflecting metallic deposits. The sun blinds allow a clear view, whilst cutting down heat and glare, and they can be mounted within the opening frames of pivoting windows, providing both partial ventilation and protection from the sun. Manual control is normal, but some blinds of this kind — the Reflex-Rol, for example — can be worked by small 24V electric DC motors. As with any other blind sited close to the window, the air trap adds to the insulation properties of the window glass.

If you want a blind mainly for the purpose of making a room dark enough to view films, TV or slides during daylight, roller blinds capable of blacking out nearly all outside light can be obtained. The Durashade is a typical example, made from polyester fabric, double coated with PVC and fitted in a matt black head box and side channels. Concealed cords, crank-rods or electric motor operation are all possible.

Rigid insect screens consist of woven glass-fibre mesh coated with PVC and sealed into aluminium alloy frames. Rigid-frame screens can be a nuisance to take down and put up, so unless they can be left conveniently in place all the time, roller insect screens are probably a better idea. They roll down from a small head box, their side edges being lined with small pips engaging in side channels to ensure an effective seal. Rigid screens can be mounted in the form of hinged or sliding panels.

High and wide internal windows can be attractively glare-protected by vertical blinds, which are similar to Venetian blinds in that they have swivelling slats, but the slats, or 'vanes', are upright and swivel sideways instead of tilting. Vane widths vary from about 50mm (2in) to 130mm (5in). Vane materials may be fabrics, some of them fire-resisting types, PVC or aluminium. Swivel action controls may be standard ball-chain devices, crank-operated or worked by electric motors. To protect the mechanism against accidental damage in the event of vanes being forced out of position, leading makes such as Luxaflex have slipping-clutch swivel units, which snap vanes back into line when the deflecting force is removed.

Horizontal-slatted Venetian blinds diffuse daylight so effectively that they transform light from even south-facing windows into the clear 'north light' sought after by artists. Venetian blinds can be successfully built into sealed or coupled-sash double-glazing units, control being effected by torsion rods passing through the window frame. Inter-pane blinds like these have narrow 25mm (1in) slats, almost invisible when in the fully open position, yet capable of presenting a vivid white or coloured decorative panel when tilted.

Fine-slatted blinds now outsell the broader 35mm (1⅜in) and 50mm (2in) wide versions, even when quite large window expanses are to be covered, their lightness and lack of bulk being advantageous for big areas. Colour ranges are consequently wide — Luxaflex currently listing 45 shades with matching 'ladder-lace' supports and control cords. Some versions are produced with slat coatings designed to conserve energy by reducing windows' radiated heat losses when closed by as much as 40 per cent. The same blinds also re-radiate less heat than standard Venetian blinds do into the interior in summer.

Venetian versions of the blackout blind combine dark coloured slats with light-trapped headrails, side and bottom channels, to cut out approximately 90 per cent of a window's light when the slats are fully closed. These blinds may be operated by cord, crank or electric motor. When not fully closed, they become normal Venetian blinds.

Both wider-slatted Venetian blinds and the vertical vane type have an alternative function. Installed away from windows, they make visually effective room dividers, adding interest and variety to a large room, whilst taking up very little space.

Conservatories need particular attention to the question of shading, if they are to remain usable when the conditions outside are hot or bright, or both. Aston conservatories can have roller blinds built in as optional extras, not standard types, since they have to follow roof and wall contours, running in purpose-designed channels within the glazing bars and housed in hollow ridge and sill sections. Gable ends have separate vertically hung blinds. All large areas of glass, whatever their shape or angle of inclination, can be fitted with pur-pose-built Venetian blinds such as Luxaflex skylight blinds. Accessible vertical areas of glazing will probably be more economically fitted with standard Venetian blinds, but for large skylights, semi-circular, circular, trian-gular or other odd-shaped or inaccessible units, standard blinds are impractical. Skylight blinds, on the other hand, can be installed horizontally, vertically or at any slant between the two. They are non-retractable, though fully tiltable by means of a rack arm mechanism. Instead of being threaded into straps or on to strings, their slats are slotted into nylon clips attached to the bars of the pivoting device — and they can be easily removed from these clips for cleaning. Con-trols available include most manual and motorised systems from cord pulls to full

electronic programming, and the wide colour range caters for what the manufacturers describe as 'dim-out effects' with the option of black slats and clips.

SEALING COMPOUNDS AND JOINT FILLERS

It is well nigh impossible for two building components to fit together with total precision and to expand and contract with changing temperature and humidity in complete unison. Brick, stone, timber, metals, plastics and concrete may all seem solid and rigid enough to make a house built with them a monolithic, unchanging unit, but this is far from the case. All building materials, whether natural or manufactured, are continually on the move after construction is finished, so there is a constant need for joint- and gap-sealing compounds to make flexible bridges between adjoining units, keeping out wind and water in the process.

Not so many years ago, mortar and plaster had to serve all the joint- and gap-sealing needs in house building — which is partly why older houses can be leaky and draughty. Today, however, builders have access to a bewildering variety of materials for solving the problem of relative movement between constructional units. According to the kind of gap to be filled, the form in which the compounds containing these substances are supplied may be a paste, a strip, an impregnated board, blanket or rope, an aerosol can or, most often, a cylindrical cartridge for use in an extrusion 'gun'.

Paste compounds are mainly used for gaps round pipes and ducts where they pass through masonry or timber structures, and are mostly silicone based. Strips may be simply paste in a form convenient for application to the more narrow and awkward-to-reach gaps, but some consist of foamed resin material pre-compressed to a fraction of its natural thick-ness, so that it expands naturally to fill a gap once in place; since natural elasticity keeps it pressing outwards against both sides, it keeps the gap sealed as expansion and contraction take place. Another kind of strip used for expansion joints deliberately left in concrete structures, paving or brickwork consists of compressible but uncompressed fibre board impregnated with bitumen. Silicone-impregnated ropes have almost limitless applications, but the chief ones are sealing joints between prefabricated concrete sections and sealing manhole covers.

Aerosols are used to apply polyurethane foam to irregular gaps and joints. The foam not only adheres well to most building materials, but remains flexible when cured and has excellent thermal insulation properties. Applied with the aerosol inverted, these PU foams react with moisture in the air to expand and harden. Taking about twenty minutes to set, they can be sawn or cut after one or two hours and are fully cured after five to seven hours. They can be used to seal holes in roofs, plumbing joints and general gaps and cracks, and will also protect delicate electrical connections — though they should not be applied whilst these are live.

Cartridge guns are crude mechanically, but simple and effective. Each squeeze of the trigger pushes a metal rod a short way forward, a pad on the front of the rod connecting with a disc in the base of the cardboard cartridge, so that the sealant is extruded out of a nozzle at the cartridge front. Silicone rubber and acrylic compounds are applied in this way, mainly for bathroom and kitchen joints between tiles and baths, shower trays and sinks. Most of the general outside jobs — sealing gaps round door and window frames, for example — are done with the cheaper oleo-resin mastics, but there are many applications which demand tougher compounds. Rainwater gutter joints are usually sealed with rubber/bitumen products, which also have advantages for roof- and basement-sealing work. Polysulphide compounds are favoured for basement floor joints, joints in cladding materials, and glazing seals. Being powerful adhesives, they are used extensively for fixing dry-lining boards to inner wall leaves as well. Plasticised butyl rubber sealants are used for sealing round

metal window frames and for bedding in ancillary components for these, such as timber subframes and sills. Silicone rubber outdoor sealants find applications in high-movement joints in concrete, stone and marble, and in other joints where high flexibility is valuable, such as where lightweight glass-reinforced plastic or uPVC components are involved.

Not all sealing applications are concerned with gaps. Often it is necessary to seal a concrete or masonry surface — either against moisture, as in outside walls subject to driving rain, or against water leaking through it, as in underground basements. It is possible to seal outside wall surfaces completely against water getting in, using acrylic or other synthetic resins, but this is inadvisable where a risk occurs of interstitial condensation being trapped. In these cases, a silicone sealer is better, keeping water out but allowing moisture already in the masonry to evaporate away. Liquid sealing solutions for protecting concrete floors from water and oil, and stopping the surface from dusting at the same time, are mostly polyurethane based.

Bitumen-based sealers for damp-proofing masonry below ground level, which may be subject to damp under pressure, need special application techniques. A typical example is the procedure recommended by the National Coal Board's waterproofing products manufacturing company, Thomas Ness, for its Dry-Ness interior waterproofer, which can be applied to walls and floors subject to damp pressures. Existing wallcoverings and plaster have to be removed and the wall surfaces underneath smoothed level with a sand/cement skim coat. Floor preparation for the waterproofer consists of thorough cleaning and degreasing, any gross unevenness being treated by a levelling compound which is not adversely affected by moisture, such as a latex cement screed. Every angle between wall and floor, or between adjoining walls, is given an extra reinforcement against damp penetration in the form of two successive coats of waterproofer applied in strips about 180mm (7in) either side of the line of intersection, with a

135

glass-fibre membrane brushed into the angle with more waterproofer and sealed with a second full coat. Three coats are then put on the walls, right up to and connecting with the damp-proof course if there is one, but in any case extending to a height which takes the treatment well above ground level. Floors are given two coats, continued a minimum of 150mm (6in) up the walls. Both wall and floor final coats are sealed ('blinded') by sprinkling them with sharp sand whilst still tacky.

When the waterproofing treatment is absolutely dry, the floor is resurfaced with a 50mm (2in)-plus screed of sand and cement. Walls are refinished with plaster at least 15mm (⅝in) thick — which may well take six months to dry properly. This drying-out time underlines the difficulty of making below-ground or partly below-ground rooms habitable, however effective the waterproofing treatment adopted.

ADHESIVES

All the mastics and sealant compounds already mentioned are *ipso facto* adhesives, but apart from these there are three main types of adhesive widely used in general building work. Perhaps the most versatile is the white liquid PVA (polyvinyl acetate) based product, which not only sticks almost anything to almost anything else, but mixes with mortar and plaster to enable thin layers to adhere better and, at suitable dilutions with water, seals off bitumen-based coatings to allow them to accept normal paint finishes. It needs at least one of the surfaces joined to be porous when used as an adhesive. Not totally waterproof, it is nevertheless very water resistant, once set, and also has the distinct advantage of setting quickly, attaining high strength within a couple of hours in normal drying conditions. Versions of PVA adhesive formulated purely for woodworking contain fillers to make them thick enough to fill less-than-perfect joints.

PVA adhesives incorporating fungicides are produced for tiling and mosaic fixing, but waterproof tiling adhesives for use in areas subject to extremes of wetness, such as those round baths and showers, are usually based on acrylic resins.

The third group of adhesives is based on neoprene rubber. All of the principal formulations are instant-sticking contact products. Brush-on versions for big-sheet and tile sticking may be solvent based and waterproof, or water based and not waterproof. Water-based contact adhesives were developed to overcome the problems associated with the heavy, toxic nature of the solvents necessary for the heavy-duty waterproof rubber-based adhesives. They are more than adequately water resistant for most common applications, especially if it is possible to protect the join edges with paint. Cartridge versions of neoprene rubber adhesives are used to produce thick beads for fixing decorative, insulating or flooring panels, plasterboard, timber battens, architraves or skirtings. Being waterproof, they can be used for fixing materials either internally or externally, and as they are applied in thin strips they avoid the degree of solvent inhalation risk of the brush-on types. This risk is serious only when solvent adhesives are used without good through-ventilation arrangements to keep the air moving. In an enclosed space, where the air is stagnant, the heavier-than-air vapour cannot disperse properly, so could possibly be inhaled in harmful concentration.

FIXINGS FOR MASONRY, WOOD AND METAL

Nails are still the most widely used fixings in general building work, and for many applications connected with timber or timber-based materials remain the most cost-effective type of fixing. They depend for their effectiveness on the strength and condition of the wood, as their grip is provided by friction, derived from the compressive reaction of the fibres they have separated, which try to return to their natural position. Wood contains water, and unless it is very thoroughly sealed can absorb moisture from the air. For this reason, stainless steel nails are increasingly specified, especially for timber-frame work.

Masonry nails

Masonry nails are extremely hard, almost as hard as a good-quality hammer head's striking face, so that they can be tapped straight into brickwork and other forms of masonry, without previous drilling and plugging operations. For manual fixing of materials such as wall battens, they can save a lot of time and trouble.

Woodscrews

Unless a professional power screwdriver is used, all but the smallest woodscrews need guide holes in timber, and drilling and plugging before they can be driven into non-wood materials. Screws are considerably stronger than nails, size for size, and have the advantage that they can be taken out and put back in again, instead of being permanent fixtures. By and large, they are slower than nails to put in, bearing in mind that nails can also be power driven, but in recent years the twin-thread type of woodscrew has speeded screw fixing up. This kind of screw has two separate, parallel helixes, each of them winding up the shank from the point twice as quickly as a single helix would, so the screw is twice as quick to put in and take out, and gives better grip since the threads are closer together than with a normal screw.

Common woodscrews are made from mild steel wire. Consequently they can rust just as nails can, and their slotted or cross-point heads are relatively soft and all too easily damaged. There are better quality screws on the market — cold-forged from boron steel wire, which can be hardened right through, and with threads that are rolled instead of being cut, to give additional sharpness and accuracy. Bright zinc plate and other protective finishes are available, and for special applications there are also screws made from stainless steel.

One tried and tested form of woodscrew which is still useful for heavy-duty fixing work is the coach screw. This has a fatter shank than a normal woodscrew and a square head so that it can be driven home by a spanner or socket wrench.

Masonry plugs and hammer screws

Plugs for anchoring woodscrews in masonry are almost invariably plastic now, nylon being favoured for building applications. The use of nylon has brought about an interesting development saving a great deal of time and trouble — the hammer screw. Drilling and plugging are carried out as normal, but the screws are then tapped in with a hammer. The resilient nylon allows the screw threads to slip through on the way in, springing back to grip them once the hammering stops. This system still allows the screw to be taken out afterwards

A professional rotary hammer like this Spit 330 makes light work of all masonry drilling and anchor setting. Unlike a normal hammer drill, this type of tool produces hammering action by 'firing' a pneumatically driven piece of metal at the bit-holding assembly. The operator is not directly connected to the action, so feels less vibration and can drill more holes without getting tired (*Spit Fixings Ltd*)

137

if necessary, using a screwdriver. While what the manufacturers refer to as the 'pull-out values' for hammer screw fixings are only about half those for ordinary screwed-in plug fixings, they are still more than adequately high for most building purposes — including the anchorage of door and window frames. For this there is a special type of 'frame anchor', designed to fit into a single hole drilled through the frame into the surrounding masonry, so that the screw can be tapped straight in. These fixings usually have neat plastic caps for the screwhead.

Expanding anchors

There are two main types of expanding metal anchor for solid masonry. One is a galvanised or stainless-steel cylindrical plug, with a built-in internal thread. This plug is inserted into a pre-drilled hole and power-hammered to make its casing expand against the hole sides, 'set-

External insulation slabs being fixed to masonry with Spit ISO universal expanding insulation anchors (*Spit Fixings Ltd*)

ting' the anchor. The matching bolt is then screwed home. An alternative is the Rawlbolt type of fixing, which consists of a steel bolt fitted inside a soft iron sleeve. The 'nut' at the bottom end of the bolt is conical in section, so that after the bolt has been inserted into the hole, and the top end nut is tightened down, the sleeve is both compressed lengthways and splayed outwards to bear against the hole sides. A similar system is used by Hilti with conical nuts at either end of a long bolt, to make a dual-action tie for strengthening cavity walls whose original ties have collapsed or otherwise failed. Their expanding Perfix bolts go into holes drilled right through one leaf and part way into the other, tightening of the accessible nut with a socket or box spanner producing expansion grip in both to hold the leaves in a firm relationship to each other.

Chemical anchors

A heavy-duty fixing particularly suitable for carrying loads that may exert dynamic stresses, but equally suitable for static ones, is the chemical or resin anchor. With this, the bolt is held in the masonry, not by expanding a mechanical sleeve, but by a chemically cured resin, supplied in sealed cartridges of various diameters and lengths, according to the size of hole required for the bolt. With an appropriate cartridge lodged in the hole, the bolt is driven in on top by a rotary hammer drill, fitted with a drive adaptor — normally a hexagon socket or rod. This breaks the cartridge, allowing resin to fill the gap between bolt and hole completely. At this stage, the bolt is left until the resin has hardened; the time for this to happen varies from ten minutes at 20°C (68°F) to five hours at freezing point.

The Tapcon construction fastening system

Tapcon is the trade name of a type of self-tapping screw anchor for concrete, brick, pre-cast panels, building blocks, stone and other masonry. Tapcon screws have alternate high-and low-profile threads, the high ones notched to assist waste clearance and to facilitate the cutting action of the threads in the masonry.

They have to have a precisely sized guide hole, but they do not need a plug. Attachments have been developed by the manufacturers to enable the drilling and screwing operations to follow each other without the delay of changing tools. There are two different versions of these Condrive attachments, which work with any power drill having a standard chuck, one for Tapcon anchors with washered hexagon heads and the other for those with cross-point, countersunk heads. Simpler and slightly faster of the two is the version for hexagon head anchors, because the hexagon drive sleeve can be left in place round the masonry drill, ready to slide forward into action as soon as the hole is completed. In the countersunk-head version, the drive sleeve holding the cross-point screwdriver bit is removed for the drilling operation, and snapped back into place to drive the screw anchor home.

The range of building fixings is almost endless. Here are some of the 400 or more made by Fischer Fixings (*Fischer Fixings Ltd*)

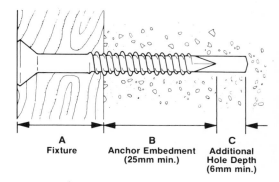

| A | B | C |
| Fixture | Anchor Embedment (25mm min.) | Additional Hole Depth (6mm min.) |

A + B = ANCHOR LENGTH
B + C = LENGTH OF DRILLED HOLE IN MASONRY

Fig 46 The Tapcon anchor screws straight into masonry without any form of plug (*Buildex/ITW Ltd*)

139

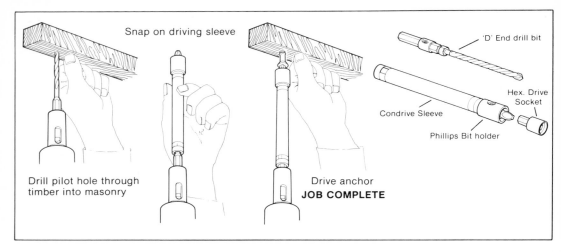

Snap on driving sleeve

'D' End drill bit

Hex. Drive Socket

Condrive Sleeve

Phillips Bit holder

Drill pilot hole through
timber into masonry

Drive anchor
JOB COMPLETE

Fig 47 This is the simple Tapcon anchor fixing sequence. The Condrive tools illustrated fit standard power drills (*Buildex/ITW Ltd*)

Expanding anchors cannot for obvious reasons be sited close to an edge, but with the Tapcon fixing this can be done with impunity. Provided they are installed in accordance with the manufacturer's recommendations concerning hole diameter and depth, and length of thread engagement in the masonry, Tapcon anchors are strong, reliable and readily removable or re-usable. Holes should be at least 6mm (¼in) deeper than the length of screw inserted and there must be at least 25mm (1in) of thread in contact with the masonry.

Cast-in sockets

Internally threaded bolt-holding sockets can be cast into concrete, where the precise position required is established in advance. The sockets are simple, thick-walled, corrosion-protected tubes of hardened steel, with a bolt thread cut into the inner face and a solid steel dowel inserted across the bottom end to provide additional anchorage.

Self-tapping and self-drilling screws

Self-tapping screws are not as widely used in building as they are in cars and domestic appliances, but they are valuable wherever anything has to be attached to thin metal or to plastic. They are case hardened, with sharp threads that cut into the sides of holes prepared for them, very similarly to Tapcon screw anchors' threads. They can be taken out and put in again, but not too often. Heads may be slotted, hexagon drive or cross-point.

For thicker metals, self-drilling screws offer a stronger fixing system, more resistant to vibration. As their name suggests, these screws not only cut their own thread, but have a point that pre-drills the hole to be tapped, so they are very quick to insert, even in steel as thick as 6mm (¼in).

Shot-fired fixings

Shot-fired fixings are nails that can be 'hammered' into concrete, brick, any other hard masonry or even into steel joists, using a tool called a cartridge hammer. This is effectively a gun, using explosive charges to fire 'nails' into suitable materials at point-blank range. There is nothing particularly complex about the system, which is as safe as the person using it — and extremely quick and efficient. The hammer unit will not fire until positive pressure against the nose of it has pushed the spring-loaded 'barrel' back against the body, so it is not possible to point it at anything, or anybody, and shoot. Cartridges are colour coded to indicate the depth of penetration which each will achieve. If the operator were stupid enough to try to put shot-fired fixings

A cartridge hammer being used to fix concrete shuttering to a wall (*Spit Fixings Ltd*)

into thin board, the nail could become a short-range bullet; but short of that, the cartridge hammer is as safe as any other fixing tool. Nails are not necessarily plain studs, but can be threaded at one end to take nuts. Shot firing is a method widely used for fixing timber framing to concrete foundation slabs.

Plasterboard and thin wall fixings

Plasterboard, chipboard, hardboard and other light wall and ceiling panel materials will not support normal nail and screw fixings as well as solid timber does. Modern flush doors also have a thin facing sheet unable to hold screws carrying much weight. Toggle fasteners work reasonably well, having wide 'wings' which spread the load across a broad area of board, but they have the disadvantages of requiring a large diameter hole to admit the folded toggles and of not providing an anchorage which is permanent; if the screw is removed, the toggle is lost behind the panel.

Where many fixings have to be made to thin boards (which form most of the interior wall surfaces in timber-frame houses) it is desirable to have screw fixings which allow screws to be withdrawn and refixed in the same places time after time. This facility can be provided for lighter loads by simple plastic plugs, but the metal fixings known a little confusingly as 'cavity wall anchors' are the best solution to the problem. They usually have a small flange at the front and a split sleeve at the back which collapses symmetrically on to the back of the panel board, forming a broad-based pyramid shaped 'nut' as the screw is tightened. Since this back support is tensioned against the front flange, the screw can be taken out and put back in again without the anchorage being lost or weakened.

CLADDING MATERIALS

On traditional brick- and stone-built houses, cladding is more of a cosmetic facing than a necessity, except in the regions where severe driving rain is a constant problem. On timber-frame houses, however, there are several forms of cladding which are viable alternatives to a single brick skin, either all over the exterior walls or on parts of them.

Natural timber

Cedar shingles and shiplap softwood boarding have been used for many years as cladding materials. Properly impregnated and sealed, softwood can be durable, weather resistant and attractive in appearance, and can provide useful additional thermal insulation. Cedar needs no impregnation, but is sometimes treated with oil/wax compounds to preserve its original red colour, since left untreated it weathers in time to a silver grey.

Plastic

Rigid polyvinyl chloride is made in three main forms as a cladding material. The Marley and Tufflex systems use thin-walled but strong, single-thickness planks, extruded from solid PVC and profiled to look like shiplap boards. Both systems use secret-fixing clips and extruded-edge, corner and other finishing profiles to give a neat finish and take up

panel dimensions

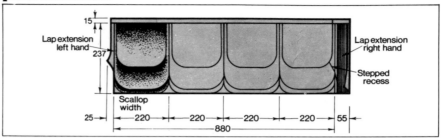

details

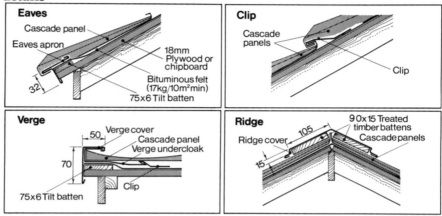

installation sequence

Fig 48 Although giving the authentic appearance of scalloped roof tiles, Cascade copper and steel 'tiles' are in fact profiled, pressed panels, each four tiles wide. The interlocking panels are fitted, not on to timber battens as are concrete or clay tiles and slates, but on to special clips fixed to a solid moisture-resistant chipboard base (*IMI Broderick Structures*)

hermal movement. In common with most cladding materials, solid PVC boards are fixed to vertical battens, about 25mm (1in) thick, which are themselves fixed direct to masonry or over breather paper to timber-frame studs.

Kufa Plastics produce hollow, webbed construction planks, with the profile of tongue-and-groove boarding. The air trapped in the compartments formed by the webs gives good thermal and sound insulation properties. This system features push-fit fixing clips. When used internally, wood-grain finish planks can be substituted for the white used for outdoor cladding.

The third main type of plastic cladding is that made by Celuform, consisting of a uPVC skin over a rigid, low-density, cellular foam plastic core. It is made in both open V-joint and shiplap tongue-and-groove profiles, and can be sawn and nailed almost as if it were solid timber. Having no internal cavities, it can be installed with the joints lying vertically, as can the solid Marley and Kufa planks. The insulation properties of Celuform are rather better than those of solid timber of equivalent thickness.

Slates and tiles

Natural slate, asbestos-cement simulated slate, clay and concrete tiles can all be fixed to vertical and near-vertical surfaces, using the same horizontal batten supports which hold them on roofs; but nailing is obligatory, as the lugs on clay and concrete tiles will not give adequate support as they do on pitched roofs in sheltered areas, where nailing is often largely dispensed with. Breather paper is usually laid under the battens for tile-hung claddings, in place of the waterproof sarking felt installed on pitched roofs.

Profiled metal tiles

One product both traditional in appearance and technically advanced is Broderick Structures' Cascade tile. Equally well suited to pitched roofing and vertical cladding applications, the Cascade system is based on pressed metal panels, which are secret-fixed by special clips, interlocking and profiled to look realistically like individual, scalloped tiles. Copper and coloured steel versions are made, each panel comprising four 'tiles'. Although strong, the metal is extremely light because it is thin, deriving its strength from the contoured folds. Cascade panels are generally mounted on 18mm (¾in) thick moisture-resistant chipboard panels, but even taking the weight of these into account, the total weight of a Cascade installation is less than half that of a batten-mounted concrete tile facing. Once clipped in place, the 'tiles' can be removed only with a special tool, so they are vandal resistant. They are also storm-proof, being certified for use in typhoon conditions. Copper may seem an unlikely material to suggest for roofing and cladding in a housing context, but the metal does weather gracefully, acquiring a soft green patina as the surface oxydises.

Coloroc lightweight concrete cladding units

These cladding units are coloured right through to look like brick or stone. Measuring 600mm wide by 100mm deep (2ft x 4in), they are flat at the front except for a concave shallow profiled top edge, which is designed to tuck neatly under the unit mounted above. Coloroc units are fixed on to hooked aluminium battens nailed to the wall vertically with their centres 300mm (1ft) apart, so that the staggered vertical joints between adjacent units lie along the centres of the U-shaped support battens. A hooked recess at the back of each unit locates its lower edge firmly, its top edge being retained by the next unit up. Finishing trim strips are fitted at the upper and lower limits of the area covered by the cladding. The system is suitable for installation in even the most severe exposure zones, with the single proviso that in these zones the tongs which the units hook on to are protected by bitumen paint. As units are not nailed or clipped in place, any individual units accidentally damaged can be removed simply by pushing them slightly upwards and levering them gently out. Coloroc installations have a 15mm (⅝in) gap between the backs of the cladding

143

Coloroc precast concrete cladding blocks are supported by a special system of aluminium hooked battens (*Forticrete Ltd*)

MANUFACTURED BOARDS AND LAMINATES

Natural timber boards sawn from a tree have always had the disadvantages of warping and shrinkage under changing atmospheric conditions. Although the ease with which they can be worked and their often attractive appearance compensate for these problems, which can anyway be partially overcome by careful selection and treatment, natural timber is becoming increasingly scarce and expensive, so that even where it would be the most suitable material to use, a substitute often has to be found amongst the range of manufactured boards available. By no means are all of these second-choice substitutes for real wood. Many are made for specific purposes for which wood is unsuitable, and are useful or beautiful in their own right.

Wood-based boards

One result of the scarcity and cost of high-grade wood has been the development of boards which are made of wood, but use it in economical ways. Chipboard is a prime example, using fine, evenly sized particles formed into boards under heat and pressure, with adhesive incorporated to bind the chips together. Chipboard therefore has no grain, so needs to be fairly thick to give it strength, but the lack of grain enables it to be cut and laid in any direction and gives an inherent monolithic quality. As already explained in the section dealing with flooring and fire-resistant grades, most types of chipboard may move a little in response to moisture-content changes, but there are moisture-resistant versions, such as the Norwegian Orkla Elite, used for roofing applications, and the Aqua Elite internal cladding panel faced with Formica laminate. Unless badly stacked or otherwise maltreated, chipboard has the virtue of being extremely flat. Some kinds are of layered construction, either to stiffen them by producing a laminated effect in the board centre or to produce a specially fine surface on one or both sides.

Blockboard is stronger than chipboard, thickness for thickness, needing support at

units and the breather paper fitted under the battens, to help the system remain weatherproof. Timber-frame walls clad with the system carry the Timber Research and Development Association's half-hour fire rating against external fire.

Masonry-walled buildings can also be clad, either for appearance, renovation or weatherproofing purposes. Sand/cement rendering and pebbledashing are forms of cladding designed primarily to improve walls' resistance to water penetration. Thin, reconstituted stone cladding systems are possible alternatives to renders or pebbledash, serving both cosmetic and weatherproofing purposes. Both the Bradstone and Stonetex systems include architectural dressings for window frames, cast to look like smooth-sawn, stone-mullioned units.

less frequent intervals when used in large spans, but it is more expensive. Its core consists of parallel strips of timber — which may be hardwood or softwood, according to the grade and origin — and its facing is of a constructional (thick) veneer. Some boards are three-layer types, with the facings running at right angles to the core timber, others five-layer, with additional facings running parallel to the core. Blockboard is used in building only where its unsupported strength is of paramount importance and its dimensional stability is useful.

Plywood shares the strength and stability of blockboard, and has the advantages of being cheaper in many grades and of being available in a variety of thicknesses. It can be cheap or expensive, depending on the grade, and it can be flexible or very stiff, depending on the thickness. Types resistant to fire, water and insect attack are made, perhaps the best known being WBP (water- and boil-proof). Plywood has an almost limitless variety of applications in building work, because of its versatility: flat-roof boarding, timber-frame construction, concrete shuttering, interior door facings and decorative panelling are a few of its many uses.

All kinds of boards used for panelling can be faced with decorative wood veneers, from the less expensive, rotary-cut sheets to the most exotic and highly priced matched facings. Real wood veneers can effectively camouflage otherwise flat and uninteresting utilitarian panelling materials, perhaps chosen for their fire-resistant or thermal insulation properties.

Wood fibres, as opposed to chips, are used to manufacture a vast range of building boards broadly classified as 'fibre boards'. Hardboard is only one of them. Fibre insulating board can be used under timber or chipboard rafts on solid floors, as wall or ceiling panelling, where it can be plastered or painted, or (in its bitumen-impregnated form) as timber-frame panel sheathing, as roof sarking board or in strips as concrete expansion joint filler. Plain, perforated and other textured insulating boards are used in the form of interlocking

tiles to insulate walls and ceilings against heat and sound. Both medium density and bitumen-impregnated boards are vapour permeable and resistant to water penetration, so they have two advantages as timber-frame panel sheathing materials. In the construction stages, they are not over-sensitive to being left unclad for reasonable periods and after completion they allow moisture vapour to pass through, helping to avoid the interstitial condensation to which the timber-frame system can be liable if mismanaged. Where bitumen-impregnated insulating board is the sheathing material, breather papers under cladding materials can be dispensed with.

Ordinary plasterboard consists of gypsum (calcium sulphate) sandwiched between sheets of cartridge paper. It is also available with a backing of polythene or aluminium foil as a vapour check, for situations where it is used in front of thermal insulation materials, as in timber-frame construction. Even in its standard form, plasterboard is highly fire resistant, but there are special fire-resisting grades containing glass fibres and vermiculite. Plasterboard can be backed with urethane or polystyrene foam insulation to improve its thermal insulation properties. Wide building boards for making partition walls often consist of plasterboard facings, with rigid foam or honeycomb centres. Not all plasterboards need plastering, some having a pre-finished face, ready for decorating. These normally have tapered edges, which are designed for invisible jointing, two adjacent tapered edges forming a shallow dish, so that they can be taped and filled.

The combination of plasterboard and insulating foam backings is not always chosen to improve plasterboard's thermal insulation properties, but to provide an insulation board with adequate fire resistance. Not all foams are alike, some kinds having better fire ratings than others, because they do not give off smoke at a high rate when subjected to heat or flame. Two of the major low-smoke-emissivity foam insulants are used in Plaschem Aerowall PF laminated lining board and by Coolag with-

145

out plasterboard in its Purlroofer insulation board for flat roofs.

Fibre-reinforced cement boards and sheets are now available with glass- and other non-asbestos-fibre reinforcement, typical examples being Glass Reinforced Concrete's Northwich building board and Turner & Newall's Tac-board. Rather easier to cut, drill and fix than the older asbestos products, they are equally non-combustible, waterproof, frost resistant, maintenance free and even stronger, without the tendency of asbestos cement to shatter when struck sharply. Their main uses are flat-roof decking, wall and ceiling lining, partition construction and soffit lining. Although they are technically suitable for external cladding and used for that purpose in prefabricated housing designed for export, the many more visually attractive cladding materials available are generally preferred for housing.

Plastic laminate and melamine-faced or wood-veneered boards may have many different kinds of core material, but the low cost and flatness of chipboard makes it the first choice for most shelving, cupboard construction and kitchen or bathroom counter work. Veneers and laminate surfaces not only provide decorative and/or hard-wearing qualities, but also add considerably to the strength of a core material, which can be made thinner for a given job than if it were used unfaced. Where a wood or plastic facing is stuck on to an existing board or panel, both sides should be faced at the same time, to stop the pull of the applied layer distorting its flatness. Even doors can be slightly warped by unilaterally applied facings. The one exception to this rule is the heavy, laminate-faced counter top based on 30mm (1¼in) thick or thicker chipboard.

Plastic laminates like Formica and Warerite are in fact 'plastic' only on the protective surface, which is clear melamine. Colours and wood-grain, abstract or pictorial designs are printed on paper under the tough surface and the dark brown backing consists of many layers of resin-impregnated paper pressed together to form a solid sheet. Laminates have totally revolutionised kitchen and bathroom

design since they were introduced, and will almost certainly continue to be used for a wide variety of applications for many years yet. What has always limited their use outside the kitchen, bathroom and utility-room context, however, is the thin, dark line of backing material left showing through wherever edges meet at an angle smaller than 180°.

Formica brought out in late 1983 a totally new surfacing material, which promises to take plastic into design fields well away from the utility scene. Called Colorcore, the new product is just as tough as the familiar laminate, even tougher in some respects, but the same colour throughout its thickness, so there is no perceptible join, giving anything surfaced on all sides with it the appearance of being made from a solid block of the material. Striking visual effects are obtainable by routing or engraving designs into the surface, whether these are made in single layers or in two or more laminated together so that different colours show through at different cutting depths. Colorcore has a delicately grained, velour finish free from obtrusive specular reflections. Heat, stain, scratch and scuff resistant, it is normally cleanable with mild soap or detergent solutions, but abrasive powder cleaners can be used on it. Handling the new material in the standard 3.05m x 1.22m (10ft x 4ft) sheets requires some care, since it is stiffer than ordinary laminate and a little thinner.

STAIRCASES

Straight-flight staircases, both with and without turns, feature two main types of construction. Enclosed stairs consist of boards forming the treads and risers let into substantial housings in the side timbers, known as 'strings' or 'stringers'. The slots do not have parallel sides, but are tapered on the undersides of treads and the backs of risers, to allow these to be cramped by wedges when the staircase is assembled. Straight stairways with open treads are supported by single or twin 'spines' under the treads, let into notches cut

A modern-style domestic spiral staircase — the 20H by Crescent of Cambridge. This unit is of traditional centre column design, so can easily support floor joists or landing in addition to carrying its normal load (*Crescent of Cambridge Ltd*)

metal-and-wood types on a steel base plate screwed to the floor. This is usually made the same thickness as underfelt, so it should be adequately concealed when mounted on the floor surface, by cutting the felt to fit round it and laying the carpet up to the core pillar. If you want the plate to fit flush with a solid floor, your staircase will have to be chosen far enough in advance to allow a suitable dish to be left for the plate when the floor is cast.

At the top, all spiral staircases must have a quarter landing, which forms the top step, so that a staircase needing a total of twelve rises

This elegant spiral staircase features a West African Sapele spiral and period-style spindles. Burbidges also make the staircase with modern-style spindles (*H. Burbidge & Son Ltd*)

into them if the construction is a timber one. Both these and their concrete and metal equivalents are usually assembled on site from precast or prefabricated components.

Concrete and metal staircases may be installed externally, not necessarily for fire escape, though they do serve that purpose. They can equally well provide separate access to a first- or second-floor flat. Although spiral staircases are not as convenient as straight-flight ones for outside access to upper floors from the point of view of getting furniture in and out, they may present a solution to a limited space problem in this context, and can be very attractive visually.

Spiral staircases are based on a central core, round which the prefabricated or precast treads are sleeved. Concrete types are supported at the base on a concrete pad, metal or

to span the vertical distance between the two floors it connects will consist of eleven treads and a landing. Most spiral staircases are made to measure from standard components which are reversible, in the sense that they can be used to form either left- or right-handed spirals. Standard stair diameters vary from about 1.2m (4ft) to well over 2m (6ft 6in). The usual number of treads per revolution is sixteen, but different types of tread may sometimes give a smaller, and not necessarily whole, number. Spiral stairs can, however, start or finish out of parallel with floor or wall lines at top or bottom, and need not be at right angles to them. The stair can be set at any angle that suits the situation. For stairs with more than sixteen rises, it is advisable to have a rest landing similar to a quarter landing part of the way up. In plan view, this will take up the same space as three or four treads.

The question of headroom needs to be taken into account when a spiral staircase is being considered. The position of the staircase should be organised so that only the higher treads project into the lower room's floor space, since there is not enough height for a tall man to walk underneath until the eleventh step counting upwards is reached. Headroom above the stair's pitch line is normally required by building regulations and by the local building control officers interpreting them to be 2m (6ft 6in), so if there is not this much room between the eleventh step counting downwards and the underside of the quarter landing, some readjustment will be needed. In another respect, too much space can be a problem. Where it is known that children under five years old are going to use the staircase, the vertical spacing between open-rise treads and the horizontal spacing between baluster uprights should not be greater than 99mm (37/8in). The tread space difficulty can be overcome by fitting half-risers under the tread nosings or above the back edges of the treads. To fit additional balusters at intervals as short as 99mm (37/8in) would give a cage effect; so manufacturers have evolved more graceful solutions to the spacing problem, including

balusters which feature loops or trident forms in the danger area, but do not have all their vertical sections stretching uninterrupted from tread to handrail.

DRAINAGE

Most houses in the UK are connected to a public drainage system by branch pipes ranging in outside diameter from 82.4mm (31/4in) to 160mm (61/4in), according to the maximum amount of flow theoretically likely, calculated by a complex formula based on national average water consumption figures. The smaller drains are not automatically specified when the formula says they are big enough, because they tend to block easily, and because of the need to maintain a safety factor big enough to allow pipes to cope with maximum foul water flow rates with about a third of their diameter clear of waste.

Drains have to clear away foul water and surface water (off the roof and possibly pathways and driveways) by gravity, reliably and continuously, and everybody wants them well out of sight and out of mind, so they are buried

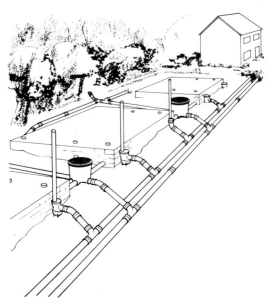

Fig 49 A typical plastic drain installation (*Bartol Plastics*)

Laying plastic drainpipes (*John Wickersham*)

A drain collection chamber made up from prefabricated concrete sections (*John Wickersham*)

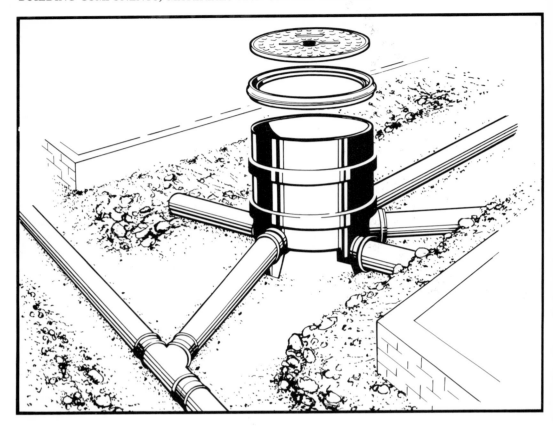

Fig 50 A Plastidrain collection chamber and man-hole cover *(Bartol Plastics Ltd)*

in deep trenches. This is partly to avoid damage and partly to facilitate the process of laying them at an appropriate gradient, usually 1 in 70 for a branch drain. Trenches are 300mm to 400mm (12in to 16in) wider than the pipe, so that the pipe-run can be supported by gravel and concrete up to the top of the pipe and then buried, using the soil which came out of the trench when it was dug. There is normally a collection point under a manhole cover somewhere near the house. This consists of a watertight inspection chamber, which may be built up in brick, precast concrete sections or moulded plastic components. Essentially, it acts as a bowl, connected to loo, sink, bath, shower and washbasin outlets — unless they are too far away, in which case

there may be the odd individual branch pipe — and also connecting with the branch pipe leading to the main sewer. In the event of the branch becoming blocked, rods or power-rotated cables can be inserted through the manhole to unblock it. Sometimes separate unblocking facilities are built into a system, in the form of obliquely connected backward facing pipes a little way down the branch pipe. These run up to ground level, terminating in 'rodding eyes', which are sealed when not in use.

Before 1970, almost all household under-ground drain pipes were in ceramic materials like vitrified clay or in heavy cast grey iron, soil pipes were of cast iron and bath/sink/shower waste pipes of lead. Vitrified clay is still the most widely used drain-pipe material below ground, but the socket-and-spigot jointed cast-iron system with its heavy bell-end joints,

The Polydrain soil/waste pipe manifold has blanking plugs for unused connections (*IMI Yorkshire Imperial Plastics*)

The Polydrain universal drain adaptor has a flexible gasket which accepts many different shapes and sizes of branch pipe (*IMI Yorkshire Imperial Plastics*)

which had to be sealed with molten lead or lead rammed down by hand to ensure adequate caulking, is now too labour intensive to be worth considering. The modern version of this system uses ductile iron pipes without any spigot ends, joints being made by a simple nitrile rubber seal, retained by a single-bolt compact collar which allows adjoining pipe sections to lie up to three degrees out of line with each other. Cast iron, the strongest of all the available materials, has particular advantages where drains have to be run under buildings. PVC pipes now account for over 20 per cent of the market for house underground drain systems, and for 90 per cent of new domestic rainwater and soil pipe systems. It is interesting to compare the breakage allowances made by quantity surveyors on large contracts in relation to the different drain-pipe materials — up to 20 per cent on ceramic, 2½ per cent on PVC, and nil on ductile iron, which is virtually unbreakable.

As recently as 1960, rainwater gutters and downpipes were made of wood, asbestos cement

or cast iron. Cast-iron ones are still made, but unless continually and thoroughly inspected and painted their life is the time it takes them to rust through. Although this can be a long time, the pieces that eventually drop off can be large and heavy. Plastic gutters avoid this problem, as do aluminium ones. Some aluminium gutters are prefabricated in standard lengths, but one type can be formed on site with special machinery. The advantage of this is that joints are required only at corners, since almost any length is produced, at the rate of 10m (32½ft) a minute, though the practical limit is around 30m (98ft), this being easily fixed by three men. Supplied and fixed by a firm called Gutterfast of Horley in Surrey, this seamless guttering is guaranteed against leaks for ten years, and features out-of-sight fixings which will carry normal ladder-leaning loads, snow and ice. Paint finishes available are white, brown or black, all guaranteed for twenty years, and the system as a whole has a normal life expectancy of thirty years.

Plastic-coated steel is the other main material currently used for gutter systems. The sections can be supplied in standard lengths or made to order, are lightweight but strong and come in a wider range of colours than the seamless aluminium type. These pressed steel gutters are made by Dales Fabrications of Ilkeston in Derbyshire.

PLUMBING MATERIALS

A domestic hot and cold water supply system is, or should be, separate and distinct from any 'wet' central heating system, except insofar as the same boiler is used to heat the water circulating in the space heating units and that for bath, sink and appliance taps. Even then, the water circuits are as a rule separate. Both take their water from the mains supply, and for this reason water boards lay down regulations to ensure that their water reaches taps used for drinking in a condition uncontaminated by any of the fittings or appliances in the circuit.

It is useful to know the location and diameter of your mains supply pipes, especially if you want to fit a water softener, which requires a feed pressure above a certain limit. If you look down the street, there should be a small but prominent metal plate somewhere along it with a large letter 'H' on it and two figures, one inside the top of the 'H' and the other inside the lower part of the letter. A figure 3 above and a 5 below would indicate that the main pipe was 3in in diameter, and 5ft away from the plate carrying the sign. Each house along the street will be connected to the main by small branch pipes with an internal diameter in the region of 16mm (⅝in). Older systems will have iron main pipes and thick-walled lead branch feeds, modern systems normally using plastic for both. Mains and branch pipes are buried at least 450mm (18in) below ground level to protect them from freezing.

Sometimes there is a stop tap in the mains branch outside the house, access to it being provided by a vertical tube with a lid on it. If there is not another one inside the house, your extension work should certainly include having one fitted, because outside taps can be very difficult to find and turn off when the ground is covered with snow.

From the point at which it enters the house, the mains supply branches off in various ways to do different jobs. Drinking water taps are supplied direct from the mains, even where a water softener is fitted in many cases, though it is quite possible and legal to connect drinking water taps to the mains via a softener. Provision is made in the pipework feeding a softener for the mains supply to bypass it, so that in the event of the unit having to be taken out of service for any reason at all, the mains supply need not be interrupted. Other appliances often connected direct to the mains are toilet cisterns, single or multi-point instantaneous water heaters ('geysers'), dish- and clothes-washing machines and electric shower heaters. Where appliances are available in high- and low-pressure versions, the high-pressure ones are for mains pressures and the low-pressure ones for water piped down from a high-level storage cistern under atmospheric pressure — 1 bar (15lb/sq in).

Older houses often have galvanised steel roof space storage tanks, which tend to rust in time and are usually of too small a capacity to cope with a houseful of modern equipment, let alone an extension containing even more water-consuming items — probably a complete kitchen and/or bathroom. If the storage tank is too small, it will at times empty faster than the mains supply can fill it, allowing uncomfortable interruptions in flow and perhaps letting air into the system, causing air locks which can be hard to dislodge. Modern reinforced plastic tanks are light in weight for their size when empty, but they may need support underneath at closer intervals than the steel type. They are more easily cleaned, however, have lids to keep out dirt and insects and can be obtained in bolt-together, knock-down form for situations where there is plenty of room to site a big tank but limited access.

A 15mm ($\frac{5}{8}$in) pipe usually carries mains water up to the tank, feeding it through a ball valve, which opens as the tank's water level drops and closes as the floating hollow sphere rises on the water surface, raising the lever rod it is attached to and pushing a plunger home to close off the supply. Ball valves may be made of brass or plastic, but both types are subject to wear and tend to be noisy. In 1983, a revolutionary new type of cistern valve was brought out, with a single moving part, much quieter, more reliable and free from adjustment and wear problems. Versions of this should be available by the time this book is published. Inlet valves are normally mounted about 75mm (3in) from the top of a tank, and an overflow pipe leading outside, usually at eaves level, is mounted at about the same height. Offtake outlets are not fitted into the base of the tank, because any dirt in the water will collect there, so the outlet pipes are fixed into the sides about 75mm (3in) from the tank bottom.

The main job of the high-level storage tank is to feed a hot water cylinder. In most systems this normally occurs through a 22mm ($\frac{3}{4}$in)

pipe leading into the side of the cylinder at a very low level, via an elbow fitting incorporating a short stub-pipe called a 'spigot' for draining it when the system has to be emptied for any reason. Hot water is taken to the taps from the very top of the cylinder, where the water is hottest; the pressure at which it is supplied, and therefore the rate at which it flows, is proportional to the height difference between the cold storage tank and the hot tap supplied. An additional pipe is teed off the hot supply pipe, and taken straight up above the storage tank, terminating in a hook bend to allow any abnormal flow to vent itself into the tank. This pipe is fitted through the tank lid and is open to ensure that the hot supply pressure does not exceed atmospheric. It is usually 22mm ($\frac{3}{4}$in) in diameter.

In older systems, boilers — including fireback boilers — used to heat the water in cylinders direct, via quite large-diameter — typically 25mm to 38mm (1in to 1$\frac{1}{2}$in) — flow and return pipes let into the cylinder sides so that the boiler and cylinder contents mixed freely. This was fine until the lining of the fire-warmed boiler became corroded with age and occasional overheating, and the dirty metal oxide particles began to appear through the taps, either as discoloration or as sediment. Modern cylinders are mostly of the indirect type, with flow and return pipes connected inside them by a pipe coil, which forms a heating element allowing the water to be warmed up without actually touching the boiler water circulating to warm it. The total area of this coil's outer surface in contact with the cylinder water determines the speed with which it can heat the contents, so a long, medium or short coil gives a high-, medium- or low-recovery cylinder. The higher the rate of recovery, the greater the cost of the cylinder.

Both direct and indirect systems can be supplemented by a separate heating element, inserted through and fixed into a screw-threaded boss in the domed cylinder top. If no supplementary heater is to be fitted, the blanking-off plate which closes off the boss is simply not removed. But since no one wants boilers or

153

fires going in hot weather, most cylinders have an electric immersion heater fitted into the cylinder, for summer use and for topping up the water heating at times of exceptionally high demand. Ideally, the immersion heater should be of the dual-element type, with one short element at the top, to heat just a few litres or gallons of water for kitchen or bathroom sink, and a longer one to heat the whole cylinder full for baths or dish- or clothes-washing machines plumbed into the hot water circuit.

Hot water cylinders are almost universally made in copper, some types being coated with insulation material at the factory, others left uninsulated, so a 75mm (3in) glass-fibre filled jacket should be fitted when all pipework has been connected. Next to a sphere, a cylinder shape has the largest surface-to-volume ratio of any, so it loses expensive heat at a high rate if not insulated. Most houses can accommodate a cylindrical hot water storage tank without any difficulty, but where space is tight, or a tank has to be fitted into an awkwardly shaped area, special shaped tanks can be made — tall and narrow, rectangular, short, fat or irregular. One of the chief applications for hatbox- or attaché-case-shaped hot water tanks is in the manufacture of all-in-one contract plumbing packs, which can comprise a cold and hot water storage tank mounted together as a single unit, pre-plumbed except for external connections. These sometimes have metal angle or tube frames,with space for mounting a boiler or for use as an airing cupboard. There are even packs which incorporate a central heating boiler, and whose cold cisterns have a separate feed/expansion tank built in for the heating system. Not all these space- and time-saving packs have odd-shaped cisterns and tanks.

One interesting hot water cylinder of conventional shape is Uttley Ingham's Pennine Gemini, so called because it has separate coils for heating small amounts of water in the top of the unit and for heating the whole water content. The two coils, fed by a boiler's flow and return pipes, are connected to each other by a three-port, two-way valve. This may be manual (controlled by a handwheel) or motorised (controlled by a push-button). It directs the flow of boiler-heated water into one coil or the other according to the valve setting chosen, so only a small amount of water is heated when demand is low, reserving the larger coil for times of greater demand. This twin-coil cylinder is pre-insulated with foam. It is possible to convert existing cylinders to twin-coil operation, but not by inserting a second coil. Uttley Ingham effects the conversion by adding a secondary cylinder, shaped rather like the dome of a mosque and called the Pennine Satellite. It does not have to be right on top of the existing cylinder, but can be installed at any convenient height above it, since the two units are connected only by pipework.

Several types of weater heater are designed to work straight off a mains water supply. The simplest of these is the non-pressure storage heater, which heats and keeps at a fixed temperature a small reservoir of water — normally from 30 to 50 litres (6½ to 11 gallons). This usually has an outlet pipe that swivels to a limited extent, so that it can serve two sinks side by side, but not a washing-machine hose, or any other pipe or fitting. Heater elements are quite small, only about 3 kiloWatts, or about the same power as a good electric kettle, so they need to be turned on in advance of demand for hot water and left on to ensure its replenishment. This type of heater is more efficient than an electric kettle, being well insulated with polyurethane foam. Thermostat setting is normally adjustable, roughly between 30° and 90°C (86° and 195°F). Pressure-type electric water heaters capable of supplying taps plumbed directly into them are usually fed from a cold storage tank, not the mains, and hold more water — up to 230 litres (well over 50 gallons). These are floor, not wall mounted, and have elements rated at around 6kW. Some wall-mounted electric heaters can be suplied by the mains water feed, because they have their own built-in feed tanks, with inlets controlled by ball valves, but this means that their outflow is purely gravitational, so

that they have to be mounted with their bases at least on a level with the highest tap to which they are connected, and preferably somewhat higher.

Instantaneous units, which heat water on the run, have very low water contents — just the volume in the coils heated by the electric elements or gas flames. Comparatively rarely are electric units used for multi-point water heating, but gas heaters for the purpose are at a high stage of development. Most of the electric instantaneous heaters are made for providing temperature-controlled water for shower heads. These are powerful units, often 7kW or 8kW, but they work very economically because of the smallness of the quantities of water heated and the low temperatures to which they heat it. They have the advantages for bathroom installation that they produce no flames or fumes and are easy to control auto-

This Leisure Tahiti shower cubicle has been built into a row of wardrobes in a bedroom to save space (*Leisure-Glynwed Consumer & Building Products Ltd*)

matically to make them fail-safe. They are normally supplied from the water mains, since a tank feeding one would have to be some 10.5m (34ft) above the unit to produce adequate water pressure. Electrical connection has to be made to a 240V, 30 amp supply — equivalent to that for an electric cooker — via a double-pole link switch that cannot be reached by a person using the bath or shower, but is otherwise readily accessible and is easily identifiable. (A double-pole switch is one that breaks both live and neutral connections when turned off, not just the live one, as light switches do.) Both water inlet and electrical connections are well shielded behind the wall-

155

mounted shower unit casing, which is itself shower-proof, and made from very tough plastic.

Not all electric shower units are heaters fed off the mains water supply. Triton Aquatherm, for example, also make two models which use the normal tank-fed hot and cold supplies. One is a simple booster pump, fitted into the flexible hose rising from a bath tap/shower mixer unit. This can make possible an acceptably good flow rate when the header tank cannot be placed high enough to provide it unassisted. It also reduces or eliminates the problem of the the shower temperature rising or falling sharply where there is no thermostatic control on the mixer and people downstairs turn taps on whilst the shower is in

A hydraulic pipe bender makes light work of forming heavier copper and stainless steel tubes (*Hire Service Shops Ltd*)

use. The other Triton unit, called the Powerflo, is also a booster pump, but this one is fed directly by the hot and cold supply pipes, acting as a mixer unit and booster pump at the same time. Being designed for low-pressure hot and cold supplies of roughly equal force, these booster units cannot be connected to a mains-pressure cold feed, which would both upset their efficiency and damage their works.

Pipes and fittings

Copper is now the standard material for plumbing and heating pipes, as lead used to be. The metal is non-corroding, easy to cut, bend and solder and — down to 15mm (⅝in) nominal diameter pipe size — is rigid and damage resistant when installed. Being solid drawn, copper tubes have no seam welds. The stiffer tubes from 15mm (⅝in) upwards are not stiff purely because of their thickness, but because they are mostly of 'half-hard temper',

which is equally suitable for water and gas pipeline installations. Pipes of 12mm (½in) diameter for minibore heating and the 10mm, 8mm and 6mm (⅜in, ⁵⁄₁₆in and ¼in) pipes for microbore heating are soft tempered. Both half-hard and soft-tempered copper tubes up to 22mm (¾in) in diameter are bendable by hand, deformation in the process being prevented by inserting special springs in them down to 15mm (⅝in), or using springs which fit outside the tube at lower diameters. All diameters can be bent using bending machines, which may be hand powered, working by simple mechanical leverage or by means of a hydraulic cylinder, or motorised. These machines do not need bending springs, because they bend the tube round formers which maintain their roundness in cross-section.

It is often necessary to bury pipes in concrete, plaster or soil, all of which may contain substances liable to attack metals. To avoid the necessity of wrapping pipework up in protective tape before burying it, manufacturers can supply it sheathed in polythene sleeving. Where buried pipes form part of a heating circuit, or even carry domestic hot water, the sleeving needs to provide thermal insulation as well as corrosion protection. IMI Yorkshire Imperial Kuterlex Plus tube achieves this ingeniously by using sleeving with a crenellated profile on the inside, to produce permanent insulating air pockets. The same company makes tubes covered in polythene without air pockets. This protects against corrosion, prevents condensation forming on cold pipes and is made in different colours, so that pipe-runs carrying different substances can be colour coded — green for drinking water and yellow ochre for gas being among the accepted conventions under BS 1710.

There are hard-drawn copper tubes, which cannot be bent or manipulated. These are thinner walled than the more usual half-hard and soft-temper tubes, and there are some fittings that cannot be used for joining them, but they have special pressure resistances which are useful in some applications, and

they can be used for sanitation as well as gas, water and heating services.

Although copper tube can be supplied in continuous coils up to 25m (82ft) long, in the widely used range from 8mm to 22mm (⅝in to ¾in) diameter, non-minibore/microbore sizes are normally supplied in 3m (10ft) straight lengths. In any case, cutting and jointing have to be effected at some point. There are three main systems of joining copper tube to itself. One involves belling out one of the two ends to be jointed, just sufficiently to allow the other end to be slipped inside it. The joint is then soldered. Soldered joints take advantage of the capillary attraction principle — the tendency of small voids to draw in liquids. So long as a close-fitting pipe joint is cleaned free of its natural oxide film and coated with flux to keep it clean as it is heated, solder applied at the pipe end will obligingly run into the slight gap between the belled and un-belled ends, hermetically sealing it. Bell-end jointing is an economical method of connecting pipe lengths of equal diameter in a straight line, but there its usefulness ends. To join pipes of different sizes, or to make a pipe run round a corner, follow an obtuse angle, connect to an appliance or tap, or enter another pipe from the side at an angle, supplementary pipe fittings are needed. There are two soldered kinds, both essentially sleeves that fit over both pipe ends to be joined. The more widely used and the cheaper of the two is the end-feed fitting, so called because the solder is applied to the ends of the fitting after it has been heated, just as in the case of the bell-end joint. About three times more expensive is the solder-ring fitting, which has slight bulges pressed into its sleeve ends during manufacture. These are filled with solder, which melts when the fitting is heated, running up the joint gap to the fitting end instead of down from it. The result is the same, and both kinds of fitting are known as capillary fittings. Solder-ring fittings have a convenience advantage over end-feed types, but although they make it theoretically unnecessary to carry solder about, it is common practice to end-feed a little into them as a

157

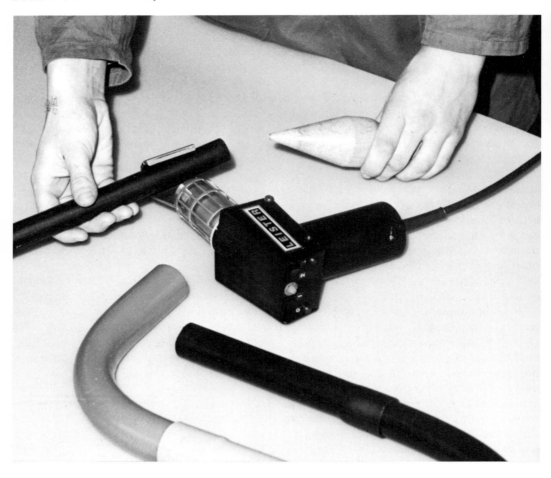

Professional hot-air blowers can be used for plumbing applications, including soldering, instead of blowtorches. Here a Leister unit is softening the end of a copper tube so that it can be belled out to make a joint (*Welwyn Tool Co Ltd*)

precautionary measure.

Considerable controversy has existed for many years concerning the possibility of significant amounts of lead from capillary fittings leaching out into drinking water, since ordinary solder does contain quite a high proportion of the poisonous metal. Small though the risk is, fittings manufacturers are beginning to make available solder-ring fittings which are totally lead free, the solder used in them consisting of approximately 3 per cent silver and 97 per cent tin.

In between the attachment ends, fittings are pressed into an enormous variety of forms — elbow with a sharp right angle or slow bend, tee, cross, corner (angled tee), corner cross (angled cross) and sweep tee, with the branch formed as a slow bend, being amongst the commonest.

More expensive than either end-feed or solder-ring fittings are compression joints, which make their seal mechanically by means of threaded collars called 'capnuts', tapered inside to make them compress a soft metal ring on to the tube and also compress it lengthways between the capnut and the body of the fitting, forming a total seal. Some plumbers use a tool to form a bulge on the actual pipe, to serve the same purpose as a ring. Compression joints are much bulkier and heavier than soldered fittings, but equally permanent and very strong. Their advantages are that they are quick to put on and can be taken apart and remade as often as necessary without any loss of efficiency. In most installations, soldered fittings are used for the majority of the joints in the pipework and compression joints in situations near cylinders, taps and appliances, where their screw-off facility is useful.

Some composite fittings have a solder sleeve on one end and a compression joint on the other. These are cheaper than all-compression fittings. Both solder and compression fittings can have one end with a male or female 'iron' thread for connection direct to appliance bosses or tap spigots. Most stopcocks, radiator valves and gate valves feature compression ends where they connect with pipes.

Compression fittings have another valuable feature, in that they can be used with stainless steel or plastic pipes, as well as with copper ones. Softer plastic pipes, such as polythene ones, need special flanged copper inserts to give the equally special compression rings a firm base to grip on, but the collars and threads remain the same; so, given the appropriate rings at each end, the same fitting can accommodate copper or stainless steel at one end and plastic pipe at the other.

Stainless steel tube, intrinsically tougher than copper, is thin walled and light, but extremely strong. In addition to standard compression fittings, stainless steel tube can be jointed by rather more compact special ones, which work without rings, compressing stainless steel sleeves so tightly on to the tube ends that they deform slightly, locking sleeve and tube together; only straight couplings of this type are available. End-feed solder fittings can be used, made from the same steel as the tubes, but there are no solder-ring fittings. Whereas the standard soft solders are used, stainless steel does need a special flux, and it takes a little more time and care to make a joint than it does in the case of copper, stainless steel being a less efficient conductor of heat. End-feed fittings can alternatively be silver soldered or

brazed on, but there is little point in using these more costly methods for domestic applications. Fittings can, however, be bonded to tubes with a special adhesive, which sets in two minutes, but which takes 2–4 hours to cure sufficiently to allow the tubes to be pressurised.

Once installed, stainless steel pipework is highly rigid and damage resistant. The material has been competitive in price with copper since the Zambia copper crisis put prices up some years ago, but stainless steel tube and fittings are still not quite as widely available as copper. This does not mean it is impossibly difficult to obtain, merely that it will not be as readily available as copper tube at the average builders' or plumbers' merchants.

Plastic tube and fittings have been around for many years, but did not become really serious competition for the metal systems until Bartol Plastics introduced Acorn high-performance polybutylene pipe and push-fit connections and fittings. Both pipe and fittings are

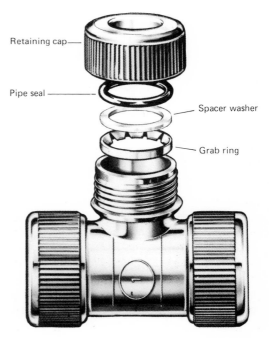

Retaining cap

Pipe seal

Spacer washer

Grab ring

Fig 51 An exploded diagram showing the parts of the Acorn push-fit joint for polybutylene water supply and heating pipes (*Bartol Plastics Ltd*)

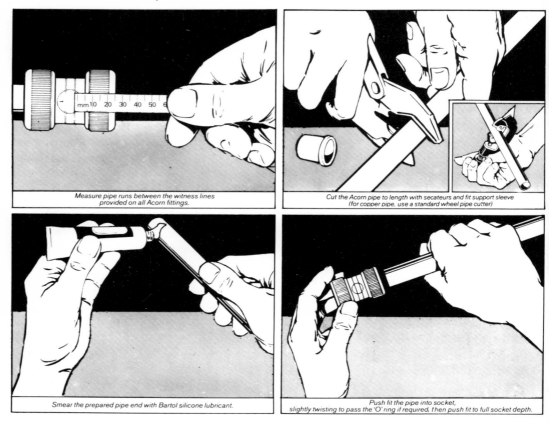

Measure pipe runs between the witness lines provided on all Acorn fittings.

Cut the Acorn pipe to length with secateurs and fit support sleeve (for copper pipe, use a standard wheel pipe cutter)

Smear the prepared pipe end with Bartol silicone lubricant.

Push fit the pipe into socket, slightly twisting to pass the 'O' ring if required, then push fit to full socket depth.

Fig 52 The simple jointing process for Bartol's plastic plumbing/heating system (*Bartol Plastics Ltd*)

suitable for hot and cold water supplies and wet central heating applications, and the pipe can also be connected via standard brass compression fittings to taps and appliances, though the company makes its own brass and composite plastic/brass connectors to suit most situations. Polybutylene pipe is not made in such a wide range of sizes as copper and stainless steel, since its chief market is in the housing field, where 15mm, 22mm and 28mm (⅝in, ¾in and 1in) cover the majority of needs. It comes in 3m (10ft) straight lengths and in 50m or 100m (164ft or 328ft) coils, and can be cut with pipe secateurs. There are no corrosion problems with the material, and pipes made from it resist the build-up of scale in hard water areas rather better than metal pipes, and are totally non-toxic. Because of the inherent thermal insulation qualities of the plastic, polybutylene pipes take longer to freeze than metal ones, and are less likely to burst than either metal or rigid plastic pipes when freezing does occur, because they are quite flexible.

Oddly, the flexibility of polybutylene pipe gives it better resistance to impact damage than has copper or rigid plastic pipe. It also has high dent and puncture resistance and stands up to abrasion extremely well. Its natural toughness is indicated by the minimum service life expected of it, which is fifty years. Polybutylene pipes will accommodate temperatures up to 90°C (194°F) under continuous pressure, way above the normal requirements of hot water and heating systems.

Although polybutylene pipe is flexible, it

will not pull out of brass compression fittings or out of Acorn push-fit joints and fittings, provided the standard stainless steel support sleeve insert is used. Acorn push-fit joints look very similar to brass compression fittings, having knurled capnut ends, but these need not be unscrewed to make a joint, each pipe end being simply sleeved, smeared with silicone lubricant and pushed home, with a slight twist to allow it to pass the flexible O-ring which effects the seal. A stainless steel grab-ring with barbed teeth is what actually holds the pipe into the fitting, which makes a leak-tight joint for any application up to its maximum temperature tolerance. Push-fit joints will also accept copper pipes, but these of course do not need to be sleeve supported. One of the important differences between copper and polybutylene systems is that a length of copper cannot flex to allow it to be pushed into a joint in a tight corner, as can the plastic pipe. This feature saves a good deal of installation time, not only with regard to joint fitting but also in that it allows the plastic pipe to be snaked and threaded through the building structure in long continuous lengths, cutting down on the number of joints necessary and on the time needed to make bends in copper.

On the debit side, polybutylene pipe is sensitive to ultraviolet light, so needs to be stored in the shade, and painted if installed in exposed locations. It should also be kept well away from direct heat sources such as electric fires, and should not be left in contact with soldering fluxes or pipe thread sealing compounds, as it could be when joined to metal pipework by a compression or composite fitting. Being flexible, it will not support fittings or appliances.

Polybutylene pipe and push-fit joint systems are completely free from one problem which can affect brass fittings in certain areas — that of joint failure caused by chemicals leaching out the zinc content of the brass. The process is known as 'dezincification'. The Copper Development Association publishes an information sheet on the subject, No 36. If you find you are in an area susceptible to the trouble, you have to use dezincification-resistant fittings wherever compression joints are required. They are made of an alloy which does not disintegrate in the presence of the aggressive water that causes the problem. There is a symbol marked on the resistant fittings — a prominent logo made up from 'D' and 'R', with the 'D' reversed right to left.

Fittings put up the cost of a plumbing installation, so unless you want the very minimum incorporated in yours, you should specify at the outset any that you particularly want. It is very convenient, for example, to be able to shut off the water supply to your cold tank without drying up every tap in the house. This means an extra stopcock or valve in the supply pipe near the tank. It can also be useful to have the facility of cutting off, say, the upstairs and downstairs parts of a wet central heating system separately, so that modifications or repairs can be carried out without draining the entire circuit. Stopcocks work like taps, achieving total shut-off by means of rubber washers. They do not allow a full-bore flow through a pipe, however, when fully open, as a gate valve does. Gate valves shut off the water using a metal shield which slides down in a groove across the pipe, portcullis fashion. When this is raised, the pipe bore is completely free of obstruction. There is a possible disadvantage to gate valves, in that the water seal depends entirely on metal-to-metal contact, which is not always close enough to stop some water getting through. A further problem with them is that they tend to become very tight, or even jammed, when left open or closed for long periods — as they inevitably are in most situations. One honourable exception is the Nibco design of gate valve, which not only seals well, but can easily be released after being left screwed down tightly, for no matter how long. With resilient-seal ball valves, you can have the best of both worlds, as they allow a good through-flow, yet shut off completely when the perforated ball that gives them their name is turned through 90°. Some have metal balls and others nylon ones, turning at either end against ring seals made from various kinds of rubber.

One item of plumbing equipment worth considering if you have a domestic hot water system which cannot be properly temperature controlled — perhaps because it is being heated by an Aga-type cooker which cannot be switched on and off by a cylinder thermostat — is the thermostatic mixer. This has a knob for setting the temperature at which you want your bath and sink hot tap water and three ports for connection to the cylinder's outlet, the cold main and the tap feed. When a hot tap is turned on, the unit adjusts the proportion of hot water to cold to produce a tap supply at the required temperature level. Faral Tropical have one of these, the Aquamix, and another is made by Tour & Andersson and marketed by TA Controls as the TA-Mix.

Drayton make a thermostatic valve which fits into the return pipe near the hot water cylinder. This cuts off the flow mechanically when the preset temperature is reached, opening again when it has dropped again. This unit is useful for cylinders heated by otherwise uncontrollable systems such as gravity circulation from solid-fuel boilers whose main job is central heating, but it is not advisable to fit them where the heat source is a backboiler in an open fire unit or an Aga-type cooker. In these cases, an explosive situation could be created by closing off the secondary circuit.

HEATING EQUIPMENT

When you build an extension, you increase the volume of living space which will need to be heated during the average thirty-three weeks of the year in which it is colder inside than out in Britain — a period referred to by heating engineers as 'the heating season'. If your present heating system has just enough power to cope with your pre-extension needs, consideration will have to be given to the question of how best to provide the extra heat required by the new space. Where this is going to be used only occasionally and is relatively small, it may be better to fit an individual heating unit — a gas fire, perhaps, or a wall-mounted electric fan heater — than to add extra radiators or

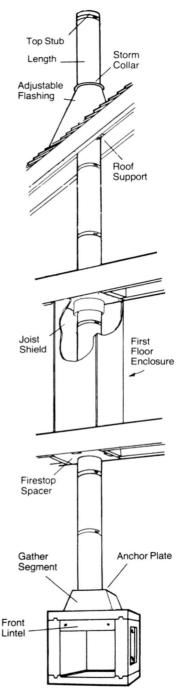

Fig 53 Diagram showing a Selkirk prefabricated SC chimney routed through a typical house structure. The chimney need not be near a wall unless a false chimney breast is required (*Selkirk*)

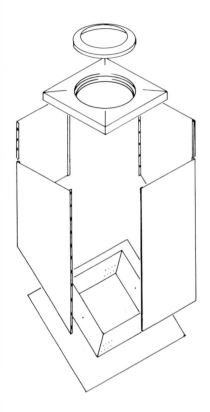

warm air outlets which could strain your central system. If, on the other hand, your present system has more than enough spare power to cope with the extra load, it would be silly not to use it.

An alternative might be to join the movement back to open-fire heating. It is no longer necessary to build a massive chimney stack to provide a flue for an open fire; modern twin-wall insulated chimney systems like the Selkirk SC are both cleaner and infinitely more efficient in terms of establishing and maintaining optimum draught conditions. The SC chimney consists of two stainless steel tubes, one inside the other, the space in between filled with mineral fibre insulation. The reason for its good performance lies in its having no great mass of material to warm up, as a masonry chimney has, so instead of taking a long time to get hot enough to produce a good draught — which is created by the difference

Fig 54 This is Selkirk's square chimney housing unit, designed to give the appearance of a traditional stack at roof level to a cylindrical chimney (*Selkirk*)

between flue gas temperature and outside atmosphere temperature at the top of a chimney — the insulated tube heats up quickly and stays hot. A hot, smooth-faced inner surface is not conducive to flue gas condensation, so deposits of tar and creosote are kept to a minimum, as is any likelihood of a chimney fire which these steel chimneys withstand cheerfully in any case.

As the outer tube does not get very hot at all, and as a 150mm or 200mm (6in or 8in) inside diameter chimney (which is all that is needed) places no inordinate load on a building's structure, twin-wall insulated chimneys are greatly favoured for providing open-fire facilities in timber-frame houses. They are prefabricated

Modern prefabricated chimney systems can be used to put fires or other heating appliances in places where there is no existing chimney. This is part of the Selkirk system, using a fire chamber built up from sections designed to slot together and twin-wall stainless-steel chimney sections with dense insulation between the walls. Chimney sections push-fit into each other, a toggle-lever locking band producing a gas-tight joint. Specially fabricated units at intermediate floor and roof-level ceiling penetration points ensure safety. Note use of elbows to adjust line of chimney to suit joist arrangement (*Selkirk*)

in sections which interlock, fastening with simple toggle straps, so can be installed quickly. At ground-floor level, a typical installation starts with a fire chamber made up from prefabricated concrete slabs and standing either on a solid floor or, if the floor is a suspended timber one, on a concrete plinth built up from the foundations. For an open fire, the chamber has a pyramidal central protrusion on its 'lid' which helps funnel the exhaust fumes smoothly into the chimney tube fitted to it via a connector plate. At ceiling and upper-floor penetration points, the chimney has to be kept at least 50mm (2in) away from any combustible material. Selkirk's system includes metal aperture liners for this purpose, which not only give the required clearance, but also shield the inner surfaces of the apertures completely.

At roof level, a combined chimney support and flashing arrangement takes the chimney through the tiles, and a square section chimney housing unit can be added to give the appearance of a traditional stack to the cylindrical terminal where it would look out of keeping with the style of the house. To finish off the chimney section inside the house, the usual method is to box it in using plasterboard on a timber batten frame to form a chimney breast which can be tiled or given any other form of decoration. Some architects specify a single-brick skin for the enclosure. For closed stoves or open-fire units which are free standing and decorative in their own right, insulated chimneys are often left unenclosed, stoved finishes being available in various colours if the bright stainless steel fails to harmonise with the rest of the interior.

Insulated chimneys are also fitted as flues for appliances other than open fires — particularly central heating boilers burning gas, oil or solid fuel and cookers of traditional Swedish pattern, typified by the Aga/Rayburn and Wamsler models. In these cases, they are normally taken through the wall and up to roof level outside, held to the wall by brackets; weather is no problem to stainless steel. Some of the cookers of the Aga type do not have

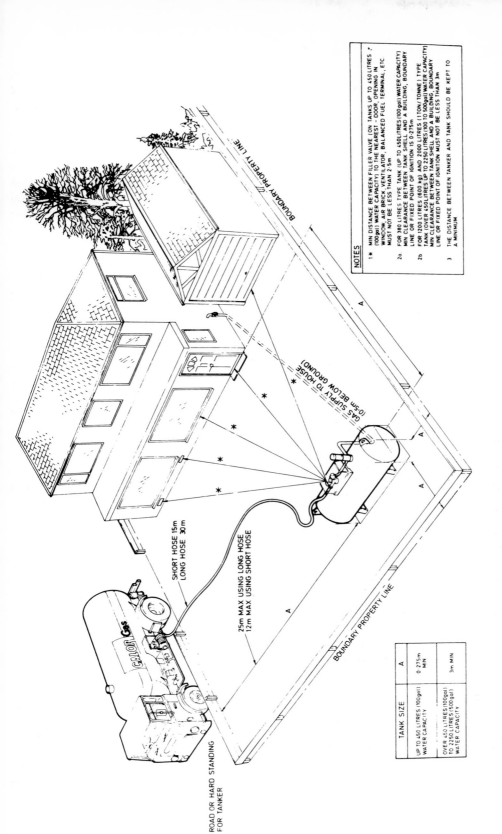

Fig 55 The regulations governing bulk tank lpg (butane/propane gas) installations are clearly set out in this pictorial site layout drawing (*Calor Gas Ltd*)

chimneys, but balanced flues instead, taking their combustion air and venting their exhaust fumes through a single terminal on the outside of the wall. If they are going into a biggish kitchen which is not well insulated, Aga-type cookers can make economic sense, since they provide a lot of hot water, a comprehensive cooking facility and a generous amount of space heating into the bargain. They last indefinitely with little maintenance, and their cast-iron ovens burn themselves clean. Unfortunately, the amount of heat let out by their poorly insulated casings can be uncomfortably great in hot weather, or even in mild weather in a small kitchen. Versions of these cookers fired by solid fuel, gas, oil and wood, are now made, though not all by all makers.

Solid floors can have hot water pipes or electric elements buried in them to provide underfloor heating, which has the advantages of invisibility and of taking up no living space. Some people find it tiring on the feet, and it can be wasteful in that response to thermostat control is not as quick as that of other systems. Certainly, to make it at all economic, the slab containing heating sources needs to have an effective layer of thermal insulation material underneath the heated one. Another invisible system, used extensively by the electricity boards, is ceiling heating, powered by low-temperature strip elements installed between the plasterboard and the ceiling joists. These elements are backed by a layer of mineral-fibre insulation at least 125mm (5in) thick. Houses heated by the system also have to be heavily insulated in the walls and double glazed to make the heating economic.

Whereas electric underfloor and ceiling heating systems have to work for some two-thirds of the time on full-price electricity, storage heaters present an intrinsically more economical proposition, since they work almost entirely on off-peak power, charged at favourable rates under the white meter system; full-rate power is used only for topping up on particularly cold days. Storage heaters are very simple units, consisting of electric elements buried inside high-density heat storage blocks. These are completely enveloped in high-efficiency ceramic-fibre insulation material which allows stored heat to escape only at a very low rate until a damper flap is opened by a thermostat to let air flow over the storage blocks and transmit heat to the house. In the event of the weather taking an unexpectedly warm turn, there could be a certain amount of waste with storage heaters, since they will have consumed fuel the previous night which with hindsight was unnecessary, but over a heating season wastage of this kind has little effect on overall running costs. With all electric heating, remember that the fuel conversion losses have already taken place at the power station and have been taken into account in the pricing system, so that you receive virtually 100 per cent of the energy paid for. In a well-maintained fossil-fuel fired heating unit, up to 20 per cent of the heat the fuel produces as it burns is lost with the exhaust fumes, and in an old, badly set and serviced unit conversion losses could well represent more than half of your fuel costs.

Solar heating
Free heat from natural sources has already been discussed in connection with heat pump installations, but there is another way of tapping the resources of the environment, though again not cheap to install. This consists in utilising the heat of the sun, which can be collected in diffused form when the sky is overcast as well as on brighter days. Solar collectors act like central heating radiators, but in reverse, since the sun's radiant rays warm them up so that the liquid — or in a recent experimental system, air — inside can be circulated to warm space or water. An ordinary steel radiator panel, painted black for maximum heat absorption, will work as a solar collector, but the purpose-made units, designed for mounting on a south facing roof, wall or terrace at an angle of 15° to 50° to the horizontal, are more sophisticated. One high-performance unit, made by Solar Economy, uses a copper tube grid, 22mm (¾in) headers connected by parallel 8mm to 10mm (5/16in to

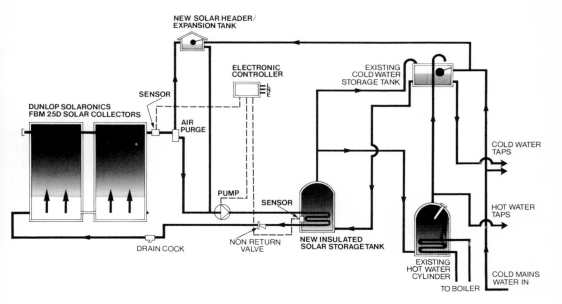

³⁄₈in) risers — the risers being continuously bonded to black-plated copper fins. A 60mm (2³⁄₈in) layer of insulation with reflective aluminium foil on its upper face goes under the collector grid and, to keep weather and cooling winds at bay, the whole aluminium-framed unit is sealed by clear plastic film on top and opaque plastic film underneath. Dunlop Solaronics adopt a different approach, preferring transparent, non-conducting materials around the heat-transfer fluid, which is coloured very dark to enable it to absorb radiant energy directly.

Solar collector systems designed to supplement normal household tap water heating normally use a closed circuit incorporating a pump to circulate sun-heated water-and-antifreeze mixture round indirect coils in an insulated storage tank (a second hot water cylinder). The pump can be controlled by a device which senses temperature differences between collector liquid and stored water, starting it up when there is a significant difference and stopping it when there is a negligible one. The 'hot' outlet of the solar storage tank is used as the 'cold' feed for the existing hot water cylinder, so reducing the heating load whenever there is enough sun-ray energy

Fig 56 How solar collectors are integrated into a domestic hot water supply system (*Dunlop Solaronics*)

around. Bigger systems with larger areas of collecting surface could be linked to a heat pump circuit, possibly via a 'heat sink'. Houses designed to take advantage of solar energy often have either a tube-warmed concrete block foundation, deep and well insulated, or an enclosed, equally well insulated water tank of massive proportions. In a really efficient set-up, summer heat can literally be saved for winter.

One increasingly popular use for solar collectors is to heat indoor or outdoor swimming pools. Here there is little point in a closed circuit, unless the system is to remain in use in the cold weather. In a direct system, the pool water itself is simply circulated through non-corroding matt black plastic panels and back into the pool, whenever there is enough sun heat to make use of.

Although maintenance is minimal with solar systems, and the heat is free except for the cost of running an electric circulation pump, the initial installation cost is still fairly high, in relation to the amount of heat available. Even

167

a small DIY system with only 4sq m (43sq ft) of collecting surface will cost something over £800, but as conventional fuel prices go up — which is almost certain — the value of free heat rises, reducing the payback period of the investment.

Central heating systems

Fanned warm air central heating units are available in gas-fired, oil-fired or electric-powered versions. Their warm air output is delivered to the different parts of the house needing it through ducts or large diameter tubes; these are quite sizeable, need to be planned into the structure of the house to keep them out of sight, and need to be insulated to maximise the system's economy. If your existing house has a warm air system, it should not be difficult to extend it into the extension, but there is no point in doing this unless its overall power can cope with the new, higher heating load in freezing conditions. Warm air systems are extremely good at bringing the air inside a house quickly up to a comfortable temperature, but not quite as good as radiator systems at warming up a masonry structure which has a high thermal storage capacity. Consequently, they are at their best where inside wall surfaces are well insulated, as in timber-framed and dry-lined constructions. The heat output into any given room is dictated by the speed at which the air is passed over the heat exchanger, the drop in its temperature as it passes along the duct(s) and the total sectional area of the duct(s) serving the room. These factors determine the maximum heat available, but reduced output at any given exit grille can be achieved by manual adjustment of the mechanical dampers behind. Any obstruction near a grille can affect the amount of warmth coming out of it — furniture, for example. Even a cat can make a significant difference, sitting right up against a grille, which seems to be the only way with warm air heating for a cat to get as warm in winter as it likes to be. This stricture apart, warm air systems, being highly responsive to thermostat controls, can be both comfortable and economic to run in the right kind of building.

All 'wet' central heating systems work on the same basic principle — that wherever a temperature difference exists in a given mass of liquid, convection currents will be set up, flowing from the warmer parts of the mass to the cooler ones, until the whole mass is at the same temperature. Natural convection is pretty slow, so systems relying on it need large-diameter pipes to achieve a rate of heat transfer high enough to be useful. It is perfectly adequate for circuits where heat transfer needs to be steady and continuous, rather than fast and intermittent, such as those installed between Aga/Rayburn cookers and domestic hot water cylinders. Here water heating is a secondary, not a primary function.

What makes modern wet heating systems such neat, unobtrusive and responsive affairs is the artificial acceleration of convection currents by electric pumps placed in circuits. This enables small-diameter pipes to carry large amounts of heat, even a 6mm (1/4in) diameter microbore tube being able to carry up to 600W of heat effectively along a 7.5m (25ft) distance. Pipes of nominal 22mm (3/4in) diameter will carry up to 15kW, enough for most small-house heating systems, and 15mm (5/8in) (smallbore) pipe about half that load.

The simplest of the accelerated circulation systems is the single-pipe loop, taking the output of the boiler at the flow connection and leading it through one radiator after another, the final one in the chain being connected back to the boiler's return terminal. This means that each radiator after the first one receives water at a temperature slightly lower than that of the boiler flow, since it has been cooled a little by the previous radiator in the series. Single-pipe systems are consequently not over-quick or efficient, but they are cheaper to install than the more efficient two-pipe systems, and are perfectly adequate for well-insulated houses.

In a two-pipe system, one pipe is led from the boiler flow to the flow connection of the final radiator in each loop or series, intermediate radiators being connected to this pipe by short feed pipes teed into it, so that every radiator receives water at the full flow temperature — given proper insulation of the pipe *en route*. Pipe No 2 is taken from the final radiator's return connection to that of the boiler, all the other radiator return pipes being teed into it. Individual radiators can be turned on, off, up or down without affecting the performance of any of the others, as the water can always move along the main flow and return lines.

'Microbore' is the term used for central heating systems which make the maximum possible use of tubes with nominal diameters of 12mm (½in) or smaller, the most widely used being 8mm and 10mm (5/16in and 3/8in). A microbore pipe network offers several advantages over minibore (or smallbore) ones. The tubes are longer, so there are fewer fittings, are easier to bend and manipulate, do not need such big notches when they have to cross joists and have so little surface area that they can be left uninsulated in most situations. Whereas with a smallbore system a certain amount of time has to be spent adjusting the lockshield valve on each radiator, to regulate the water flow rate to produce the intended output, with a microbore system this is unnecessary because the network is self-balancing. Radiator valves can be neater, not because they are any smaller than with minibore, but because it is possible to use double-entry types, only one valve being needed per radiator, as both flow and return pipes go into it. A double-entry valve has a short length of flexible tube screwed into it, to carry the flow water well inside the radiator; but provided this is at least 180mm (7in) long, the twin-pipe valve works just as well as one at either end, and makes for less floor cutting during installation.

In its simplest form, a microbore network loop — usually serving a whole floor in a small house — has fairly short main flow and return pipes of perhaps 22mm (¾in) diameter connecting the boiler terminals to separate flow and return 'manifolds'. These are metal boxes or tubes from which the microbore tubes

sprout, one from the flow manifold and one from the return manifold to each radiator in the circuit. No microbore loop can be longer than 15m (49ft); this means 15m of pipe, not linear distance from manifold to radiator — 7.5m (24½ft) out and the same again back. Some tube manifolds have the microbore connections on the side, like Brussels sprouts, and others have them coming straight out of the end like the tentacles of an octopus. It is quite common to have an all-in-one manifold — a longish tube with a separating shield in the centre, flow and return manifolds stuck together back to back, in effect.

Manifolds need not be used at all, and over longer distances it may not be practical to use them. Each loop can be worked out on the basis of using the smallest possible diameter of pipe to the greatest extent possible. There may be short legs of 22mm (¾in) with longer legs of 15mm (5/8in) teed off them, tee, elbow and cross fittings being used to take microbore tubes off the 15mm (5/8in) tube to the various radiators *en route* — the 15mm tubes acting as long manifolds. They would need to be insulated to ensure that the boiler's heat arrived where it was needed, at the radiators, instead of warming the space under the floor.

Pumps are often integral parts of cental heating boilers, but even as separate units they are normally mounted close to the boiler, to ensure efficient circulation. It does not matter whether a pump is in the flow line, pushing water out of the boiler, or whether it is on the return, pushing it in, but there should be no sharp pipe bends or elbows near it. Most pumps have at least two speeds to choose from, to help to establish the ideal differential between the boiler flow and return temperatures, which is 11°C (52°F). If the return water is coming back to the boiler without having dropped to about 11°C lower than when it left, it is going through the radiators too quickly to allow them to deliver their rated output, so the boiler has an easy time, but the house is not as warm as it should be. If it is coming back having dropped much more than 11°C, the house will be inefficiently warmed because the

169

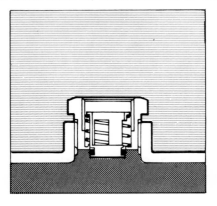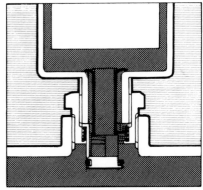

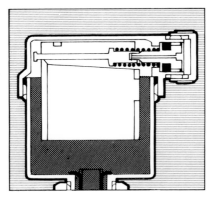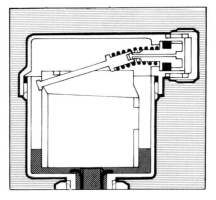

Fig 57 The working sequence of the Barlo R88/1 automatic air vent: a) the shut-off valve in closed position; b) inserting the valve the shut-off valve opens; c) in the closed position; d) when air enters the chamber the float sinks and opens the outlet (*Barlo Products Limited. Redrawn for publication by Brian Wilkins of London*)

boiler has a hard time putting the heat back into the water.

Most boilers are designed to heat domestic hot water as well as radiator circuits. Larger, free-standing boilers with fairly high water contents usually have a gravity (natural convection) circuit to warm the storage cylinder up and pump-assisted circuit for the radiators. Except where the boiler is a solid-fuel type, which must have some work to do when idling, both hot water and heating circuits can be controlled by thermostats, but it is unnecessary to have a cylinder thermostat for a gravity circuit, as the boiler has a built-in thermostat to control the output water temperature, unless you want your tap water at a lower temperature. Wall-hung boilers are very small in relation to their heating power because they do not have a high water content, heating water rather as a geyser does, in a pipe coil round a sheet-metal 'chimney'. They are extremely responsive and efficient, but tend to need more maintenance than free-standing boilers do, as the heating coil has to be replaced every now and then. Low water content boilers cannot circulate their heat output by gravity, so when they are used to heat storage cylinders as well as radiator circuits, both operations have to be pumped, the switch from one to the other being effected by three-port diverter valves in the flow pipe. Control circuits can be wired to give the cylinder thermostat priority over the room thermostat controlling the house temperature, or vice versa. This can mean losing space heating whilst the cylinder is replenished, if the diverter valve is one which shuts one exit port completely whilst the other is open, but there are valves which allow part of the flow to circulate to each circuit simultaneously. However, with a modest cylinder stat setting and a well-insulated cylinder, domestic water heating is very quick. So if the boiler's output is only just big enough to cope with the space heating, it is better to have its whole power doing either one job or the other, rather than trying to do both unsuccessfully.

As water heats up, it has to expand. Provision has to be made for the temporary extra volume when a circuit is designed, and may be made in one of two ways. The most usual method consists in running a vertical pipe up from the boiler flow line to the heating system's feed and expansion tank, which should be a separate and smaller version of the domestic cold tank, with its own ball valve and overflow pipe. The expansion pipe is left unstopped, with its top end bent over the tank, so that any excessive flow up the pipe will be directed harmlessly into it. Since the expansion pipe is open to the atmosphere, the whole system works at atmospheric pressure. It is possible to have a pressurised feed and expansion tank instead of a gravity-feed type. Instead of being open to the air, this has a flexible diaphragm with an air- or gas-filled chamber behind it. The feed pipe acts also as an expansion pipe, so that the expanding water presses against the diaphragm, which returns to its original position when the water goes cool and its volume shrinks again. With a pressurised tank, the pressure of the air or inert gas in the expansion void dictates the pressure under which the system operates, which is usually a bit higher than atmospheric, for one of two alternative good reasons. Either the tank has been installed to provide a head of water impossible to achieve by gravity, because it cannot be placed high enough — in a bungalow, for example — or it has been put in to allow a high working temperature to be maintained without risk of the water evaporating at a high rate. There are advantages in having a higher than normal boiler thermostat setting, in terms of heating efficiency and

therefore of economy. Radiators, however, need to be of a convector design such as that of the Thermalrad, which features a tube network inside a multi-slotted steel casing. Though the tubes become very hot, the casing remains safe for children, and everyone else, to touch.

Not all convector radiators have different water and surface temperatures. Some are designed purely to increase the heat output available in relation to the wall area occupied. Hudevad Plan radiators are a good example, with corrugated fins behind the front plate which are not simply strips of metal but hollow ribs forming part of the water jacket. They are also deeper than conventional panel radiators. The total effect of the extra radiating surface is a two and a half times increase in output for a given frontal area over that of a single flat panel. All radiators induce convection currents in the air; those described specifically as being convector types have some device for increasing the rate at which they warm the air. Skirting radiators are interesting convectors, having been around for longer than most of the others. Their heating element is a single tube with many small fins on it, mounted where the skirting would normally be, inside a neat metal shield with slots at top and bottom to direct the air flow. Skirting radiators are especially good at cutting draughts and at providing a pleasantly warm atmosphere at lowish thermostat settings. They are rather expensive to install, partly because, to give a uniform appearance to each room or hallway, it is necessary to fit shield sections as dummy skirtings, even where there is no finned tube to cover — the heat output required for a given room dictating the length of the tube installed, since the height and depth cannot be varied, as they can with panel radiators.

Some convectors have motor fans to accelerate convection. The fans are room-thermostat controlled and so capable of providing a stable environment with economy. As the rate of air movement is high, motorised convector radiators can be sited above doors or in other out-of-the-way places where space is limited.

The conventional, though not the ideal, method of controlling whole-house space heating is to site a single room thermostat either in the hallway or in the main living room — about 1.5m (5ft) off the floor, out of the way of any window or door draughts and not too near any sources of heat. This is a system which works reasonably well if the radiator in each room, hall or landing is the right size for the job it has to do. A one-thermostat system, however, can make no allowance for incidental heat losses — perhaps through someone leaving a door open for a few minutes — or heat gains when lights are turned on, or several people occupy the same room, or the sun comes out. Thermostatic radiator valves (TRVs) can sense quite small changes in room temperature and respond to them quickly, whether they are of the all-works-in-the-knob type or the slightly more efficient remote-mounted sensor kind. Putting TRVs on all radiators, then, seems a sensible idea — as indeed it is, capable of saving anything up to 25 per cent of your space heating costs.

With all radiators controlled by their own valves, the problem arises of finding a satisfactory way to control the boiler and pump. You could leave the pump on all the time and set the hall thermostat high, so that the boiler would always come on when a radiator valve opened itself, relying on the boiler thermostat to turn it off when the demand and the flow stopped, but this would be unnecesssarily wearing on the pump, which would be vainly trying to pump water along valve-blocked pipes half the time; and it would also entail leaving a constant live power supply to the boiler, which in a conventional system is cut off, together with the pump's supply, when the set roomstat temperature is reached. A unique device for dealing with all these difficulties has been developed by Salamander Electronics. It is called a TRV flow sensor controller. The flow sensor component is a sensitive electronic switch, mounted in a short compression-fitted housing which is installed vertically in the boiler's flow pipe. It senses the slightest movement of water through the heat-ing system — even one caused by a thermostatic valve opening — transmitting a signal to a separate electronic monitoring control box, which turns the boiler and pump on until the sensor again signals to indicate that the movement has stopped, the valve having closed again. An individual thermostatic radiator valve, anywhere in the house, can therefore switch on the boiler and pump to obtain heat, quite independently of any other part of the system.

The benefit of being able to have different parts of the house at different temperatures can be had only if the doors between the parts kept warm and those kept cooler are closed, since warm air, like warm water, has a natural tendency to move to cooler areas.

Humidifiers and dehumidifiers

With the exception of solid-fuel fires and room heaters and that of radiant gas fires, most heating systems tend to dry up the air in a house. Where the dryness causes discomfort or respiratory problems, where it causes older furniture to become a bit loose in the joints due to the wood shrinking, or where it makes musical instruments go quickly out of tune, there are two principal methods of putting the moisture back. The cheaper is to hang humidifiers on radiators. These are simple devices, consisting of small water reservoirs and some form of wick to produce the required degree of evaporation. Electric humidifiers are far more effective and, if your system lacks the radiators, these may be the only remedy available. An electric humidifier consists of a fairly large water reservoir — typically 4.5 litres (1 gallon) or more — and a small heater controlled by a humidistat, which as its name suggests turns the vaporising heat on and off according to the moisture content of the air, the actual level being pre-selectable with most models. Some can be plumbed in, so that you do not even have to refill them with water.

In the reverse situation, where there may be a combination of poor ventilation and a high moisture content in the air inside a house — perhaps due to cooking, washing, bathing, gas room heaters or inadequate general heating, or perhaps to high insulation — a dehumidifier may be necessary. This works rather like a refrigerator, drawing air over a cold 'radiator' to condense out the water, which can be either collected for periodic emptying or permanently and continuously drained away through a tube. The heat drawn out of the cold radiator is transferred to a hot one, over which the dehumidified air is passed, so that it returns to the house very much drier and several degrees warmer than when it entered the dehumidifier. The amount of electricity used is quite small, typically about the same as that consumed by a 100W light bulb for a unit capable of keeping the average small house dry. Larger, more powerful versions are used during construction to dry out the water contained in plaster and cement.

HEATING COSTS

Human bodies lose heat in two ways. A certain amount is lost by radiation to nearby cold surfaces, which is why you feel chilly when you pass near a single-glazed window in cold weather. For the most part, however, body warmth is conducted away by the surrounding air, so heating systems are designed mainly to raise the temperature of the air enclosed by the house's shell. If all a heating installation had to do were to warm up the house's air to a comfortable level, heating costs would be much lower than they are, but air loses its heat to floors, ceilings, walls, doors and windows — all of which in turn lose heat to the air outside during the thirty-three weeks referred to by heating engineers as 'the heating season'. The rates at which the various parts of the building shell let the heat pass through have a considerable effect on the amount of heat you have to put back into the air inside.

Air contains oxygen, which is used up as people breathe and as heating or cooking flames burn, so you cannot simply keep on heating and reheating the same old air. It has to be changed to maintain the oxygen level. This means letting some warm air out and

colder, fresh air in all the time, inevitably increasing the heating load. In a well-draught-proofed house, in which nobody leaves doors and windows open unnecessarily, the number of air-changes an hour should be about 1½ in living rooms and bedrooms and 2–2½ in bathrooms and kitchens.

Assuming that a heating system is thermostatically controlled, producing heat only when needed, you can work out with the aid of a calculator approximately what a proposed extension will cost to heat, and also establish whether or not an existing boiler or other heating unit will be able to cope with the extra load, or whether it will need to be replaced by a more powerful one or supplemented by additional heat sources. A heating calculation is not particularly complex for a house, being based on straightforward concepts.

U-values

A U-value is a measure of the rate at which heat passes through a building component, from the air on one side of it to the air on the other. In the case of solid items such as floors, doors, windows, walls and roofs, it is expressed as the number of watts which will pass through 1sq m every hour for each degree centigrade of temperature difference between the air on one side of it and the air on the other. A watt is one joule per hour, so the watt unit already contains the time element. Consequently a U-value is expressed as a number of watts per square metre per degree centigrade, usually written as $W/m^2\,°C$. Something with a low U-value is a good insulator against heat loss, because it lets heat through at a low rate.

The amount of heat needed to warm air up is also expressed as a U-value, though strictly it is not one. It is 0.34W per *cubic* metre per degree C — $0.34W/m^3\,°C$.

Design heat loss

'Design heat loss' means the amount of heat your house's shell loses every hour when the inside is at the temperature you want to live at and the outside temperature is $-1°C\,(30°F)$. It includes an allowance for heating up the air changed by ventilation. What the calculation gives is the net amount of heat a boiler (or whatever) has to be capable of producing at full blast to cope with the average winter.

Seasonal heat loss

This is the total amount of heat your system will have to produce in the heating season to keep your house at the design temperature. It is usually worked out on the basis of a sixteen-hour day, with the average temperature outside being 6°C (43°F). You may use your heating for only four hours a day, but that does not necessarily mean that your seasonal heat requirement will be a quarter of the sixteen-hour figure, as you will have to warm the house up from colder levels, using more fuel than you would if the heat were on for a greater proportion of the day. Some engineers recommend leaving the heat on twenty-four hours a day, setting back the night thermostat level a few degrees, so as to avoid heavy warm-up loads. The seasonal heat loss figure will give you an idea of your running costs.

Heating appliance efficiency

All heating appliances which burn fuel, be it coal-derived solid, gas or oil, inevitably waste a certain amount of the heat produced in burning it via the hot gases and air exhausted through flues or chimneys. Modern units waste less than older ones, but most conversion losses are around 20 to 30 per cent — lower in the case of a well-maintained and adjusted appliance than with a neglected one, which may be fouled up and inefficient. Manufacturers are very honest about this efficiency factor, advertising and selling their appliances on the basis of rated output. The importance of the combustion loss percentage to you lies in its effect on heating fuel costs, since you have to buy enough fuel to satisfy the appliance's heat *input* requirements to obtain the benefit of its rated output.

Both figures normally appear on the nameplate, usually in British Thermal Units per hour (BTU/h) or in kiloWatts, often both. It makes no difference what the units are, as the difference between the stated input and output ratings in any given unit system represents the heat you pay for but cannot use for every continuous hour the appliance operates at full capacity.

Calorific values of fuels

There is rather more logic to the definition of units of heat than there is to the older units of weight and measurement. The important thing is not the basis of a system, but its universality, so that we all know what the various units mean and can compare like with like when considering the merits or suitability of different items of equipment. Unfortunately, the UK is at present in a prolonged and confusing state of transition between imperial units and those of the Système Internationale (SI), commonly but incorrectly called the 'metric system'.

Heat is a form of energy, so the base unit of the SI heat measurement system is the joule, which may seem abstruse when described as the amount of force required to give a mass of one gramme an acceleration of one gramme per second per second, but becomes more interesting when applied for one second to produce the unit we know as a watt. In the imperial system, the basic unit of heat energy is the British Thermal Unit, defined as the amount of heat required to raise one pound of water through one degree Fahrenheit. This is a very small unit, its smallness being one reason for its continued popularity. It is much more impressive, for example, to call a particular model of boiler the 'XY 90,000' than the 'XY 26.3', the two figures being its output in BTUs per hour and kiloWatts, respectively.

When you buy electricity, of course, you are not buying a fuel that needs to be burnt, but the output of a power station that has already done the burning for you, so every kiloWatt hour you pay for is available as useful heat, conversion losses at the power station being taken into account when the price per kWh (Unit) is worked out. If your heating system is electric — whether a wet one powered by a Maxton boiler, an all-electric warm air blower or a series of storage heaters — you can convert your seasonal heat loss total into a space heating cost estimate simply by multiplying the kWh total by the unit rate you pay and adding in standing charges.

With other fuels, you have to turn your seasonal heat requirement into a fuel quantity on the basis of the fuel's calorific value, the amount of heat produced by a given quantity of it. The figure you start with is the input total, not the output, because that represents the amount of fuel you expect to have to buy to produce the estimated output needed. There is quite an assortment of units. Solid-fuel calorific values are normally quoted in kWh per tonne (1,000kg), a typical manufactured smokeless fuel value being 7,500kWh/T. Gas is charged by the therm, which is 100,000 BTUs, but your bill is calculated by converting the number of cubic feet recorded on your meter into therms, on the basis of the gas's calorific value, given on your bill in BTUs per cubic foot and megajoules (MJ) — millions of joules — per cubic metre (m³). The value for North Sea gas (butane) is 1035BTU/cu ft, or 38.6MJ/m³; that for propane gas — widely used in bottled form — being nearly 150 per cent higher at 95MJ/m³. Manufacturers of bottled gas usually also state the calorific value of their product in MJ per liquid litre — 25.5MJ/l in the case of propane — and this is the figure that you work on for bottled gas — also known as LPG or liquefied petroleum gas — because it is sold by the liquid litre.

Calorific values for fuel oils are usually stated in kWh per litre, but are occasionally quoted in kilocalories per litre. The lighter '28 second' grade oil used in wall-flame boilers has a value in the region of 10.2kWh/l and the heavier '35 second' oil used in pressure-jet boilers is rated at around 10.6kWh/l. Although the values are normally quoted in the SI units, the oil may still be charged for by the gallon, which is 4.546 litres. A set of conversion factors is given on page 199–201.

Working out heat losses

If you know the composition of the various components of your house, you can measure the areas of wall, ceiling, floor, door and window and multiply them by the relevant U-values, temperature differences and number of heating season hours to obtain an approximate seasonal heat loss. With a calculator, the process is not too laborious. Having made the calculation for the existing house, you can do a similar one for the proposed extension, remembering that it will not only increase the existing area of heat-leaking surfaces, but also reduce it to some extent, because outside walls are being made into interior partition walls. You need to bear in mind that, even if your existing house has badly insulated walls and roof, the new parts will have to conform to current building regulation minimum standards.

Suppose you want to keep your house at an inside temperature of 21°C (70°F) for the whole of the 33-week heating season, turning the heating off at night. Seven 16-hour days for 33 weeks gives a total of 3,696 hours, during which the average temperature outside will be 6°C (43°F), so the average temperature difference between inside and outside air will be $21 - 6 = 15$°C $(70 - 43 = 27$°F$)$. This is the temperature differential used for calculating the likely fuel consumption of your heating system. If you are working out what the output of a new system needs to be, or what the radiator or heating duct size should be for a particular room, you would work on the bigger differential between the temperature you want the inside to be and −1°C (30°F) outside.

Whether you want to work out the whole house losses or just those for individual rooms, the process is much the same for each section of its structure with a different U-value:

area x U-value x temperature difference.

When calculating design heat loss, this would give you a figure in kWh or BTUs representing the hourly heat leakage through the structure. You would add to that a figure relating to the air volume that has to be warmed up:

volume x U-value x temperature difference x number of air changes per hour.

175

Some typical U-values for various types of
structure $W/m^2°C$

230mm solid brick wall, unrendered	2.50
Same, rendered	2.34
Brick/brick cavity wall	1.50
Brick/breeze cavity wall	1.30
Brick/aerated concrete block cavity wall	1.00
Timber-frame panel with weatherboard facing	1.70
Same with brick skin	1.50
Solid concrete floor	0.53
Suspended timber floor over airspace	0.43
Timber doors, or parts of doors	2.84
Single glazed windows or doors (or parts of them)	5.68
Double-glazed windows or doors (or parts of them)	2.90
Plasterboard ceilings under 30° pitched roof, unsarked	2.05
Same, with sarking felt between tiles/slates and rafters	2.01
Lath and plaster ceilings under pitched roofs, unsarked	3.16
Flat concrete roofs	2.72
Timber-boarded flat roofs	1.52

These figures are for the structures without any additional insulation.

Example

To arrive at the design heat loss (hourly loss with interior at design temperature and $-1°C$ or 30°F outside) of a postwar semi-detached house with a pitched roof, brick/breeze block cavity walls and single-glazed windows, with a ground-floor are of 45sq m:

Walls 77m² x 22° x 1.3W/m²°C	2,2202.2W
Doors 4m² x 22° x 2.84W/m²°C	249.92W
Windows 15m² x 22° x 5.68W/m²°C	1,874.4W
Ground floor 45m² x 22° x 0.43W/m²°C	425.7W
Roof 45m² x 22° x 2.05W/m²°C	2,029.5W
Kitchen and bathroom air/ventilation 38m³ x 22° x 0.34W/m³°C x 2 air changes	568.48W
Rest of house air/ventilation 178m³ x 22° x 0.34W/m³°C x 1.5 air changes	1,997.16W
Total design heat loss and system power needed:	9,347.36W

Just under 9½kW, then, would keep the house up to temperature in freezing conditions, though the system would need to be a little more powerful if it also had to heat water.

Two factors would have to be changed in the calculation of overall seasonal fuel consumption. The temperature difference would be 21 minus 6 and the number of hours in the heating season would be used by which to multiply the hourly watts consumption. If you divide the design heat loss figure by 22 and multiply by 15 and 3,696, you have the estimated seasonal output required by the system, in watts. Divide by 1,000 to get kWh:

$$\frac{9,347.36 \times 15 \times 3,696}{22 \times 1,000} = 23,555.346\text{kWh}$$

Rounding off the overall consumption figure to 23,555kWh, you then need to adjust it upwards to allow for fuel conversion losses, if your system is to be gas, oil or solid-fuel fired. It is wise to make some allowance for a falling off in efficiency as the boiler or other heating unit gets older; so let us assume that the manufacturer rates it as 78 per cent efficient and work on a realistic overall 70 per cent efficiency. The net requirement of 23,555kWh plus, say, 3,000 kW for water heating comes to 26,555kW. Since your heating unit is giving you only 70 per cent of the heat in its fuel, you will have to buy and burn enough of it to produce a gross output of:

$$\frac{26,555 \times 10}{7} = 37,936\text{kWh}$$

Using calorific values, this means:

$\frac{37,936}{7,500}$ = about 5 tonnes of solid fuel, or $\frac{37,936}{10.2}$ = 3,719 litres (x 0.22 = 818 gallons) of '28 second' fuel oil, or $\frac{37,936}{29.3}$ = 1,295 therms of gas. If you were in the countryside with no mains gas supply and were using propane LPG, the calculation would be $\frac{37,936}{7.08}$ = 5,358 litres of liquid propane gas.

INSULATION AND ITS EFFECT ON HEATING SYSTEMS AND COSTS

Insulation reduces heating costs to a remarkable degree. It may take a few years to recover the initial capital outlay, but the savings go on year after year, and their cash value increases with rising inflation. Suppose our typical house used in the example had 100mm (4in) of cellulose-fibre insulation blown into its roof space to bring the roof U-value down to 0.31W/m²°C, its windows double glazed to halve their heat loss rate to 2.9W/m²°C and its outside walls' cavities filled to produce a value of only 0.54W/m²°C. These three improvements would bring the design heat loss down to 5,420 watts, as opposed to 9,347 watts. Allowing 3kW for water heating, the total output need now be only 8,420 watts = 12,029 watts gross input. Using this reduced figure to calculate running costs, we get a fuel consumption estimate of only 21,218kWh — only 56 per cent of the uninsulated house's heating requirement. It might even be possible to put in a smaller, cheaper boiler or other heating unit, and it would certainly be possible to reduce radiator or duct sizes, if the insulation measures were taken before the heating system was installed. Although on a gas or electric mains tariff the savings are all made at the cheaper unit end of the scale, and although standing charges remain, a 44 per cent saving in fuel consumption is still very worth while. At the time of writing, a therm on a typical central heating tariff gas bill costs 33.5p, at which price the difference between the cost of 1,295 therms for the uninsulated house and of 724 therms for the insulated one was worth over £191 a year.

Looking at the question of fuel savings through insulation from another viewpoint, imagine a two-storey extension increasing the house's ground-floor area and total volume by 50 per cent, with similar proportions of wall taken up by doors and windows. Insulating both this and the existing house to the standard just outlined would allow you to heat both original house and extension for less than it cost to heat the uninsulated house. The gross heat input required for the extension would be 11,332kWh or 387 therms, with insulated walls and roof and double-glazed windows, compared to a saving on the older part alone of 16,718kWh.

Cavity walls can be insulated in a variety of ways. They can be dry-lined with insulating board faced with plasterboard, the usual method of adhesion being plaster dabs, so that there is a small air gap between wall and board to add to the insulation of the board itself. Dry lining produces U-values within the current building regulation stipulation of 0.6W/m²°C with almost any brick/block wall construction, leaving the cavity unfilled. Obviously this is an insulation method better suited to new constructions than to existing ones. It enables heating systems to warm a house up very quickly, so is especially well suited to warm air equipment, though you lose the heat storage facility which the inner leaf provides with a cavity insulation fill, and which adds greatly to a building's thermal stability.

Not all cavity insulation methods involve filling the gap between the inner and outer leaves completely. Expanded polystyrene or the denser mineral- or wood-fibre boards are often fixed to the outside of the inner block leaf by studs. The board is only about half as thick as the cavity is wide, so there is nothing going right across except the standard wall ties. Some foam cavity fill systems gave a little trouble at one time, because narrow fissures caused by uneven drying out encouraged water to cross the cavity by capillary attraction, but no system applied in accordance with its Agrément certificate stipulations will give such problems. An increasingly popular cavity fill system uses polystyrene beads, lightly bonded together with an adhesive. Beads and adhesive are blown in simultaneously, the setting time of the adhesive being artificially extended so that bonding does not take place before the beads have settled into position. They consequently pour in like Rice Krispies, filling the cavity completely, and once in place form a stable mass which does not compact or migrate to leave uninsulated gaps. Nor is there any loss of insulating fill if the wall is subsequently cut for alterations such as the insertion of doors or windows, or for building extensions. The granular structure of the fill ensures that any water penetrating to the inside of the outer leaf runs downwards through the beads, since they do not absorb

177

moisture and do not produce capillary paths across the cavity, which can breathe almost normally.

Dry mineral fibre may be blown into an existing cavity wall, or built into a new one in the form of batts sized to fit snugly between wall ties at standard spacings. The fibres of the batts are bonded together with a water-repellent resin and the lie of the fibres is arranged so that none of them stretch across the cavity, but are aligned parallel to the masonry's vertical surfaces to ensure that water cannot cross the gap between leaves.

Most cavity fills produce overall wall U-values in the region of 0.52 to 0.54, well below (meaning better than) the minimum building regulation requirement. Older, solid brick or stone walls are more difficult and therefore more expensive to insulate, but they are much more thermally inefficient to start with, so savings through insulation are very noticeable. As with cavity walls, interior dry lining is one possibility, but causes considerable disruption in an occupied house. Cavity filling is out of the question because there is no cavity to fill.

The only viable option with most solid-walled houses is to apply insulation to the outside, protected by a coat of crack-resistant and weatherproof material. All the technical problems related to external insulation have been solved, so it is perfectly feasible to bring a cold house leaking heat through its walls at the rate of $2.11W/m^2°C$ or more up to the current standard of $0.6W/m^2°C$ or better. The total thickness of the insulation/protection layer to do this, however, may involve a drastic change in the appearance of the house which may, by destroying the character of a period house, be unacceptable to the planning authorities, even if not to you.

There are currently three systems of external insulation on the market, all using expanded polystyrene board as the insulating layer. The Disbotherm System 600 uses adhesive to stick EPS panels up to 100mm (4in) thick to the masonry. Door and window reveals are extended by aluminium sill plates and metal angle strips are inserted to protect the insulation boards where they meet on outside corners. One render coat is applied direct to the insulation, a woven glass-fibre reinforcing mat being embedded in it. A second coat of adhesive render then goes on, followed by a final decorative, weatherproof render, which is a maintenance-free finish.

Purlmac external wall insulation consists of 25mm (1in) thick Coolag Thermafoil board (aluminium vapour-check liner towards the masonry), protected either by a sand/cement render coat pressed into expanded metal lathing and covered with a decorative finish, or by uPVC board or Coloroc cast-concrete cladding units fixed to battens. For uPVC cladding, the battens are normally vertical and fixed to the masonry on top of the insulating panels. For the Coloroc units, they are fixed horizontally between the insulation panels, the cladding's hooked support profiles being nailed to the wood. Specially moulded EPS insulation panels are used in the Unidri system, panel edges being tongued and grooved to fit into each other, avoiding any risk of cold entering through joint gaps. Channels are also moulded into the backs of the panels to allow them to slide over moulded plastic shoes fixed to the masonry. These shoes not only hold the insulation in place, but hold it slightly away from the wall surface to provide a small air gap which connects with the outside atmosphere via perforated trims at the wall base and at the heads of door and window apertures to provide a vapour pressure release route, allowing the masonry to breathe without the insulation performance of the system being affected. Expanded stainless steel lathing is hung against the insulation and secured through it to the supporting shoes by plastic fasteners.

Unidri finish off the insulation process by applying a mortar render in two 10mm (3/8in) coats. The mortar is modified by Ronacrete additives unique to the system to make it crack resistant, waterproof and capable of withstanding temperatures from $-20°C$ to $+80°C$ ($-4°F$ to $+176°F$). Insulation panel thickness

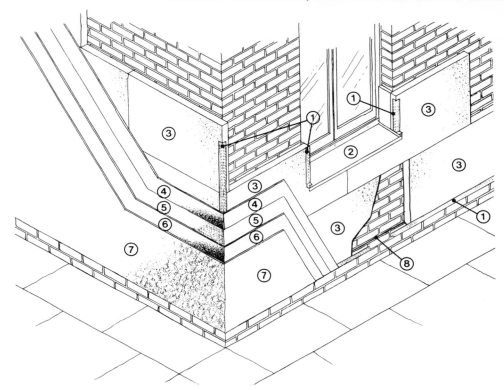

Fig 58 This isometric view of a typical installation shows the components and the build-up of the Disbotherm System 600, with treatment at windows, corners, damp-proof course and over-sills: 1 Edge rail; 2 Aluminium over-sill; 3 Disbotherm EPS panels fixed with adhesive; 4 Adhesive render; 5 Disbotherm Fabric 650 woven glass fibre; 6 Second coat adhesive render; 7 Disbotherm plaster/final render coat; 8 Damp-proof course (*Disbotherm Ltd*)

can be varied in the Unidri system, but the current building regulation minimum of $0.6W/m^2°C$ is achievable in most cases with a 75mm (3in) panel. As with the Purlmac system, Coloroc or uPVC claddings can be used in place of the Unidri render finish.

All three of the external insulation systems described can be applied to any of the precast concrete component and other system-built houses, including the Airey, Woolaway, Unity and Orlit types, just as they can to stone or brick. They have been used on occasion to improve the insulation properties of timber-framed walls, in cases where it was inconvenient to remove interior wall linings to insert insulation material between the timber studs; but for most houses — and certainly for all new timber-frame constructions — it is far cheaper to insulate the frame section hollows.

A standard timber-frame wall section with the usual single brick skin has a U-value of $1.23W/m^2°C$ without any insulation material

in it. A mere 50mm (2in) of mineral-fibre or equivalent insulation will bring its heat-leakage rate down to the BR minimum of $0.6W/m^2°C$, but for the small amount of extra material (and no extra labour) required to double the thickness, filling the hollow, the wall structure's U-value can be reduced to $0.32W/m^2°C$. In our example of a 45m² semi, a 50mm (2in) insulation layer would save each year 2,690kWh and a 100mm (4in) layer would save 3,885kWh. Translated into cash terms, worked out at 33.5p a therm (29.3kWh), these

179

savings are respectively £31 and £45, in round figures. If the studding was deepened to allow thicker insulation to be put in, it might well pay long-term dividends to have 160mm (over 6in) of insulation, producing a U-value of 0.22W/m²°C and a saving of 4,312kWh or 147 therms worth £49. This example underlines an important point about insulation — that the heat-loss reduction is not directly proportional to the thickness installed. In other words, you do not save twice as much by putting in twice the thickness.

Roof insulation — next to draughtproofing the most cost effective of all the steps you can take to save heat in a pitched-roof house — provides perhaps the best illustration of the principle of diminishing returns in this context. Starting with a totally uninsulated plasterboard ceiling under a sarked and tiled pitched roof, you can cut out 60 per cent of the roof loss by putting down a mere 25mm (1in) thickness of mineral-fibre or cellulose-fibre insulation, by no means enough to satisfy current BRs, but nevertheless a substantial saving. You would have to double that thickness to achieve a saving of 75 per cent and quadruple it to reach one of 85 per cent (and satisfy the current BRs minimum for roofs of 0.35W/m²°C). The 200mm (8in) thickness common in the United States saves about 92 per cent of the uninsulated heat loss and the 400mm (16in) layers frequently applied in Sweden save about 96 per cent of it. Savings at the top end of the thickness scale are marginal, albeit worth while where winter temperatures regularly dive 30°C or more below zero (32°F) and where the heating season lasts longer. Even in the comparatively mild UK, remember that rising fuel prices also make marginal savings useful. Not so very long ago the economical level of roof insulation was 25mm (1in), which would be ridiculously low today.

Insulation and water vapour

For most of the time in Britain, as in any cool temperate climate, the air inside occupied buildings is both warmer and moister than the air outside. The water carried in the air is in the form of an extremely fine vapour — so fine that it behaves exactly like a gas. Since the warm air containing it has a natural tendency to expand, there is a constant 'vapour pressure' indoors which forces the gaseous water to migrate through the building shell. An uninsulated wall will usually stay warm enough to let it pass through, but when you insulate the wall on the inside, the vapour cools rapidly because the insulation is not letting heat through, so the vapour condenses, either within the thickness of the insulation itself, wetting it and reducing its efficiency, or more damagingly still within the masonry, where it can freeze and cause cracks. This is why a vapour-check membrane is needed — always on the warm side of the insulation — usually in the form of a polythene or aluminium foil backing on lining boards. In timber-frame structures, it is often provided by a polythene or Kraft bituminous building paper lining on mineral-fibre insulation rolls, the lining being slightly wider than the insulation so that the side flanges can be used to overlap each other on the studs for fastening by nails or staples. Alternatively, separate rolls or sheets of the membrane material can be fixed over the insulation before lining is carried out.

With closed-cell insulation materials which do not let water vapour through, such as cork and expanded polystyrene, a vapour check is not always necessary, but is sometimes provided as a precaution with materials which have a slight tendency to transmit vapour. Even with quite thick layers of insulation over ceilings beneath pitched roofs, no check membrane is normally needed, as the moisture can evaporate away freely.

Well-insulated walls, roofs and floors will help to keep a building cool when it is warm outside, just as they keep in available warmth during winter. In the UK, this heat shield facility is for the most part just a comfort bonus, which cannot be valued in cost-saving terms as fuel savings can in the colder weather. In hotter countries, however, it can cost as much to cool a building in summer as it does to heat it in winter, using heat pumps in reverse, as it were, to provide air conditioning. In these circumstances, insulation saves money the whole year round.

When working out heat losses, remember that a U-value is an air-to-air heat loss rate index. Where there are large areas of glass you have the benefit of considerable heat gains on sunny days, even when it is cold outside, because radiant heat warms up what it is focused on without heating up the air in between source and target directly. In a conser-

vatory, the air is warmed up, not by the sun's rays, but by the walls, floor, furniture and other objects inside, after they have been warmed up directly. The U-values quoted for single, double, triple or any other kind of glazing simply indicate their air-to-air insulation performance, their resistance to, or their ability to transmit, radiant energy being indicated by a solar energy reflectance percentage.

To translate SI units into imperial, or vice versa, there is a list of factors on page 199, which enable a calculator to switch between the systems without too much trouble.

8
Extension Work Affecting Mains Electricity, Gas and Water Connections

ELECTRICITY

Your local electricity board owns and controls the cable bringing power into your house, and also the meter to which it is connected. Any work involving interference with the meter or its supply lines — moving it to another place, for example, or replacing it by one with a higher amperage rating to cope with a larger installation — can be carried out only by the board itself or by its approved contractors.

The whole of your electrical installation beyond the meter belongs to you and is under your control; you can do, or have done, whatever you want with it, subject to the wiring regulations. These are a set of inevitably complex rules designed by the IEE (Institute of Electrical Engineers) to ensure the safety of electrical installations. In Scotland, they have the force of law, but no properly qualified electrician is likely to disregard them elsewhere in the UK. Since he might well be blamed for any accident involving faulty wiring after he has worked on your circuits, he is within his rights to refuse to alter or add to wiring he considers unsafe, unless he is allowed to remedy the faults in the process.

Electricity boards do not insist on carrying out wiring inspections, but they will give your circuits a very searching once-over on request; the cost is not inconsiderable, but the peace of mind is well worth the price. An 'NIC approved' contractor has been vetted by the NICEIC — the National Inspection Council for Electrical Installations Contractors — and will also probably be a member of the Electrical Contractors' Association (ECA). Both organisations demand that contractors under their aegis work to IEE standards.

GAS

Meter ownership and responsibility for gas supplies are the same as those applying in the case of electricity. Since it is quite easy for a plumber with no special knowledge of gas to make connections and alterations, the jointing and pipe manipulation skills being the same, you should make sure that the fitters or firms dealing with gas connections are 'gas registered', a status usually advertised as 'CORGI registered'. CORGI stands for the Confederation for the Registration of Gas Installers, an organisation supported and controlled by British Gas and a number of relevant trade bodies.

With a gas-registered installer, you are at least certain that full technical competence was achieved before registration was allowed, and that the work of the installer is liable to random inspection by the organisation, to which complaints can be directed in the event of unsatisfactory performance.

Gas meters, like electric ones, are designed for a given throughput, so if your extension entails changing your boiler or other heating unit for a model using considerably more gas than the old one, your meter may have to be changed for one able to cope with the added flow. Another point to bear in mind when changing to a larger output unit is that it will not give its full performance unless the gas pipe feeding it is adequate in diameter. The manufacturer's installation instructions always specify this, up to a point about 600mm (2ft) from the unit, the final connecting length usually being allowed in smaller tubing.

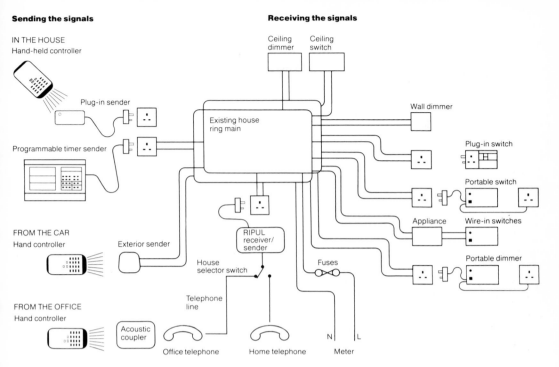

Sending the signals

IN THE HOUSE
Hand-held controller

Plug-in sender

Programmable timer sender

FROM THE CAR
Hand controller

Exterior sender

FROM THE OFFICE
Hand controller

Acoustic coupler

Office telephone

Telephone line

House selector switch

RIPUL receiver/sender

Home telephone

Existing house ring main

Receiving the signals

Ceiling dimmer

Ceiling switch

Wall dimmer

Plug-in switch

Portable switch

Appliance

Wire-in switches

Portable dimmer

Fuses

Meter

N   L

WATER

If you do change the main supply pipe from an ancient lead one to a modern heavy-duty plastic type, remember the old habit of using water mains pipes as electrical earthing connections. Make sure that anything that was by some oversight relying on the lead main for an earth is earthed properly to the electricity board's earth point, to which metal heating and water piping may have to be connected where an electrical system is of the protective multiple-earth type.

Extension work frequently involves additional outdoor tap installations. Water boards usually make an extra charge on the water rates for these, somewhat higher for those used with sprinkler equipment than for those used only with hand-held hoses. Boards may also charge extra for water used for building work.

Fig 59 In the house of the future, you will be able to control the electrical appliances without touching a switch. This circuit shows what is technically possible, using 'sender' units which can operate plug-in and other switches anywhere on the same ring main by means of coded pulses. Everything shown in the diagram was actually in existence at the time of writing, only the office or other outside telephone-linked sender remaining to be perfected (*Home Automation Ltd*)

9
Raising the Wind

There are various ways of financing an extension. The cheapest one — open to a fortunate few — is simply to have the money and spend it. For most of us it is a case of turning either the capital represented by a paid-for existing house into money, or borrowing on the basis of a regular income, with a partly paid-for house as ultimate security for the loan.

BUILDING SOCIETIES

Except in times of mortgage famine, building societies are more than willing to lend money for home extensions. The Woolwich, for example, the fifth largest of the UK's 200 societies, granted over £64 million during 1983, about 30 per cent of its loan total for that year, by way of 'further advances' to existing borrowers. You almost invariably have to be an existing borrower or a first-time one to be given a loan for an extension from a building society, and preference is at least ostensibly given to people wanting to extend their homes for more or less utilitarian reasons. Having been founded to help the less wealthy become home owners (in the fullness of time), the building societies have an understandable reluctance to finance luxuries like swimming pools and saunas; however, one society's spokesman has been known during a mortgage glut to refer wryly to 'borrowers driving round in their kitchen extensions', so there is no need to write the societies off as sources of funds for the jacuzzi without asking. It may be the right time to apply.

Building societies lending to a borrower with part of an existing mortgage outstanding will normally add the second loan to the first,

so that the augmented mortgage is scheduled to be paid off within the period envisaged for the original loan, but they can be flexible about arrangement details, provided their traditional criteria relating to the value of the extended house as security for the extended loan, and relating to the borrower's ability to meet the repayments, are satisfied. Naturally, they would not want to establish a loan repayment period stretching out beyond a likely retirement date.

Although the withdrawal of tax relief on endowment and other life assurance premiums in the 1984 spring budget has made endowment policy secured loans less attractive than before the axe fell, with-profits policies issued by the top ten insurance companies may still be capable of producing enough profit over a fifteen- or twenty-year term to compensate for the higher interest outgoings on an insurance-based mortgage. If you had a policy in existence before 14 March 1984, you continue to pay net premiums as long as the contract remains in force as originally drawn up; so if you happen to have such an endowment assurance policy, unassigned and of suitable value, you can use it to advantage. Some building societies will accept the totally tax-allowable personal pension scheme insurances instead of endowment policies as security for mortgage loans.

The only two building societies which charge a flat interest rate, whatever the total size of a loan, at the time of writing are the Nationwide and the Woolwich. Some start charging rates half a per cent or more higher when loans reach only £10,000; others make the threshold £20,000 or £25,000. The extra percentage mostly varies from ½ to 1½ over the normal house-price range, but can exceed 3 per cent on really large amounts.

As regards the method and timing of an agreed mortgage advance, most societies are flexible, but you will need to establish at an early date how you need the money paid — the entire sum at the end of the building work for a small job, or in instalments against an architect's, surveyor's or architectural technician's certificates at the completion of recognised stages of construction.

You will be expected to insure the building shell in its extended form. In fact, the society will insist on doing this on your behalf, charging you with the premium. The amount insured should be for the cost of rebuilding from scratch, probably higher than market value, and should be revised in line with building cost inflation each year. If you fail to do this, you could conceivably find yourself without enough money to replace your home if the unthinkable happened.

BANKS

Banks are well entrenched in the home improvement loans market, which includes finance for extensions, currently advancing about a third of the net lending in the housing finance sector. The National Westminster Bank's 1983 mortgage lending book of well over £3 billion, for example, would place it within the top ten building societies if it were one. Barclays, Coutts, Lloyds, Lombard North Central, the Midland, the National Westminster, the Bank of Scotland and Williams & Glyn's all lend money for home improvement and extension purposes.

Most of them like you to be a customer, but some will accept applications for building finance from non-customers, looking on them as prospective ones. Some make unsecured loans, whilst others lend on a second-mortgage basis, staking a claim on what is left of your house when the building society has taken its cut, in the event of otherwise irrecoverable default on repayments. All pay far more attention to your basic ability to make repayments out of normal cash flow than they do to the question of security. Several have standard home-improvement schemes, with stated loan limits ranging from as little as £500 to as much as £25,000 and repayment periods from six months to a usual maximum of ten years.

The better a loan is secured, generally speaking, the lower the interest rate. With most banks, the rate is fixed from the start, remaining unchanged throughout the loan period, some of the finance houses with variable rates allowing the monthly repayments to remain fixed and adjusting the repayment period to accommodate fluctuations. Finance houses such as Barclays' subsidiary, Mercantile Credit, provide a great deal of the finance for extension and improvement work carried out by specialist contractors, in many cases paying the contract price to them direct on receipt of your satisfaction note or contract supervisor's certificate.

Bank interest paid on a home improvement or extension loan is eligible for tax relief, as building society loan interest payments are, but you have to produce a certificate from the bank each year at tax return time to get it.

Setting-up fees, inspection fees and insurance premiums may or may not be charged as part of a bank's loan deal, so make sure you have all the facts so that you can work out the net cost of the borrowed money, taking tax relief into account, before signing on the dotted line.

10
Survival on Site

With the best will in the world, extension work cannot be relied on to go completely as planned. Equipment may not arrive and inspectors may not inspect on schedule, so there may well be uncomfortable periods when there are draughty gaps in walls, gaping trenches, dust if the weather is dry, mud if it is wet, and, if you are very unlucky, days on end with no heating or hot water. Builders should be able to forecast such difficulties and keep them to the minimum, but they inevitably have to regard as a building site what you see as home, so you should plan for the odd short-duration siege, just in case.

Carpet protector strips do not work well for long stints. It is far better to take up carpets and other vulnerable floor-coverings in areas subject to builders' traffic or mud and dust from the family's feet, until the mess has subsided. Extra doormats outside the rooms you live in whilst the building work goes on can save a lot of work. Draughtstrip the doors and windows of your living quarters, to keep dust entry to the minimum, and put ornaments, photographs and similar items in sideboards or cupboards as far as possible, covering each unit with plastic sheeting. Books can go in cardboard cartons, as can records and tapes.

Food storage is a particular problem if the kitchen is affected by the alterations, as it often is. If the fridge is electric, you can probably move it into your pro-tem 'kitchen'. Any form of camping equipment and experience comes into its own in siege living conditions — with stringent fire precautions if you have to use camp cooking stoves. Large polythene bags can be used to keep blankets or sleeping bags clean.

Half the fun of having an extension built lies in talking about the traumas after it is all over. You may be surprised how quickly the discomforts are forgotten. Taking a few photographs helps you to enjoy them later, even if it is impossible to revel in them at the time.

Appendix 1:
Relevant Organisations

Architects whose work is featured in the book:
ATP Group Partnership
Queens House
Queens Road
Buckhurst Hill
Essex IG9 5BP (01 505 4413)

William Binney Associates
The Cloisters
Appleby
Cumbria CA16 6QN (0930 51395)

Browne & Martin
32 Meades Lane
Chesham
Buckinghamshire HP5 1ND (0494 786218)

TACP — The Anthony Clark Partnership
27–29 Grosvenor Road
Wrexham
Clwyd LL11 1DH (0978 364161)

G Parry Davies and Associates
4 Bridge Street
Denbigh
Clwyd LL16 3TG (074 571 2413)

Norman R Harrison RIBA
Lennox House
Lennox Street
Bognor Regis
West Sussex PO21 1LZ (0243 821799)

Wyn Jones, Paul Andrews and Associates
222 High Street
Haverfordwest
Dyfed SA61 2DA (0437 5156)

Christopher Morton M Arch ARIBA
Summers Place
Whitbourne
Worcester (0886 21644)

Simpson & Brown
179 Canongate
Edinburgh EH8 8BN (031 557 3880)

Speakman Architects
Lumb Holme
Broughton Mills
Broughton-in-Furness
Cumbria A20 6AX (065 76 579)

Bathroom, kitchen & electrical furniture/ equipment manufacturers
AEG-Telefunken (UK) Limited
217 Bath Road
Slough
Berkshire SL1 4AW (0753 872101)

AGA-Rayburn
Glynwed Consumer & Building Products
Limited
PO Box 30
Ketley
Telford
Shropshire TF1 1BR (0952 51177)

Aidelle — Division of Airflow Developments
Limited
Lancaster Road
High Wycombe
Buckinghamshire HP12 3QP (0494 25252)
(*Extractor fans*)

B & R Electrical Products Limited
Temple Fields
Harlow
Essex CM20 2BG (0279 443351)
(Switches)

Electronic Hygiene Limited
2 Junction Road
Harrow
Middlesex HA1 1NL (01 863 9066)
(Insect-killing lamps)

Elektrak International Limited
45 High Street
Kingston upon Thames
Surry KT1 1LQ (01 546 7799)
(Trunking-mounted safety power points)

Emerald Stainless Steel Limited
Chapelfield
Radcliffe
Manchester M26 9JF (061 766 8211)
(Kitchen waste disposal units, sinks, taps)

Fordham Plastics Limited
Fordham House
Dudley Road
Wolverhampton
Staffs WV2 4DS (0902 59123)
(Sinks, accessories)

Formica Limited
Coast Road
North Shields
Tyne & Wear NE29 8RE (0632 57566)
(Decorative laminates, boards, composites)

Gilflex-Key Limited
Old's Approach
Tolpits Lane
Watford
Herts WD1 8XT (0923 720177)
(Clip-together electrical conduit system)

Glendale Furniture Company
Glendale Avenue
Sandycroft Industrial Estate
Deeside
Clwyd CH5 2QP (0244 533724)

Greenwood Airvac Ventilation Limited
PO Box 3
Brookside Industrial Estate
Rustington
Littlehampton
West Sussex BN16 3LH (09062 71021)
(Extractor fans)

Home Automation Limited
Pindar Road
Hoddesdon
Herts EN11 0ET (0992 460355)
(Automatic remote control switching equipment)

Ideal-Standard Limited
PO Box 60 National Avenue
Hull
HU5 4JE (0482 46461)
(Baths, taps, 'Whirlpool' bath system)

Ideal Timber Products Limited
Broadmeadow Industrial Estate
Dumbarton G82 2RG (0389 61777)
(Kitchens)

Kingcraft
39B Market Street
Chapel-en-le-Frith
Stockport
Cheshire SK12 6HP (0298 812528)
('Easibath' bathing device for disabled people)

Heinrich Läger (UK) Limited
Läger House
Swan Mews
Lichfield
Staffordshire (05432 57755)
(Kitchens)

Leisure
Glynwed Consumer & Building Products
Limited
Meadow Lane
Long Eaton
Nottingham NG10 2AT (06076 4141)
*(Kitchen sinks, bathroom vanitory basins &
shower cubicles)*

Nordic Saunas Limited
Nordic House
31–33 Lesbourne Road
Reigate
Surrey RH2 7JS (073 72 49451)

Peak Technologies Limited
Dayson Works
Warwick Road
Borehamwood
Herts WD6 1NA (01 207 0020)
(*Infra-red detecting security lighting*)

Peglers Limited
St Catherine's Avenue
Doncaster
South Yorkshire DN4 8DF (0302 68581)
(*Taps, shower systems*)

Southway Contracts Euro Kitchen Centre
63 Brent Street
London NW4 2EE (01 202 4777)
(*Mini-kitchen and pre-assembled multi-function units*)

J W Swain Plastics Limited
Byron Street
Buxton
Derbyshire SK17 6LY (0298 2365)
(*Shower systems for disabled people*)
Also — Northern Ireland Division
      Balloo Way
      Balloo Industrial Estate
      Bangor
      County Down (0247 50497)

Teisseire Cuisines (UK) Limited
252 Watford Way
Hendon
London NW4 4UB (01 203 4250)
(*Kitchens*)

Toshiba (UK) Limited (Air Conditioning Division)
Freepost
Frimley
Camberley
Surrey GU16 5BR (0276 62222)
(*Heat-exchanging extractor fans, heat pumps*)

Building component, equipment & fixings manufacturers

Allmat Limited
Selsdon Road Industrial Estate
232 Selsdon Road
South Croydon
Surrey CR2 6PL (01 680 0666)
(*'Furfix' wall extension profiles*)

D Anderson & Son Limited
Stretford
Manchester M32 0YL (061 865 4444)
(*Roofing felts, insulating rooflights*)

Andrews Industrial Equipment Limited
Dudley Road
Wolverhampton WV2 3DB (0902 58111)
(*Building dryers and heaters hire service*)

Armstrong Screws & Fixings
72 Great Barr Street
Birmingham B9 4BJ (021 772 4334)
(*'Dril-Kwick' self-drilling screws*)

The Atlas Stone Company
(Division of Eternit Building Products Limited)
Whelford Road
Fairford
Gloucestershire GL7 4DT (0285 712128)
(*'Dryangle' precast concrete tiles for wet basement floor surfacing*)

Buildex
Division of ITW Limited
Suttons Industrial Park
Reading
Berkshire RG6 1HF (0734 61044)
(*'Tapcon' fastening system*)

Butterley Building Materials Limited
1 Bow Street
London WC2 (01 240 2267)
(*Bricks*)

Catnic Components Limited
Pontygwindy Estate
Caerphilly
Mid-Glamorgan CF8 2WJ (0222 885955)
(*Lintels, ties, hangers & associated products*)

Cavity Trays Limited
Vale Road
Penn Hill Trading Estate
Yeovil
Somerset BA21 5HU (0935 74769)

Celcon Limited
289–293 High Holborn
London WC1V 7HU (01 242 9766)
(*Insulating building blocks*)

AB Celloplast
PO Box 297
S–60104 Norrköping
Sweden
(*'Tenoarm' age-resistant building film*)

Agent: Graphica Advertising & Marketing
13 Dover Street
London W1X 3PH (01 935 0902)

Dufaylite Developments Limited —
Clayboard Division
Cromwell Road
St Neots
Cambridgeshire PE19 1QW (0480 215000)
(*'Clayboard' void former for foundations*)

Euroroof Limited
Denton Drive
Northwich
Cheshire CW9 7LU (0606 48222)
(*'Dragon Wagon' torch trolleys for hot bitumen
application on large surfaces*)

Artur Fischer (UK) Limited
Fischer House
25 Newton Road
Marlow
Bucks SL7 1JY (062 84 72882)
(*Fixings*)

Forticrete Limited
Hill Head Quarry
Harpur Hill
Buxton
Derbyshire SK17 9PS (0298 79191)
(*'Coloroc' cladding system*)

P C Henderson Limited
Tangent Works
Romford
Essex RM3 8UL (04023 45555)
(*Garage doors, door gear, general sliding and
folding door gear*)

Hire Service Shops Limited
(Head Office)
31 London Road
Reigate
Surrey RH2 9PZ (073 72 49441)
(*Tools and equipment hire shops —
in 75 mainland UK centres*)

Brian Hyde Limited
Stirling Road
Shirley
Solihull
West Midlands B90 4LZ (021 705 7987)
(*Importer of 'Stabila' levels and other tools*)

I G Lintels Limited
Avondale Road
Cwmbran
Gwent NP44 1XY (063 33 66811)
(*Weldless steel lintels and associated products*)

IMI Broderick Structures
Forsyth Road
Sheerwater
Woking
Surrey GU21 5RR (04862 21411)
(*'Cascade' copper and steel roofing tiles*)

Ibstock Building Products Limited
Ibstock
Leicester LE6 1HS (0530 60531)
(*Chamfered clay paving setts*)

Kay Metzeler Limited
Wellington Road
Bollington
Macclesfield
Cheshire SK10 5JJ (0625 73366)
(*Plastics, insulation, 'Regupol' rubber/
polyurethane roofing*)

V L Martin & Company Limited
Witley Works
Witley Gardens
Southall
Middlesex (01 574 1145)
(*'Marcaddy' industrial cable reels*)

Mason Master Limited
Braunston
Daventry
Northamptonshire NN11 7HX (0788 890351)
(*Masonry drills, masonry saws*)

Plasmor Limited
PO Box 44
Womersley Road
Knottingley
West Yorkshire WF11 0DN (0977 83221)
(*Insulating building blocks*)

Rabone Chesterman Limited
Whitmore Street
Birmingham B18 5BD (021 554 5431)
(*Measuring tools, levels*)

Ruberoid Building Products Limited
Brimsdown
Enfield
Middlesex EN3 7PP (01 805 3434)
(*Insulated and general flat-roof covering systems*)

Rytons Ventilation Equipment Limited
68 Rockingham Road
Kettering
Northamptonshire NN16 8JU (0536 511874)
(*Structural ventilation units*)

Spit Fixings Limited
Old Brighton Road
Lowfield Heath

Crawley
West Sussex RH11 0QN (0293 23372)
(*Fixing systems and power tools, including
cartridge hammers*)

Vulcanite Limited
(Ruberoid Group)
Trident Works
Seven Stars Bridge
Wigan
Lancashire WN3 5AF (0942 46292)
(*'Grün' propane gas fired bitumen boilers*)
Also at: Lockview Road
          Stranmillis
          Belfast BT9 5FP (0232 669444)

The Welwyn Tool Company Limited
Stonehills House
Welwyn Garden City
Hertfordshire AL8 6NJ (0707 96 29121)
(*Plastic welding/repair/seam sealing equipment*)

Willan Building Services
2 Brooklands Road
Sale
Cheshire M33 3SS (061 973 6262)
(*Structural ventilation units*)

Winn & Coles (DENSO) Limited
Denso House
Chapel Road
London SE27 0TR (01 670 7511)
(*Sealants, water proofing and caulking materials*)

Building systems specialists
Calders & Grandidge Limited
London Road
Boston
Lincolnshire PE21 7JH (0205 66660)
(*Timber-frame components*)

Gang-Nail Limited and
Redland Construction Software Limited
The Trading Estate
Farnham
Surrey GU9 9PQ (0252 722425)
(*'Alpha 2000' system for timber-frame
manufacturers and 'Gamma 2000' system for
house builders*)

F Pratten & Company Limited
Charlton Road
Bath
Avon BA3 4AG (0761 412441)
(Timber-frame systems)

Rush & Tompkins Limited
Marlow House
Station Road
Sidcup
Kent DA15 7BP (01 300 3388)
*('Speedframe' patent timber-frame low-cost
standard housing system)*

Technal UK Limited
Agents:
Garfield Lewis Systems Limited
Unit 44
Kelvin Way Trading Estate
West Bromwich
West Midlands B70 7TP (021 525 8585)
(Aluminium construction systems)

**Door, joinery, lift, staircase & window
manufacturers**
Albion Design
12 Flitcroft Street
London WC2H 8DJ (01 836 0151)
(Cast iron and timber spiral staircases)

Boulton & Paul (Joinery) Limited
Riverside Works
Norwich NR1 1EB (0603 60133)
(Timber windows, doors)

Bowater Rippers Limited
Castle Hedingham
Halstead
Essex CO9 3EP (0787 60391)
*(Softwood and hardwood windows, doors,
including garage and patio doors)*

Brockley Wood Technology
119A Tanners Hill
London SE8 4QD (01 691 2008)
(Victorian/period porches in wood)

H Burbidge & Son Limited
Whittington Road

Oswestry
Shropshire SY11 1HZ (0691 655131)
(Kitchens, staircases)

W H Colt (London) Limited
Havant
Hampshire PO9 2LY (0705 451111)
(Roof windows)

Consort Aluminium Limited
Unit 1
Newtown Industrial Estate
Green Lane
Tewkesbury
Gloucestershire GL20 8SL (0684 297393)

Crescent of Cambridge Limited
130 Hills Road
Cambridge CB2 1PS (0223 67835)
(Spiral staircases)

Gimson & Co (Leicester) Limited
Vulcan Road
Leicester LE5 3EA (0533 21425)
(Stair, personal and open/enclosed shaft lifts)

Juno Roplasto Limited
3 Kimber Road
Wandsworth
London SW18 (01 874 9146)

Minivator Sales Limited
Englands Lane
Dunstable
Bedfordshire (0582 65961)
(Stairlifts)

Pilkington Flat Glass Limited
Prescot Road
St Helens
Merseyside WA10 3TT (0744 28882)
Also offices in Altrincham, Birmingham,
Dublin, Glasgow, Leeds and Rickmansworth

The Velux Company Limited
Lizanne House
Mount Sion
Tunbridge Wells
Kent TN1 1UE (0892 44055)
(Roof windows)

Also at 27 Mespil Road, Dublin 4
(0001 609635)

The Wessex Medical Equipment Company
Limited
Unit Two
Budds Lane Industrial Estate
Romsey
Hampshire (0794 518246)
(Lift and vertical seat for disabled people)

Westland Engineers Limited
Yeovil
Somerset (0935 75200)
*(Garage doors and automatic control gear for
them)*

Governmental, official & statutory bodies
Architects Registration Council of the United
Kingdom
73 Hallam Street
London W1 (01 580 5861)

DHSS — Department of Health & Social
Security
Alexander Fleming House
Elephant & Castle
London SE1 6BY (01 407 5522)

DOE — Department of the Environment
Historic Buildings Council
25 Savile Row
London W1X 2BT (01 734 6010
Extension 650)

DOE — Department of the Environment
(Planning Appeals — England)
Tollgate House
Houlton Street
Bristol BS2 9DJ (0272 218811)

HMSO — Her Majesty's Stationery Office
HMSO Books — Enquiries
PO Box 276
London SW8 (01 211 8815)

HMSO Books — Retail Counter Service
Holborn Bookshop

49 High Holborn
London WC1 (01 928 6977)

National Home Improvement Council
26 Store Street
London WC1 (01 636 2562)

Planning Appeals Commission
(Northern Ireland appeals)
Carlton House
Shaftesbury Square
Belfast BT2 7LD (0232 244710)

Scottish Office
(Scottish planning appeals)
New St Andrews House
St James Centre
Edinburgh EH1 3TF (031 556 8400)

Welsh Office
(Welsh planning appeals)
Cathays Park
Cardiff CF1 3NQ (0222 825111)

Heating, plumbing and drainage equipment
Barlo Products Limited
Barlo House
Foundry Lane
Horsham
West Sussex RH13 5TQ (0403 62342)
(Convector radiators, brackets, automatic air vent)

Bartol Plastics Limited
Edlington
Doncaster
South Yorkshire DN12 1BY (0709 863551)
(Plastic plumbing and drainage systems)

Calor Gas Limited
Appleton Park
Datchet
Slough SL3 9JG (0753 40000)

Clos-O-Mat (Great Britain) Limited
2 Brooklands Road
Sale
Cheshire M33 3SS (061 973 6262)
(Automatic thermostatic taps)

Conder Hardware Limited
(Conder Pollution Control)
Abbotts Barton House
Winchester
Hampshire SO23 7SJ (0962 55250)
(Septic tanks)

Dunlop Solaronics
The Maltings Industrial Estate
Southminster
Essex CM0 7EQ (0621 773555 or
Freefone 3852)
(Solar collector/heating systems)

IMI Yorkshire Imperial Plastics
PO Box 166
Leeds
West Yorkshire LS1 1RD (0532 701107)
(Plastic drainage systems)

Marley Extrusions Limited
Lenham
Maidstone
Kent ME17 2DE (0622 858888)
*(Plastic drainage systems, baths, shower trays
and enclosures)*

Maxton Boilers (Marketing) Limited
Consort House
Jubilee Road
Burgess Hill
Sussex RH15 9TL (044 46 47626)
(Electric central heating boilers)

Strax Distribution Limited
41B Brecknock Road
London N7 0BT (01 485 7056)
*(High-efficiency fireplaces with retractable doors,
stoves, chimney extractor fans)*

Thermal Radiators Limited
Shepherds House Lane
London Road
Earley
Reading
Berkshire RG6 1AE (0734 62641)
(Convector radiators)

Transbyn Limited
Benford House
Bury Street
Ruislip
Middlesex HA4 7TL (08956 30336)
('Saniplus'/'Saniflo' smallbore sanitary system)

The Wednesbury Tube Company Limited
Oxford Street
Bilston
West Midlands WV14 7DS (0902 41133)
(Copper plumbing pipe and fittings)

Insulation products and services
Coolag Purlboard
Heysham Works
Middleton
Morecambe
Lancashire LA3 3PP (0524 55611)
(Insulating boards)

Disbotherm Limited
12 Mount Ephraim Road
Royal Tunbridge Wells
Kent TN1 1EE (08092 44822)
(External insulation system)

Epsicon Products Limited
PO Box 12
Thorns Road
Quarry Bank
Brierley Hill
West Midlands DY5 2LA (0384 891146)
(Interlocking cavity insulation panels)

Fibreglass Limited
Insulation Division
St Helens
Merseyside WA10 3TR (0744 24022)
(Glass fibre insulation materials)

Unidri Limited
Ashgrove Works
380 Stoney Stanton Road
Coventry
Warwickshire CV6 5DJ
(External insulation system)

Professional, trade and charitable organisations

Accident Offices Association
Aldermary House
Queen Street
London EC4P 4JD (01 248 4477)
(Insurance)

Air Conditioning Advisory Bureau
30 Millbank
London SW1 (01 834 8827)

American Plywood Association
101 Wigmore Street
London W1H 9AB (01 629 3437)

Architectural Association
34 Bedford Square
London WC1 (01 636 0974)

Associated Master Plumbers and Domestic
Engineers
151–2 Plumstead Road
London SE18 7DY (01 855 1844)

Association of British Plywood & Veneer
Manufacturers
Epworth House
25–35 City Road
London EC1Y 1AR (01 628 5801)

Association of British Roofing Felt
Manufacturers
69 Cannon Street
London EC4N 5AB (01 248 4444)

Association of Builders Hardware
Manufacturers
5 Greenfield Crescent
Birmingham B15 3BE (021 454 2177)

Association of Building Centres
26 Store Street
London WC1E 7BT (01 637 1022)

Association of Building Component
Manufacturers
26 Store Street
London WC1E 7BT (01 580 9083)

Association of Consultant Architects
7 King Street
Bristol BS1 4EJ (0272 293372)

Association of Manufacturers of Domestic
Electric Appliances
593 Hitchin Road
Stopsley
Luton LU2 7UN (0582 411001)

The Brick Development Association (Brick
Advisory Centre)
26 Store Street
London WC1E 7BT (01 637 0047)

Building Employers Confederation (Formerly
the National Federation of Building Trades
Employers)
82 New Cavendish Street
London W1M 8AD (01 580 5588)

Building Societies Association
14 Park Street
London W1 (01 629 0515)

CIOB — The Chartered Institute of Building
Englemere
Kings Ride
Ascot
Berkshire SL5 8BJ (0990 23355)

CORGI — Confederation for the Registration
of Gas Installers
140 Tottenham Court Road
London W1P 9LN (01 387 9185)

Cement & Concrete Association
Information Division
52 Grosvenor Gardens
London SW1W 0AQ (01 235 6661)

Chartered Institute of Arbitrators
69 Cannon Street
London EC4 (01 236 8761)

Construction Surveyors Institute
203 Lordship Lane
London SE22 8HA (01 693 0219)

Disabled Living Foundation
380–384 Harrow Road
London W9 2HV (01 289 6111)

Electrical Contractors Association
32 Palace Court
London W2 (01 229 1266)

Eurisol-UK — Association of British
Manufacturers of Mineral Insulating Fibres
St Paul's House
Edison Road
Bromley
Kent BR2 0EP (01 466 6719)

Federation of Master Builders
33 John Street
London WC1N 2BB (01 242 7583)

Glass and Glazing Federation
6 Mount Row
London W1Y 6DY (01 409 0545)

Guild of Surveyors
33 Batchworth Lane
Northwood
Middlesex HA6 3EQ (09274 27755)

HVCA — Heating & Ventilating Contractors
Association
ESCA House
34 Palace Court
Bayswater
London W2 4JG (01 229 2488)

IEEIE — Institution of Electrical &
Electronics Incorporated Engineers
2 Savoy Hill
London WC2R 0BS (01 836 3357)

Incorporated Association of Architects &
Surveyors
Jubilee House
Billingsbrook Road
Weston Favell
Northampton NN3 4NW (0604 404121)

Incorporated Society of Valuers &
Auctioneers
3 Cadogan Gate
London SW1X 0AS (01 235 2282)

Institute of Domestic Heating &
Environmental Engineers (Formerly Institute
of Heating & Ventilating Engineers)
93 High Road
South Benfleet
Essex SS7 3BR (037 45 54266)

Institute of Plumbing
Scottish Mutual House
North Street
Hornchurch
Essex RM11 1RU (04024 51236)

Life Offices Association
Aldermary House
Queen Street
London EC4N 1TP (01 236 1101)
(*Insurance*)

NHBC — National House Building Council
58 Portland Place
London W1N 4BU (01 637 1248)

National Association of Plumbers, Heating &
Mechanical Services Contractors
6 Gate Street
London WC2A 3HX (01 405 2678)

National Inspection Council for Electrical
Installation Contracting
Alembic House
93 Albert Embankment
London SE1 7TB (01 582 7746)

National Supervisory Council for Intruder
Alarms
73–79 Rochester Row
London SE1P 1LQ (01 828 7582)

National Water Council
1 Queen Anne's Gate
London SW1H 9BT (01 930 3100)

RAI — Royal Institute of Architects of Ireland
8 Merrion Road
Dublin (0001 761703)

RIAS — The Royal Incorporation of
Architects in Scotland
15 Rutland Square
Edinburgh EH1 2BE (031 229 7205)

RIBA — The Royal Institute of British
Architects
66 Portland Place
London W1N 4AD (01 580 5533)

RICS — The Royal Institution of Chartered
Surveyors
12 Great George Street
London SW1P 3AD (01 222 7000)

RNIB — The Royal National Institute for the
Blind
224 Great Portland Street
London W1 (01 388 1266)

RSUA — The Royal Society of Ulster
Architects
2 Mount Charles
Belfast BT7 1NZ (0232 223760)

Royal Association for Disability &
Rehabilitation
25 Mortimer Street
London W1N 8AB (01 637 5400)

Royal National Institute for the Deaf
105 Gower Street
London WC1 6AH (01 387 8033)

SAAT — The Society of Architectural and
Associated Technicians
397 City Road
London EC1V 1NE (01 278 2206)

Scottish & Northern Ireland Plumbing
Employers Federation
2 Walker Street
Edinburgh EH3 7LB (031 225 2255)

Spastics Society
12 Park Crescent
London W1N 4EQ (01 636 5020)

The Steel Window Association
26 Store Street
London WC1E 7JR (01 637 3571)

TIMA — Thermal Insulation Manufacturers
Association
5 Langley Street
London WC2H 9JA (01 379 3404)

TRADA — Timber Research & Development
Association
Stocking Lane
Hughenden Valley
High Wycombe
Buckinghamshire HP14 4ND (024 024 3091)

Proofing & protective products & systems
Peter Cox Limited
Wandle Way
Mitcham
Surrey CR4 4NB (01 640 1151)
(Damp, rot and pest eradication)

Grangersol Limited
Imperial Way
Watford
Hertfordshire WD2 4JW (0923 24086)
(Masonry sealants)

London Chemical Company Limited
Batchworth Island
Church Street
Rickmansworth
Hertfordshire WD3 1JQ (0923 771366)
(Damp-proofing coatings)

Thomas Ness Limited
Cardiff Road
Nantgarw
Cardiff CF4 7YH (044 385 2511)
(Damp and waterproofing systems)

RIW Protective Products Company Limited
Tubs Hill House
London Road
Sevenoaks
Kent TN13 1BL (0732 460446)
(Damp and waterproofing systems)

Winn & Coales (Denso) Limited
Denso House
Chapel Road
London SE27 0TR
(Sealants and mastics, including 'Sylglas' products)

Specialist design & construction services
The Argos Group of Companies
8 Chase Road
Park Royal
London NW10 6QD (01 961 3900)
(Extensions)

Ark Component Buildings Limited (Ark Home Extensions)
Freepost
4 Tresham Road
Orton
Southgate
Peterborough PE2 0BR (0733 232233)

Aston Home Extensions Limited
Aston House
Hadham Road
Bishops Stortford
Hertfordshire CM23 2QE (0279 506881)
(Extensions and conservatories)

Crescourt Loft Conversions Limited
4–54 Roebuck Lane
West Bromwich
West Midlands B70 6QR (021 553 4131)
Also at: 85 Hangar Riding
         Carpenders Park
         Watford
         Hertfordshire WD1 5BH
         (01 428 9918)

Crescourt Ireland Limited
Kilronan House
Church Road
Malahide
County Dublin (0001 452 359)

DEMAND — Design & Manufacture for Disability
99 Leman Street
London E1 8EY (01 488 9869)
(Furniture/equipment)

High Speed Glass Limited
8 Stonegate Road
Leeds 6 (0532 789562)
(Agents for 'Solaire' Heatsaver conservatories made by Grosvenor Products)

LECS Housing
Sibton Green
Saxmundham
Suffolk IP17 2JX (072 877 639)
(Designers and builders of prototype low energy consumption housing)

Marley Buildings Limited
Peasmarsh
Guildford
Surrey GU3 1LS (0483 69922)
(Extensions and conservatories)

Riviera Plant Interiors Limited
Hamble House
Meadrow
Godalming
Surrey GU7 3JX
(Silk polyester artificial plants)

Appendix 2:
Conversion Factors

AREA

square inches (sq in)	×	645.2	=	square millimetres (sq mm)
sq in	×	6.452	=	square centimetres (sq cm)
sq in	×	0.0006452	=	square metres (sq m)
square feet (sq ft)	×	92,900.0	=	square millimetres (sq mm)
sq ft	×	929.0	=	square centimetres (sq cm)
sq ft	×	0.0929	=	square metres (sq m)
square yards (sq yd)	×	836,100.0	=	square millimetres (sq mm)
sq yd	×	8,361.0	=	square centimetres (sq cm)
sq yd	×	0.8361	=	square metres (sq m)
acres	×	4,046.9	=	square metres (sq m)
acres	×	0.40469	=	hectares (10,000 sq m)
square millimetres (sq mm)	×	0.00155	=	square inches (sq in)
sq mm	×	0.0000108	=	square feet (sq ft)
sq mm	×	0.0000012	=	square yards (sq yd)
square centimetres (sq cm)	×	0.155	=	square inches (sq in)
sq cm	×	0.0010764	=	square feet (sq ft)
sq cm	×	0.0001196	=	square yards (sq yd)
square metres (sq m)	×	1,550.0	=	square inches (sq in)
sq m	×	10.764	=	square feet (sq ft)
sq m	×	1.196	=	square yards (sq yd)
hectares	×	11,960.0	=	square yards (sq yd)
hectares	×	2.471	=	acres

HEAT/ENERGY

Btu/hr	×	0.2931	=	watts (W)
Btu/hr	×	0.0002931	=	kilowatts (kW) = Units of electricity
Btu/hr	×	0.2520	=	kilocalories/hr (kcal/hr)
Btu/hr	×	0.001055	=	megajoules (MJ)
Btu/hr	×	0.00001	=	therms
kilocalories/hr	×	3.968	=	Btu/hr
kcal/hr	×	0.001163	=	kilowatts (kW)
kcal/hr	×	0.004186	=	megajoules (MJ)
kcal/hr	×	0.0000397	=	therms
kcal/hr	×	1.163	=	watts (W)
kilowatts (kW)	×	3412.0	=	Btu/hr
kW	×	860.0	=	kilocalories/hr (kcal/hr)

kilowatt hour (kWh, unit of electricity)	×	3.6	=	megajoules (MJ)
kWh	×	0.03412	=	therms
megajoules (MJ)	×	947.9	=	Btu
MJ	×	238.9	=	kilocalories (kcal)
MJ	×	0.2778	=	kilowatt hours (kWh)
MJ	×	0.00948	=	therms
therms	×	100,000.0	=	Btu
therms	×	25,200.0	=	kilocalories (kcal)
therms	×	29.3	=	kilowatt hours (kWh)
therms	×	105.5	=	megajoules (MJ)

LINEAR MEASURE

inches (in)	×	2.54	=	centimetres (cm)
in	×	25.4	=	millimetres (mm)
feet (ft)	×	30.48	=	centimetres (cm)
ft	×	0.3048	=	metres (m)
ft	×	304.8	=	millimetres (mm)
yards (yd)	×	0.9144	=	metres (m)
millimetres (mm)	×	0.03937	=	inches (in)
mm	×	0.0032808	=	feet (ft)
mm	×	0.0010936	=	yards (yd)
centimetres (cm)	×	0.0328	=	feet (ft)
cm	×	0.3937	=	inches (in)
cm	×	0.01094	=	yards (yd)
metres (m)	×	3.2808	=	feet (ft)
m	×	39.37	=	inches (in)

TEMPERATURE

Fahrenheit	−	32 × 0.55	=	Celsius (°C)
Celsius (Centigrade)	×	1.8 + 32	=	Fahrenheit (°F)

THERMAL TRANSMITTANCE ('U'—) VALUES

Btu/sq ft/hr/deg F	×	5.678	=	w/sq m deg C
w/sq m deg C	×	0.1761	=	Btu/sq ft/hr/deg F

VOLUME/LIQUID MEASURE

pints (pt)	×	0.568	=	cubic centimetres (cc) or millilitres (ml)
pts	×	0.568	=	litres (l)
cubic feet (cu ft)	×	0.028317	=	cubic metres (cu m)
cu ft	×	28.3168	=	litres (l)
cubic yards (cu yd)	×	0.7646	=	cubic metres (cu m)
gallons (gal)	×	4.546	=	litres (l)

litres	×	1.76	=	pints
litres	×	0.22	=	gallons (gal)
cubic metres (cu m)	×	35.31	=	cubic feet (cu ft)
sq m	×	1.308	=	cubic yards (cu yd)

WEIGHT

ounces (oz)	×	28.3495	=	grammes (g)
pounds (lb)	×	453.6	=	g
lb	×	0.4536	=	kilogrammes (kg)
lb	×	0.0004536	=	tonnes (= 1,000 kg)
hundredweight (cwt)	×	0.0508	=	kilogrammes (= 1,000 g)
cwt	×	0.0508	=	tonnes
tons	×	1,016.0	=	kilogrammes (kg)
tons	×	1.016	=	tonnes
grammes (g)	×	0.0353	=	ounces (oz)
g	×	0.0022046	=	pounds (lb)
kilogrammes (kg)	×	2.2046	=	lb
kg	×	0.01968	=	hundredweight (cwt)
kg	×	0.0009842	=	tons
tonnes	×	2,205.0	=	pounds (lb)
tonnes	×	0.9842	=	tons

Index

Page numbers in *italic* indicate illustrations

Accident insurance, 84-5
Adhesives, 136
Aga-type cookers, 162, 166, 168
Agrément Certificates, 110-11, 177
Airbricks, 90, 93-4, 94, 102
Alarm system, electronic personal, 43
Aluminium: doors and windows, 122-4, *23, 35;* gutters, 152; tiles, 143
Aluminium Window Association, 123
Anchors, masonry, 135-41, *137-40*
Arbitration procedures, 77, 78, 80
Architect, advantage of using, 29, 42
Architects' organisations, 63-5, 67-8
Architectural technicians, 67
Asbestos-cement roofing, 100, *18*
Attic conversions, 31-2
Awning blinds, exterior, 36

Balconies, 31
Ball valves, 153, 161
Balusters, 148
Bank loans, 185
Bankruptcy of contractor, 74, 77
Bathrooms for disabled, 45-7, *46*
Bay window, addition of, 31
Bedrooms, access to, 36
Bi-fold type doors, 40
Bitumen-based masonry sealers, 135-6
Bitumen boilers, 121
Bitumen felt, 115, 121-2
'Black light' insect lures, 19, *19*
Blinds, 36, 132-4
Blockboard, 144-5
Boilers, central heating and water, 53-4, 168-72
Bolt-on door-opening units, 17
Breeze blocks, 92

Bricks and bricklaying, 90-2, 112, 113-17, *114;* efflorescence on, 115-16; sulphate attack on, 116
British Standards Specifications, 110ff
Builder, finding suitable, 68, 74-8
Building Centres, 65, 67
Building Employers' Confederation, 84, 85; guarantee scheme, 76-8
Building society loans, 55, 184-5
Buildings of special architectural or historical interest, 58

Calcium silicate bricks, 113
Calorific values of fuels, 174-5
Cartridge guns for sealing joints, 135
Cast-in bolt-holding sockets, 140
Cast-iron: drain pipes, 150-1; gutters, 152
Cavity trays, 90-2, 100, *91, 101*
Cavity wall anchors, 141
Cavity walls, 88, 90-3, *90-1* insulation, 92-3, 177-8, *92*
Ceilings, 33, 97, 166
Cement, 111
Central heating, 168-72ff, *21, 170*
Chartered Institute of Building, 68, 76
Chimneys, 163-4, 166, *163-4*
Chipboard, 93, 97, 144, 146, *142*
Cladding materials, 141-4, *144*
Clayboard, 87
Clay bricks, 113
Clayheave, 87
Collars, roof, 99
Colorcore, 146
Comb jointing, 116-17
Compression joints, 158-9
Concertina folding doors, 40
Conciliation procedures, 77, 78
Concrete, 111-12 bricks, 113 cladding, 143-4, *144*

floors, 94, 97, *94-5*
lintels, 117
sealers for, 135
Condensation, 180, *29, 91*
Confederation for the Registration of Gas Installers, 182
Conservatories, 19-29, 31, *20, 22-9, 38;* effect on rateable value, 53; shading for, 134
Contractor's insurance, 85
Contracts, making, 70-82, 85
Cookers, for disabled, 50, *48-9*
Copper pipes, 156ff; tiles, 143, *35, 142*
Cotswold traditional, 97, 99

Damage, insurance against, 83-4, 85
Damp-proof courses, 92, 115, 117, 120, 135-6
Deeds, restrictions in, 51
Dehumidifiers, 172-3
Department of the Environment, 58, 62
Design heat loss, 173-4
Designers: evaluating work, 74-5; fees, 68-9
Design of Housing for the Convenience of Disabled People, 42
Directory of Architectural Practices, 64
Disabled, designing for, 42-7, 50, *44-6, 48-50*
Disabled Living Foundation, 42
Dividing walls, removing, 30-1
DIY extensions, 78-9, *8-13, 15*
Doors, 36, 40, 122-30
 for disabled, 44-5
 folding, 40
 garage, 16-17
 glass for, 130-1
 lintels, 116-20, *118-19*
 patio, 19, 30
 performance ratings, 132

Dormer windows, 34-6, *35*
Double glazing, 131, *27*
Downpipes, 151-2
Drainage, 40-1, 148-52, *148-51*
Driveways for disabled, 43-4
Driving Rain Index, 132

Efflorescence on brickwork,
  115-16
Electrical Contractors'
  Association, 182
Electrical extensions, regulations
  for, 182, 183
Epoxy-resin-based putty, 112
Estimate, definition of, 71
Expanded metal laths, 120-1
Exposure zones, 132
Extension Manual, 79

Faculty of Architects and
  Surveyors, 63-4
Federation of Building
  Subcontractors, 76
Federation of Master Builders,
  73, 78, 84, 85
Fees, 51, 68-9
Fibre boards, 145-6
Filling and patching compounds,
  112
Financing of extensions, 184-5
Fire-heated boilers, 153
Fire regulations and resistance
  ratings, 31-2
Flat roofs, 100-2, 121-2, *101*
Floors:
  intermediate, 97
  joist and board, 93-4
  solid concrete, 94, 97, *94-5*
Folding doors, 40
Formica, 146
Foundations, 17-18, 87, *88, 104*
Fuels, calorific value, 174-5
Furfix profile wall extension
  systems, 116-17, *116*

Garages, 16-18, *17, 30, 119*;
  effect on rateable value, 52
Gas, extension affecting mains,
  182
Gate valves, 161
Glass and glazing, 29, 130-1
Glass & Glazing Federation, 130
Grab handles for disabled, 45
Gross value of property, 52
Ground floors, construction of,
  93-5, 97, *94-5*
Ground-level extensions, 30-1,
  18, 22

Guarantee schemes, 76-8
Gutters, rainwater, 100, 151-2

'Half-hour' fire standard, 32
Hammer screws, 137-8, *137*
Handicapped, designing for,
  42-7, 50, *44-6, 48-50*
Hardboard, 145
Heating costs, 172-81
Heating equipment, 21, 162-72
Heat pumps, 21, *21*, 25-6
Hot bitumen bonding, 121-2
Hot water cylinders, 153-4
House Builders' Federation, 76
Household goods, insuring, 84
Housing for the Elderly,
  information pack, 42
Humidifiers, 172
Hydraulic cement, 112

Immersion heaters, 154
Incorporated Association of
  Architects and Surveyors, 64
Inner leaves, in walls, 92-3
Insect: screens, 133; traps, 19, *19*
Inspection chambers, 150
Inspection pit in garage, 17
Institute of Registered
  Architects Ltd, 63
Insulation:
  aluminium frames, 122
  effect on heating costs, 176-81,
    179
  floor, 94, 97, 180, *93-4*
  plastic frames, 124
  rooflights, 122
  roofs, 101-2, 122, 180
  walls, 92-3, 103, 108-9, 180,
    92, 138
Insurance, 83-6:
  Building Employers'
    Confederation, 76-8
  Federation of Master
    Builders, 78
  in contracts with builders, 73
  not chargeable with bank loan,
    185
Intermediate floors, 97
Internal walls, construction
  of, 97, *119*

Joint Contracts Tribunal, 72, 85
Joint-filling compounds, 134-6

Kitchen aids for disabled, 47-50
Kitchen, doors in, 36, 40

Laminated board, 144-6, *39*

Laminated safety glass, 130-1
Lead pipes and fittings, 156, 158,
  183
Lean-to roofs, 100
Lifts for disabled, 43, *44*
Lignum plastic system, 127
Lintels, 117, 120, *118-19*
Listed buildings, 33, 58, 62
Loft rooms, 31-6

Mains water supply, 152ff, 183
Manifolds, 169, *150*
Masonry fixings, 137-41, *137-41*
Master Builder, trade journal, 73,
  78
Materials on site, insurance for,
  83-4
Microbore central heating, 168ff
Mirror glass, 131
Mono-pitched roofs, 100
Mortgage value, definition of, 52

Nails, 136-7
National Federation of Building
  Trades Employers, 73, 76
National Inspection Council for
  Electrical Installations, 182
National Register of Warranted
  Builders, 78
Neoprene rubber adhesives, 136

Open-fire heating, 163-4, *163-4*
Open-tread staircases, 146-7, 148
Outdoor tap installations, 183
Outline planning permission, 55
Ovens for disabled, 50, *48-9*

Package-deal extensions, 41
Passageways, internal, 44
Paths for wheelchairs, 43-4
Patios, 18-19, 130
Pipes and fittings:
  central heating, 168ff
  rainwater, 100, 151-2
  water systems, 152-62
Pitched roofs, 34, 97, 99-100, *27*
Pitch polymer damp proofing,
  115
Planning permission, 21, 27, 32,
  52-5, 58, 62
Plasterboard, 145-6
Pleated folding doors, 40
Plugs: masonry, 137-40; thin
  walls, 141
Plumbing: materials, 152-62;
  planning of, 33, 40-1
Plywood, 145
Polybutylene pipes, 159-61, *159*

Polystyrene-bead insulation, 177-8
Polyvinyl acetate (PVA) adhesives, 136
Polyvinyl chlorite (uPVC) windows/doors, 124-7
Porches, 14-15
Portland cement, 112
Prefabricated extensions, 29, 41
Property value, effect of extension on, 51
Pumps, central heating, 169-70, 172
Purlins, definition of, 99
Putty, epoxy-resin-based, 112

Quotation, definition of, 71

Radiators, central heating, 168-72
Rafters, pitched roof, 99
Rainwater gutters, 100, 151-2
Rateable value, 51-3
Ready-mixed concrete, 111-12, 96
Roller blinds, 37, 133
Roofing felts, 121-2
Roofs:
    flat, 100-2, *101*
    insulation, 33, 101-2, 122, 180
    lean-to, 100
    pitched, 34, 97, 99-100, *27*
    timber-framed constructions, 102, *106-7*
    windows in, 34-6, 122, 134, *27, 29, 36*
Roof space, extending into, 32-6
Rooms, rearranging existing, 29-32
Royal Incorporation of Architects in Scotland, 64-5
Royal Institute of Architects of Ireland, 65
Royal Institute of British Architects, 63, 65
Royal Society of Ulster Architects, 65

Safety glass, 29, 130-1, *22-3*
Sarking, 33, 99-100, *98*
Sash windows, 130, *129*
Scottish Building Employers' Confederation, 76
Screws, 137-40
Sealing compounds, 134-6
Seasonal heat loss, 174

Security equipment, 42-3
Self-contained suites of rooms, 41-2
Self-tapping and self-drilling screws, 140
Shot-fired fixings, 140-1
Shower units, 45, 47, 155-6, *155*
Shutters, 132-3
Skylights, 34-7, 122, 134
Slate roofs, 100, 143
'Sleeper' walls, 93
Society of Architectural and Associated Technicians, 67
Society of Surveying Technicians, 68
Solar heating, 166-8, *167*
Soldered joints, 157-9, *158*
Solid masonry walls, 88-90, 178, *89*
Stables, classed as extensions, 16
Stainless steel pipework, 159
Staircases:
    for disabled, 43
    to loft, 34
    spiral, 34, 147-8, *147*
    straight-flight, 146-7
Stair-lifts, 43, *45*
Steel: gutters, 152; lintels, 117, *118-19;* tiles, 143, *142;* windows/doors, 127-8
Steel Window Association, 127
Stop taps (cocks), 161, 152
Storage heaters, electric, 166
Storage tanks, 153
Straight-flight staircases, 146-7
Style, unity of, 15, *25-7, 38*
Sulphate attack on brickwork, 116
Surveying technicians, 68
Surveyors' fees, 51
Surveyors' organisations, 63-4, 67-8
'Suspended' timber floor, 93-4, *93*
Swimming pools, heating, 167

Tapcon masonry anchors, 138-40, *139-40*
Taps for disabled, 47, *46, 48-9*
Tax relief on borrowings, 184, 185
Theft of materials, insurance against, 83-4
Thermassic uPVC window/doors, 126-7, *126*
Thermostatic water mixers, 162

Thermostats, central heating, 172ff
Ties, cavity walls, 90, 92, *90*
Tiles, roof, 100, 143, *142*
Timber:
    cladding, 141
    floors, 93, *83*
    roofs, 99, *15*
    windows and doors, 128-30
Timber-frame construction, 102-3, 108-9, 141, 179, *103-8, 119*
Toilet aids for disabled, 45-7
Toilet units, where drain access difficult, 41

Underfloor heating, 166
Unity of style, 15, *25-7, 38*
Up-and-over doors, 17, *17*
uPVC windows/doors, 126-7, *125-6*
Upwards extensions, 29-36
U-values, 173ff

Valleys, roof, 99-100
Valuers' fees, 51
Veneers, 145-6
Venetian blinds, 36, 132-4
Vertical vane blinds, 133-4
Vitrified clay drain pipes, 150-1

Wallplates, 97, 99
Walls: construction, 80, 90-3, 97, *89-91, 103-5, 108, 119;* joining new to existing, 116-17
Warerite, 146
Washbasins for disabled, 47
Washing machines, plumbing for, 152, 154
Water heaters, 152, 154-6
Water softeners, 152
Water supply system, 152-6, 183, *167*
Wheelchairs, provision for, 43-5, 47, 50
Windows:
    aluminium, 122-4, *23, 35*
    glass for, 130-1
    performance ratings, 132
    plastic, 124-7, *124-6*
    rooflights, 122, *27, 29, 36*
    sash, 130, *129*
    steel, 127-8
    timber, 128-30
Wood-based boards, 144-6
Woodscrews, 137